GREEN WITH MILK AND SUGAR

GREEN WITH MILK AND SUGAR

WHEN JAPAN FILLED AMERICA'S TEA CUPS

———

ROBERT HELLYER

Columbia University Press
New York

Columbia University Press wishes to express its appreciation for assistance given
by the Wm. Theodore de Bary Fund in the publication of this book.

Columbia University Press

Publishers Since 1893

New York   Chichester, West Sussex

cup.columbia.edu

Library of Congress Cataloging-in-Publication Data

Names: Hellyer, Robert I., author.

Title: Green with milk and sugar : when Japan filled America's tea cups /
Robert Hellyer.

Description: New York : Columbia University Press, [2021] |
Includes bibliographical references and index.

Identifiers: LCCN 2021003017 (print) | LCCN 2021003018 (ebook) |
ISBN 9780231199100 (hardback) | ISBN 9780231216678 (pbk.) |
ISBN 9780231552943 (ebook)

Subjects: LCSH: Tea trade—United States—History. | Tea trade—Japan—History.
| Green tea—Social aspects—United States—History. | Green tea—Social
aspects—Japan—History. | United States—Civilization—Japanese influences. |
Japan—Civilization—American influences.

Classification: LCC HD9198.U52 H45 2021 (print) | LCC HD9198.U52 (ebook) |
DDC 382/.413720952—dc23

LC record available at https://lccn.loc.gov/2021003017

LC ebook record available at https://lccn.loc.gov/2021003018

Cover design: Julia Kushnirsky

Cover photograph: PAF / Alamy Stock Photo

FOR MY MOTHER,
NANCY INGELS HELLYER

CONTENTS

NOTES ON CONVENTIONS

ROMANIZATION

Japanese words, names, titles, and place names are spelled using the modified Hepburn system. Japanese words include macrons, except for commonly used ones, such as "shogun" and "Tokyo," which appear in standard English dictionaries.

Chinese words, proper names, and place names are spelled according to the pinyin system except in some book titles and in cases, such as Canton (Guangzhou), where the older romanization is more familiar to English-language readers.

PROPER NAMES

Chinese and Japanese names appear in the original order, with the family name first, followed by the given name, except for citations in English-language works where the author's name appears in Western order.

DATES

Except for those included in direct quotations from sources, dates of the Japanese calendar (used until 1873) have been converted into the Gregorian calendar. Months referred to by name (e.g., "June") are Gregorian dates, while references by number (e.g., "the fifth month") are dates according to the Japanese calendar.

PREFACE

first learned about tea in America and Japan as a boy in Tacoma, Washington, tasked with mowing the lawns of my grandmothers. My maternal grandmother lived in a small home built in the 1850s by one of the area's first European American settlers. Her red house with a white picket fence was surrounded by a large yard dotted with fruit trees. After long hours struggling with an unreliable mower, I garnered some pocket money. The real payoff, though, was luscious slices of pie, baked with the yard's bounty of apples, cherries, and blackberries. Alongside would be a pot of black tea, brewed with loose leaves. These were some of my first cups of tea. Unfortunately, I recall little of the tea's flavor, which was overwhelmed by cream and three heaping spoons of sugar.

My paternal grandmother's lawn presented a particular challenge. Rimmed by woodland, it hid teeming ant hills. As a reward for gingerly navigating these hazards, I would not only add to my week's spending money but also—to my delight—be allowed to drink all the cola I wanted. (Realizing I would overindulge, at home my mother allowed it only on special occasions.) As my grandmother and I sat on lawn chairs savoring the aroma of freshly cut grass, she often talked of her time in Japan in the early 1930s as the wife of a tea merchant.

Much of what propelled me to write this book was a desire to delve beyond the anecdotes from those summer days and to learn more about the worlds of my grandmothers.

FIGURE 0.1 My maternal grandmother, Eleanor McKee Ingels, high school graduation portrait, Toulon, Illinois, spring 1919.

My maternal grandmother, née Eleanor McKee, was a grocer's daughter from a town near Galva in northwestern Illinois. She saw off her
fiancé, Sherman Ingels, in 1917 to fight in World War I. A few months
after his return in 1919, they tied the knot—but did not stay long in Illinois. The region's frequent thunderstorms brought Sherman back to the
horrors of artillery barrages endured in trenches of the Western Front.
Following a friend's suggestion, the couple loaded up their Model T Ford
and set out across the country to settle in Tacoma, where thunderstorms
are rare and my grandfather could begin to heal. A landscape architect,

Sherman fathered a family of three daughters, the youngest being my mother, Nancy, born in 1936.

My paternal grandmother also grew up in Illinois. Née Ethel MacArthur Reagan, she was raised in the affluent Chicago suburb of Riverside. Following a brief courtship, she skipped her 1931 graduation ceremony at Radcliffe College to marry George Hellyer, who had recently moved back to Riverside after several years in Europe.

George's late father had been a partner in Hellyer and Company, a family tea-export company founded by his grandfather. His uncles offered their newly wed nephew a position in the firm's processing factory in Shizuoka, Japan, where George had spent some of his childhood. He turned out to have a discriminating palate so was trained as a tea taster. After three years in the family business, George determined to leave Japan and seek new opportunities in the Pacific Northwest, where his brother was putting down roots. He found work in Tacoma, now

FIGURE 0.2 My paternal grandparents, Ethel (first row, far right) and George (standing, fifth from right) Hellyer, sailing to Japan in May 1932.

supporting a family with a daughter and a son—my father, Harold, born in Tokyo in 1934.

My two grandmothers shared more than Midwestern roots and migration to the Tacoma area. They were fellow participants in the global commodity chain of Japanese green tea that forms the skeletal structure of this book. Not only did my paternal grandmother marry into a tea-exporting family, but my maternal grandmother—though serving black tea to her clueless grandson—kept a cache of green tea for more sophisticated guests, green tea being viewed by generations of Midwesterners as the more elegant beverage.

Today black tea is the default choice of American tea drinkers, but it was green tea that dominated for roughly the first century and a half of the republic. The story of the cultural, social, and commercial breakthroughs behind that affinity—the chain from production in Japan to export and marketing in the United States to its reign as an American prestige beverage—is little known—and thus the focus of this book.

Fragrant cups of that gentle stimulant (green, oolong, and black teas—I like them all) sustained me during the writing of this book. With a nod to my hospitable grandmothers, I have found that a surprising amount of history can be contained in a simple cup.

GREEN WITH MILK AND SUGAR

INTRODUCTION

Botanists conclude that the tea plant (*Camellia sinensis*) is indigenous to an area stretching from the Indian state of Assam; across northern parts of Burma, Thailand, and Vietnam; and into southern China. Peoples in that area first picked and consumed naturally growing tea, and it was in southern China that the tea plant was domesticated. From the first to the sixth centuries CE, Chinese elites began to drink tea as an alternative to alcohol, and Buddhist priests came to value its ability clear their minds in the quest for enlightenment.[1] During China's Tang dynasty (618–907), tea came to be consumed throughout that cosmopolitan empire and gained popularity in Japan. Chinese scholar-officials became connoisseurs, giving attention to the cultivation of the plant and processing of the leaves, the quality of water used in brewing, and the joys brought by a cup of tea.[2] Subsequent Chinese dynasties developed tea as an export good, to be exchanged for horses with neighboring Tibetans and later traded to Mongols and Russians at outposts on China's northern frontier. In the early seventeenth century, Dutch merchant ships began to acquire tea at Chinese ports, introducing the beverage to Western Europe and setting in motion tea's popularity in Britain and arrival in colonial America.[3]

Today, teas made from *Camellia sinensis* are generally grouped into three classes, based upon the level of oxidation—the amount of time leaves are exposed to oxygen after being picked. To produce green tea, the oxidation process is stopped quickly, with the resulting brew usually green but also sometimes light yellow. Some teas that fall into the green tea category produce a light brown liquid when brewed. Oolong teas are allowed to oxidize somewhat longer and therefore, when infused, range from a yellowish to a brown color. Black teas are oxidized even longer and further manipulated, often by withering, which darkens the leaves and results in a warm brown or even dark amber brew. These categories are far from fixed, and some U.S. tea retailers include others, such as pu'er, a tea produced in select regions of China.[4]

Thus, the name of a class of tea does not necessarily equate to the color of the brewed beverage—a green tea can produce a brown infusion, and the brewing of a black tea does not always result in a black-colored fluid. Such a flexible understanding of tea is valuable in approaching the history of tea in United States and Japan. Today the colors that defined teas in those two nations have flipped from roughly a century before. Americans, who now drink black teas, were once so keen to have their teas green that they willingly bought them with additives that enhanced a tea's green color. Japanese today overwhelmingly drink green teas that, when infused, produce a rich green brew. Yet in the past, a good portion of Japanese consumed green teas that yielded a brown nectar when brewed. How and why this intriguing transposition of national tastes unfolded—through interchange between the two nations and other international contexts—will be explained in this book.

———— ✧ ————

In the United States today, tea occupies a paradoxical position—less popular than coffee but in many ways denoting greater social sophistication. Meeting for coffee has informal connotations, but at a refined or formal affair, tea seems more appropriate. Exclusive hotels, like The Plaza in New York City, feature an elegant dining room or lounge where a patron can partake of afternoon tea, selecting from a menu that includes a range of teas and accompanying dishes.[5] Toy companies sell not coffee pots and mugs but tea sets, with which children can play and practice social graces.[6] Though iced coffee has grown popular in recent years, iced tea seems more elegant for summer gatherings. In the American South, "sweet tea"—iced black tea with ample sugar—has become a regional icon, suitable for family and guests.[7]

The sophisticated societal niche that tea holds in the United States can be traced to colonial times, when the beverage evoked cultural and social kinship to the British homeland. Of course, in the turbulent 1770s, tea—then onerously taxed—became a catalyst that coalesced opposition to British rule. "Tea parties," the most famous in Boston, were opening salvoes in the American Revolution. Thanks to those events, an often-repeated misconception emerged: Americans, full of patriotic ardor, turned away from tea and overwhelmingly embraced coffee, setting the latter on a path to become the quintessential national nonalcoholic beverage it is today.[8]

Beyond the colonial period, Americans are often portrayed as reluctant and uncouth tea drinkers. British writers and observers are commonly the source of such critiques, describing Americans as making egregious faux pas in the brewing and drinking of tea. Thomas J. Lipton, a Scot who established one of the world's most iconic tea brands, looked askance at U.S. tea culture. Lipton scoffed at the teas Americans consumed and with almost missionary zeal sought to persuade American consumers to drink instead the supposedly superior teas sold by his firm.[9] Historians often highlight the perspectives of other British marketers who like Lipton saw themselves as fighting to overcome American prejudices against tea and create a veritable culture of tea consumption in the United States.[10]

British marketing and advertising did, at times, influence American tastes. Yet the sense that U.S. tea culture remained static and was shaped primarily by transatlantic interactions obscures the rich and varied progression of American tea consumption.

By tracing tea from its colonial origins to its consumption in the United States today, this book will show that since independence from Britain, American "teaways"— to coin a term—emerged primarily from internal trends as well as direct ties with China and later Japan, which served as the main suppliers of tea to the United States until the early twentieth century. The most distinct American teaway—and the focus of this book—was the preference for green tea, often consumed hot with milk and sugar, that appeared around 1800 and remained woven into the American fabric until the 1940s.

I use the commodity chain—a durable historical methodology—to illuminate the intertwined domestic and international story of how Japanese green tea became so prevalent in American cups. Commodity chain shifts will also help us understand the reasons that, starting in the 1920s, American tea drinkers began to embrace black teas, then mostly produced in Ceylon and India, initiating the consumption pattern that continues to this day. Along the way, we will consider the evolution of advertising, the methods of marketing by large and small firms, and the role of the U.S. government in regulating foods and beverages. As one of the first products to face federal guidelines, tea helped form American views of what constitutes a "pure" versus "adulterated" product and illustrates the challenges of developing a regulatory regime.

Tea also presents a way to examine more closely American perspectives on East Asia and Japan in particular. In writing this book, I often encountered the misconception that Americans with a taste for Japanese green tea must have been elites swept up in the fascination with "things Japanese" that spread through much of the Western world in the late nineteenth century. Although such elite consumption was important, most American tea drinkers saw Japanese (and Chinese) green tea as an everyday, not exotic, product. As with so much of the American experience, racism also played a role. Views and stereotypes of Chinese and Japanese led Americans to choose particular types of green teas and eventually prompted them to favor the black teas that still dominate today.

Our commodity chain does not simply trace a one-way flow of tea from Japan, the producer, to the United States, the consumer. We will also examine Japanese teaways involving several types of green tea. Green tea is, of course, an icon of Japanese culture, especially in its powdered form, *matcha*. Whisked with hot water to produce a green, frothy brew, *matcha* is best known for its use in the intricate tea ceremony (*chanoyu*). Our focus, however, will be on daily habits of leaf-tea drinking

and the various factors—particularly the American shift to black teas—
that, beginning in the 1920s, made the green tea variety, *sencha*, the most
widely consumed in Japan, drunk from morning until night, so constant
a companion that it becomes an afterthought.

The Japanese end of our commodity chain—the planting, harvesting,
refining, and transport of green tea to the United States—also reveals
much about the broader course of the recent Japanese past. Japanese had
grown and consumed tea for centuries, but in the second half of the nineteenth century, U.S. demand converged with internal political and
socioeconomic developments to create a tea export industry. Exploring
Japan as a tea exporting state also provides fresh insights on the nation's
transformation as the first Asian state to industrialize and subsequently
form an empire in Asia and the Pacific.

This book's supporting "people story" of the Japanese and Americans
who facilitated the trade from production to consumption provides a
fuller picture of the roughly eighty years when Japan filled American tea-
cups. Part of that story will be told through the lives of my paternal
ancestors—first through an Englishman who, in the 1860s, developed a
tea export business based in the Japanese port city of Nagasaki. In
the 1880s, my great-great-grandfather, Frederick Hellyer, then head
of the firm, moved to Chicago because of that city's strategic location in
the U.S. tea trade. He and his children became U.S. citizens and worked
with Japanese counterparts, many of whom I will also profile, to revitalize imports of Japanese green tea into the United States in the 1920s
and 1930s.

Yet this book is not a history centered on a single family. The contributions of my ancestors form but one link in the chain of Americans and
Japanese involved in the trade—a chain that begins with the Japanese
families, some samurai and some commoners, who planted tea fields on
their small farms to take advantage of a burgeoning export trade. Their
stories are particularly important because the tea that ended up on
American tables was not produced on large plantations, as in India and
Ceylon, but on small family farms throughout Japan.

The book will also follow the contributions of Japanese brokers working as intermediaries in the shipment of teas, as well as the women who

toiled long hours in tea refining factories. The craftsmen who built the chests and the artists who made the labels attached to them are also part of this story. Next are the merchant associations and government officials who strove to expand sales of Japanese green tea by studying American tastes. They promoted their nation's teas in advertising campaigns, at world fairs, and through negotiations with U.S. government officials. Finally, readers will meet the Japanese tea retailers who marketed high-quality *sencha* to the Japanese home and imperial markets beginning in the 1920s.

On the U.S. side, in addition to tea importers, this book will discuss the large New York–based mail-order firms that helped expand tea consumption in the 1860s and 1870s, as well as the jobbers, the intermediaries who arranged shipments of Japanese green tea to retailers. It will also profile grocers who sold tea door to door, first in horse-drawn wagons and later in trucks, helping create one of the larger supermarket chains in the Midwest. Although focusing on Americans and Japanese, the book also traces the lives of others shaped by the competitive, global tea market of the late nineteenth and early twentieth centuries. Among them is a merchant from Ceylon who established his own tea import firm in Chicago, striving to break through the racial barriers that defined U.S. society and business. It will also explore the contributions of Chinese experts who aided Japanese tea farmers and provided vital knowhow for Western merchants exporting Japanese tea.

Throughout, this book shows that an examination of tea presents fresh insights on how and why cultural and social trends, as well as constructions of gender, unfolded in both Japan and the United States. In Japan, for example, teaways remained universal and largely ungendered. Americans, on the other hand, came to see many types of tea as feminine, as is revealed in newspaper articles, in literature, and in the association of tea with a grandmother or another maternal relative.

Beyond considering trends in tea consumption that spanned the United States, the book will focus on the Midwest, which in the second half of the nineteenth century was transformed by interconnected surges in population, economic expansion, and urbanization. During its age of explosive growth, the Midwest became the center of Japanese green tea consumption. Farmers and urban folk alike purchased the now lower-priced green tea, helping to "democratize" its consumption.

This challenges another misperception I often hear: Midwesterners, living in an apparently bucolic and isolated region, could not have been interested in so exotic a beverage as green tea. Such a viewpoint belies the long and varied history of tea consumption in the United States. It also ignores Midwesterners' engagement with the outside world, typified by the millions who, in the rough decade beginning in 1893, attended three world fairs—then an exciting window to the outside world.[11]

It is no doubt because of the overlooked place of tea in the American experience that I encounter amazement upon telling Americans about the now lost teaway of drinking green tea, served hot, often with milk and sugar. People from all walks of life offer a counternarrative that invariably includes an elderly relative's practice of serving black tea. These stories illustrate how much the consumption of green tea has faded from the collective American memory. Yet they also show that consuming tea, whatever the color, presents a social and familial memory marker in a nation where tea has supposedly been nothing more than an afterthought.

In writing this book, my goal is not to contradict cherished stories that emerge from the varied nature of teaways in a country as diverse as the United States. It is rather to explain how tea tells a very American and especially Midwestern story of connections with Japan and other Asian states.

In a similar vein, my Japanese friends are surprised when I describe how nineteenth-century Americans added milk and sugar to their cups of hot green tea. Yet the hardest sell is convincing them that the now forgotten American penchant for green tea helped shape today's Japanese national preference for *sencha*.

My overarching goal in this book is to break through such parochial assumptions and demonstrate that we cannot understand in isolation the histories of tea in either Japan or the United States. The forthcoming chapters thus present an entwined American and Japanese tale, spanning the Pacific in the rough century from 1850 to 1950, revealing in multiple ways how national history is inherently international.

1

THE FOUNDATIONS OF TEAWAYS IN
JAPAN AND THE UNITED STATES

I n Japan, tea has been consumed for over a millennium. Tea illustrates
a defining characteristic of the earliest epochs of Japanese history: an
initial embrace of Chinese civilization followed by the emergence of
more distinct "Japanese" practices. In the seventh century, the Yamato
court, which had come to dominate a significant portion of the Japanese archipelago, faced internal discord and threats from abroad. In
response, Yamato leaders sought to invigorate their regime by incorpo-
rating features of what they saw as a superior Chinese civilization.
They restructured court ranks along Chinese lines and implemented
Confucian modes of governance. The court and the nobility also began
to practice Buddhism, seeing it as another key to China's greatness.

Tea consumption in Japan initially developed as part of a larger
embrace of Chinese practices. In the early Heian period (794–1185 CE),
nobles offered effusive praise for tea, which was not widely cultivated and
thus an elite beverage. Mirroring their counterparts in China, they
viewed tea as "a unique and supreme device for abandoning the desires
of reality and for building a world of freedom that transcended that reality." Emperors and nobles composed verses, modeled on Chinese poetic
styles, describing the spiritual qualities contained in a cup of tea.[1]

Eisai, a Buddhist monk who traveled to China in the late twelfth century, would profoundly shape Japanese teaways. He is often remem-
bered for introducing the Rinzai sect of Zen Buddhism, a significant

contribution to Japan's religious history. Yet Eisai also returned with tea plants and seeds and a desire to share his knowledge of tea. To that end, he penned an influential treatise, *Drinking Tea for Health*. Drawing upon his observations while in China, Eisai offered instructions on how to steam and roast tea leaves to allow for their preservation in jars. He also detailed the preparation and consumption of powdered tea (*matcha*). Rather than considering it a spiritual beverage, Eisai presented tea as a health elixir, stressing that its bitter taste was beneficial to the heart and improved one's overall physical well-being.[2]

In the thirteenth century, tea came to be offered during Buddhist and Shinto ceremonies, helping further expand consumption. Court nobles and the samurai class, the latter then gaining more political and economic power, held events to choose superior teas based upon their area of production, instead of judging simply by quality, as was the practice in China. This variation formed one of the early ways that elites began to define Japanese teaways: inspired by Chinese methods but tailored to Japanese contexts.[3]

More tea fields were planted, and peasants would offer tea they had grown, along with rice and other products, as tribute payments to their feudal lords. In the fourteenth century, tea shops appeared in the capital of Kyoto. Thereafter production continued to increase until, by the sixteenth century, tea emerged as a commodity traded throughout Japan.[4]

Around that time, in an even sharper departure from Chinese practices, a group of artists and scholars developed an enduring and distinct Japanese teaway: the tea ceremony (*chanoyu*), in which *matcha* is prepared, served, and consumed in a series of intricate rituals. Samurai, both men and women, became practitioners of the ceremony, exemplifying the samurai ideal of pursuing excellence in both the martial and cultural arts.[5]

TEA DURING JAPAN'S EDO PERIOD

The Edo period (1600–1868) marked the political ascendency of the samurai class over the court nobility and the emperor. Like much of Europe at the time, Japan was not a defined nation as we understand such a political structure today. It instead existed as a diffuse polity, at the time often termed a "realm." The ruling Tokugawa house emerged as the central authority of samurai rule. Following a series of military victories in the early seventeenth century, it began to directly govern and levy taxes upon large, noncontiguous areas throughout Japan. Roughly 260 independent lords ruled the rest of the realm, controlling a patchwork of independent domains. All lords swore allegiance to the shogun, whose grand castle complex dominated the landscape in the Tokugawa capital of Edo, today's Tokyo.

The Tokugawa government, dubbed the shogunate (*bakufu*) by historians, used institutions to keep lords subservient. For example, a system of alternate attendance required lords to spend regular periods in Edo and to leave family members there as hostages to limit the possibility of fomenting rebellion. As the shogun's capital, Edo grew into a thriving metropolis, eclipsing Kyoto in size and political stature.

With the memory of the bitter internal conflicts of the sixteenth century in mind, the leaders of the shogunate also restricted the growth of infrastructure to limit possible military threats to Edo. The Tōkaidō highway served as the main thoroughfare linking the capital to Kyoto and via a spur road to Osaka, which functioned as Japan's central marketplace. Despite its importance as a transportation artery, the shogunate decreed that the Tōkaidō remain a narrow road limited to foot traffic. In addition, at strategic points, such as the crossing of the Ōi River near Mt. Fuji, the shogunate prohibited the construction of bridges to prevent their possible military use. Instead, porters ferried travelers and their belongings. Artists sketched portrayals of the crossing, including the passage of commoners and military processions of the shogun. Often disseminated in illustrated series of woodblock prints, such scenes provided artistic snapshots of life in Japan.

The political order assured Tokugawa dominance and peace within the realm. The samurai class, roughly 6 percent of the population, could thus maintain a status system with themselves at the top, ruling over the majority commoner class, which was composed mostly of rural peasants but also included merchants living predominately in cities and towns. Japan became a state with large urban centers, like Edo and Osaka, as well as smaller cities that grew around the castles maintained by

FIGURE 1.1 With Mt. Fuji in the background, porters ferry people and goods across a ford of the Ōi River on the Tōkaidō Road.

Source: Andō Hiroshige, *Shunen Ōigawa* [The Ōi River border of Suruga and Tōtōmi Provinces], from the series 36 Views of Mount Fuji (1858). Library of Congress.

individual lords. Peasants lived mainly in villages, growing rice used to pay taxes to the lords. As the Edo period progressed, they also produced more cash crops, including tea, which were shipped to urban markets.

In the seventeenth century, Uji, a town near Kyoto long known for its tea, solidified its reputation as Japan's premier tea producing region. Tea producers from Uji, an area under direct Tokugawa rule, became involved in an intriguing annual ritual. Each March, a small contingent of tea specialists, escorted by Tokugawa samurai, would depart Edo Castle headed for Uji. Traveling via the Tōkaidō, the group accompanied several large, empty tea jars, carried on palanquins, to their destination. After being filled with some of the new season's choicest teas, the jars, guarded by the small band, made their way back to Edo. Witnessed by thousands of samurai and commoners during the round-trip journey, the procession, whose members wore clothing adorned with the Tokugawa crest, publicly affirmed the shogunate as the central authority. The shogunate assigned a high rank to the tea procession among the many pageants that traveled along the Tōkaidō, such as those of the lords moving to and from Edo in the system of alternate residence. Everyone encountering the tea procession, including lords, had to stop and respect its passing. It also ritualistically presented the shogun as receiving the realm's finest tea leaves, which were ground into *matcha* and offered at numerous ceremonies conducted at Edo Castle.[6]

The Kanbayashi family, who served as the administrators of Uji, also disseminated knowledge about tea production and the tea ceremony to lords throughout the realm. For example, the Yamauchi, the ruling family of Tosa, a domain composed of a large portion of the southern island of Shikoku, welcomed a member of the Kanbayashi family on several occasions.[7]

Tosa became a well-known tea producing area. In the early Edo period, farmers began to cultivate tea on mountain slopes. Tosa peasants also produced forest commodities such as lumber, paper made from mulberry trees, and camphor used for medicinal purposes. In the 1660s, Nonaka Kenzan, the domain's chief administrator, attempted to boost domain revenue by banning the private sale of four prominent goods, including tea and paper. Under the new plan, wealthy wholesalers purchased licenses from the domain, allowing control over the market in a specific good. Amid strong opposition, fueled in part by the domain's strict enforcement of the monopolies, Nonaka's successor again permitted the free trade of tea, although he directed that a tax be levied on shipments to points outside the domain.

During the eighteenth and early nineteenth centuries, Tosa leaders continued efforts to channel profits from tea and other products into domain coffers. They made agreements with wholesalers and established a products office within the domain's administrative structure. Domain leaders were keen to control the sale of Tosa teas because of their strong reputation in many parts of the Japanese realm; some even became associated with the name of the farmer that produced them. The mountain hamlet of Ōtoyo shipped to neighboring domains various grades of green teas, along with a type of fermented tea similar Chinese pu'er tea, a variety popular throughout the world today.[8]

Tosa was one of many locales that sent teas to Osaka. Merchants from Uji as well as other areas near Kyoto, such as Yamashiro and Ise, also shipped their teas, as did counterparts from Sunpu, a province under direct Tokugawa control near Mt. Fuji. In Osaka, the number of tea wholesalers grew from thirteen in 1679 to forty-six in 1715.[9]

Edo received teas from central Honshu as well as from points to its north that remain important tea production zones today. In the early nineteenth century, the Kawagoe domain (in what is now Saitama Prefecture) began to supply Edo.[10] Sashima, located a bit further north in today's Ibaraki Prefecture, had since the mid-eighteenth century dispatched tea, often via river, to Edo wholesalers. In 1853, the Sekiyado domain, which ruled Sashima, established a domain products office to receive a greater share of the profits from the domain's tea trade.[11]

In the early Edo period, most producers throughout the realm refined tea using a Chinese stir-roasting process brought to Japan sometime in the sixteenth century. In this method, freshly picked tea leaves are roasted in a heated pan and then rolled on a mat, producing cracks in the leaves that allow the juices to flow. Several more roastings produce what is today known as *kamairi-cha*, which like other green teas has a green to slight yellow color when brewed.[12]

In the 1730s, Nagatani Sōen, an Uji tea man, pioneered a refining process that marked another milestone in Japanese teaways. Nagatani's new method produced teas with a richer green color, a process that created the *sencha* type of green tea dominant in Japan today. In Nagatani's technique, soon after the leaves are picked, they are steamed to stop the oxidation process and then quickly cooled. During the Edo and early Meiji periods, the moist leaves were then placed on a thick paper tray heated underneath by charcoal. A worker subsequently molded the tea by hand, gradually removing the remaining moisture. To produce even finer grades of *sencha*, a worker would spend four to five hours shaping a batch of tea into spindles. Other workers would then pick out stems and sort the grades of tea. The process emphasized the use of the more tender leaves that bud from tea plants in spring. Producers throughout Japan gradually embraced this "Uji method," including in Kawagoe and Sunpu. In Sashima in the early nineteenth century, Nakayama Motonari, the teenage son of a wealthy commoner family, invited an expert to teach Uji refining methods to area producers. By the mid-nineteenth century, most regions producing *sencha* as a commercial good used the Uji method, although stir-roasted teas were still made in parts of northwestern Kyushu.[13]

Early in the Edo period, Uji tea men advanced a method of covering tea bushes for part of the season, often with straw mats supported by bamboo frames. The practice produced a tea with a brighter green color and sweeter flavor. In the early nineteenth century, the finest-quality teas grown with this method were dubbed *gyokuro* (jade dew). Tea merchants in Osaka and Edo successfully marketed the new grade. Japanese would soon categorize *gyokuro* as the highest grade of leaf tea, followed by *sencha*. As they consumed more *sencha*, Japanese elites also created a version of the tea ceremony that uses leaf instead of powered tea. By the mid-nineteenth century, *gyokuro* became the standard tea for these gatherings.[14]

Yet throughout Japan, the more widely consumed variety was *bancha*, teas picked throughout the year and often composed of a mixture of stems and coarser leaves. Nakamura Yōichirō has chronicled the wide regional variations in *bancha* that still exist today, many of which can be traced back centuries. He offers, as one example, farmers from a mountainous area of Fukui Prefecture, located in central Honshu not far from the Japan Sea coast. In the late fall, farmers there harvest tea grown between rice paddies. Using a sickle, a farmer will cut branches from tea bushes, bind them into bundles with crude straw rope, and hang them to dry in a room that receives ample sunlight. In January, the farmer takes down the bundles, which are now dry and crisp, and cuts each branch into small pieces before roasting both the leaves and stems together to make *bancha* that keeps well for a year. Although classified as a green tea, when brewed, *bancha* usually produces a tea with a light brown color. Nakamura notes that the prevalence of *bancha* within Japanese society during the Edo period created a linguistic vestige—the word *chairo* (literally "tea color") is still commonly used in modern Japanese to connote the color brown.[15]

In 1859, Ōkura Nagatsune, an agronomist, penned a manual to assist farmers in producing *bancha* for domestic use and to sell as a cash crop. Recognizing it as a daily necessity, he noted that some busy farmers would purchase their tea from a shop in a nearby town. He implored them to grow their own instead and thereby save precious funds. Even those holding small plots could squeeze in four or five plants on the borders of their fields, which would grow enough tea for their family. Describing the wider market, Ōkura noted that farmers in eastern Kyushu shipped *bancha* to Osaka, where the people "consume it from morning until night." Ise also produced *bancha* and sent it via cargo ship to Edo.[16]

Residents of the shogun's capital could choose from many tea varieties in addition to *bancha*. One shop offered strong and light varieties of powdered green teas, sixteen different types of *sencha* from Uji and surrounding regions, nine varieties of lower-priced "economy" teas, and even teas made from barley and mulberry leaves.[17] The denizens of Edo, Kyoto, Osaka, and other cities consumed tea throughout the day, buying it in shops and from street peddlers. In ingeniously constructed boxes hoisted on their shoulders or conveyed by hand, peddlers carried a charcoal brazier and vessel to heat water, as well as pots and cups to serve thirsty customers. Other hawkers offered tea leaves, which they touted had been procured by searching far and wide for the best varieties.[18]

Teahouses (*chaya*) existed in many forms, at times with little relation to tea itself. In the Tokugawa-sanctioned "red light" pleasure quarters on the outskirts of Edo, some teahouses were places where clients met or were introduced to courtesans (*tayū*) and geisha, the latter a class of entertainers, skilled in dance and performing arts, that emerged in the eighteenth century. In the seventeenth century, some women working in the Edo pleasure quarters were pejoratively dubbed *sancha*, literally, "powdered tea." This differentiated them from the courtesans, the superior grade of tea in this metaphor, who unlike the *sancha*, had the option of refusing sex with a customer.[19]

The more common brand of teahouses, which centered on the serving of tea, were found especially in major cities and offered a place to sit and enjoy a cup along with a snack or quick meal. Many were also located near major temples or shrines and along major thoroughfares. On the Tōkaidō, the shogunate allowed teahouses to be set up at short intervals to meet the strong demand for tea and light meals for travelers.[20]

Now much more widely available, tea, "discovered" as a wonder drug by Eisai centuries before, had become ordinary. To cure common and serious ailments, Japanese would instead use remedies made from a range of domestically produced and imported flora and fauna, including ginseng and the skins of citrus fruits.[21] Discussions of tea and health often revolved around the pitfalls of simply missing a cup at certain times of the day. Popular poetry (*haikai*) made reference to the superstition that a morning cup of tea was necessary to forestall ill fortune, particularly for those about to embark on a journey.[22] In the early nineteenth century, prominent scholars writing about the leaf made little note of its medicinal qualities, instead focusing on how tea plants fit within frameworks of the Japanese archipelago's natural history. [23]

As the Edo period progressed, tea become truly ubiquitous in Japanese daily life, consumed at meals and throughout the day. An account penned in 1814 described a wayward traveler knocking at the door of a remote farmhouse. As a matter of accepted custom, he was welcomed and offered a cup of tea without charge. As a common, everyday beverage, tea was ingrained at every level of the Japanese social fabric, spanning class divides.[24]

FIGURE 1.2 A tea house at the entrance path to the Seiryūji Temple in the Shiba neighborhood of Tokyo in 1872. Replete with benches for customers (in the foreground), the
teahouse signs appear to advertise various types of rice cake (*hyakumi mochi*) and rice
cooked in tea (*chameshi*) as its specialties. An analysis of this image is presented in
Tokyo Daigaku Shiryōhensanjo Koshashin Kenkyū Purojekuto, ed., *Kōseisai gazō de
yomigaeru 150-nenmae no bakumatsu, Meiji shoki Nihon: Burugā & Mōzā no garasu
genban shashin korekushon* [Reviving Bakumatsu and early Meiji Japan of 150 years
ago with high-definition images: the Burger & Moser original glass photo collections]
(Tokyo: Yōsensha, 2018), 35–37.

Source: Michael Moser, Kammerhofmuseum Bad Aussee, Imagno, picturedesk.com.

CHINESE TEAS FOR COLONIAL AMERICA

Western Europeans first began consuming tea in the early seventeenth
century. Tea's progression from a luxury to a more commonplace beverage, popular especially in Britain, is a well-told story.[25] Our account
begins in mid-eighteenth-century China, which, as the sole purveyor of
tea to Western Europe and North America, formed the core of a three-
state dynamic. Thanks to a steady flow of Chinese tea into the British

Isles, Britons created their own culture of tea consumption. As colonists, Americans adopted those British practices, which formed the foundations of American tea culture. American independence at the end of the eighteenth century brought about the creation of direct U.S.-China trade, which fostered the birth of distinct American teaways.

During the latter half of the seventeenth century, the Qing, a nomadic people from Manchuria, conquered China and went on to build an expansive empire, one twice as large as the Ming empire (1368–1644) they overthrew. Under Qing rule (1644–1911), China remained the largest and most economically vital state in East Asia—and by many calculations, the world.[26]

Different from the national fiscal practices of today, the Qing imperial court maintained no central mint, and thus China used imported currencies. Silver coins and ingots—many from Japan—were common for market and tax transactions. In the late seventeenth century, the flow of Japanese silver trickled off, and subsequently China imported more Spanish silver coins, trusted by Chinese merchants because of their high level of purity.[27]

Western European merchants, such as those of the English East India Company, brought Spanish coins to obtain Chinese porcelains, silks, and, most of all, tea. In the late 1750s, the Qing court issued a series of decrees that made Canton, in southern China, the sole trading point for Western European vessels, and intercourse through the port increased in subsequent decades. British merchants bemoaned the need to bring silver to obtain tea. They also chafed under the guidelines of what historians have dubbed the "Canton system," which, for example, permitted only male merchants—and no wives or children—to reside and trade for half-year intervals in the port. Yet the British had little choice, given that China was the sole producer of tea for the world market. Britons continued to drink tea in increasing amounts, especially after the British government helped reduce retail prices by slashing duties in 1773. The English East India Company, which held a monopoly on the import of tea into Britain, also sought to sell more tea in the American colonies.[28]

In the first years of the colonies, Americans drank predominately ale and wine, but over the course of the eighteenth century, the colonists took to tea like their counterparts in the British Isles. Tea—both green and black—became widely accepted in upper-class homes; many families would share a cup or two at breakfast and later welcome guests at afternoon tea parties. A wealthy household would possess a tea table, often with a tilting top, which saved space in the home.[29] The family would keep the accepted teatime equipment close at hand: a teapot, a container for milk and cream (adding lemon was not yet common), a sugar bowl, a slop bowl (used to deposit cold tea and dregs from cups before hot tea was poured), and, of course, cups, saucers, and spoons. At an afternoon tea, the eldest daughter or youngest married woman of the house would serve the tea, and guests could sample cakes, cold pastries, sugared nuts, and preserved fruits prepared for the occasion. For younger members of the household, a tea party would often evolve into an evening of singing, dancing, or playing cards.[30]

During much of the eighteenth and nineteenth centuries, British and Americans used three main categories, adopted from those used in China, to grade and classify black tea. Much as is the case today, the categories were based upon when the leaves were picked during the year and the amount of stems present. Souchong, meaning "small" or "scarce," was the most desirable as it was made from tender—and thus more flavorful—leaves harvested in the spring. Congou came next on the quality scale because it included a greater proportion of coarse leaves. Bohea, which could be stored for a longer period, occupied the lowest rank; it had a fair amount of stems and coarse leaves harvested during the summer.

Merchants generally classified young hyson, composed of especially tender leaves gathered early in the spring, as the highest grade of green tea. Next came two varieties made from leaves also picked early in the season but hand rolled into balls by Chinese producers: the larger were called imperial and the smaller, gunpowder, because of their granular appearance. Closely behind in the quality ranking was hyson. Derived from a Chinese word for "flourishing spring," hyson was composed of leaves picked a bit later in the season and was therefore considered less flavorful than young hyson. Next came hyson skin, so named because Chinese producers made it with yellowed and other lower-quality leaves discarded, like fruit skins, when making the more valued hyson grade. Twankay, dubbed the bohea of green teas, formed the lowest grade. It was made of leaves picked later in the season, and "less care and trouble [was] bestowed on its preparation."[31]

Prominent Americans had a penchant for black and green tea varieties. In the 1750s, George Washington ordered both to be delivered to Mount Vernon. Thomas Jefferson initially enjoyed souchong black tea but later came to prefer imperial and hyson green teas.[32] Silversmiths crafted tea services with two pots of the same size, one for black and the other for green tea.[33] Bohea seems to have grown especially popular, as evidenced by its mention in the Tea Act of May 1773.[34] Colonists soon came to see that act and tea itself as symbols of perceived British oppression. Patriots in Connecticut, New York, the Carolinas, and, most famously, Boston organized "tea parties" to protest British rule. In a diary entry soon after the Boston Tea Party on December 16, 1773, John Adams recorded that the Sons of Liberty threw primarily chests of bohea into Boston Harbor, although historians have concluded that some green tea was also dumped into the sea that famous night.[35]

In tune with such anti-tea sentiments, in late 1774 the Continental Congress decreed that beginning in March the following year, a ban would be imposed on the purchase and use of any tea brought to the colonies by the English East India Company. Although the measure drew support for severing commercial ties with Britain, colonists still wanted to drink tea, and prominent merchants wished to profit from its sale. Therefore, in April 1776 the Continental Congress revised its order, allowing colonists to consume tea stored in American ports. During the late 1770s, high demand prompted smugglers to traffic in teas.[36]

The trajectory of tea consumption in the United States was especially shaped by how merchants and traders chose to pursue maritime commerce following the 1783 Treaty of Paris, which confirmed the United States as an independent nation. To obtain tea and other Asian goods, Americans could have plugged themselves into existing European networks, most being monopolies like that of the English East India Company. Yet Americans chose to capitalize on a fruit of independence: the opportunity to trade, as independent merchants, directly with valuable foreign markets such as China.[37]

By trading at Canton and returning directly to a U.S. port, American merchants would thereafter be especially attuned to shifting American tastes in tea. The newcomer Americans were aided by the fact that Canton merchants quickly took a liking to them, finding them more flexible in their approach to trade than English East India Company and other European merchant groups.[38] Canton merchants even offered American traders lines of credit to facilitate purchases of large cargoes of tea.[39] Ships from Boston, New York, and other East Coast ports brought not only Spanish silver coins to Canton but also cargoes of ginseng, which the Chinese used as a medicine and which grew naturally in New England and what is today eastern Canada. They also would stop at points along the Pacific Northwest coast to obtain sea otter pelts (prized for their lush fur) from Native Americans and in Hawai'i to acquire sandalwood (used as incense and to make fans and furniture). At Canton, U.S. traders would exchange these products for porcelains, silks, and, most of all, tea, which they transported, via the Atlantic and Indian Oceans, to ports on the East Coast.[40]

With the fledgling republic confronting serious debt, in 1789 Congress imposed a number of tariffs, including on tea, to increase revenue. It made rates higher for greens, but all types of tea incurred a lower tariff when brought on U.S. vessels as opposed to foreign bottoms.[41] During the 1790s, U.S. ships carried more black teas—especially bohea and souchong—some of which was transshipped to British and European ports.[42] Urban shops, such as the Tea Warehouse, a Philadelphia establishment operated by one Sarah Eaton, sold most of the main varieties of black and green teas.[43] As shown in figure 1.3, a Baltimore craftsman made mahogany chests with separate canisters for storing green and black teas.

As in colonial times, Americans drank tea throughout the day. George Washington, now in retirement at Mount Vernon, enjoyed several dishes (the term for cups) of tea along with cornmeal hoe cakes (aka johnny-cakes) at breakfast. For dinner, he ate a single plate of food with "five or six glasses of wine" and enjoyed a nightcap of punch or beer and one more cup of tea.[44]

FIGURE 1.3 Crafted in Baltimore, Maryland, likely between 1790 and 1810, the tin canisters of this mahogany chest were used to store various types of black and green teas. In England, the middle cannister often served as a sugar container.

Source: Collection of the Museum of Early Southern Decorative Arts,
Old Salem Museums & Gardens, Winston-Salem, North Carolina.

AMERICANS DEVELOP A PREFERENCE
FOR GREEN TEAS

After 1800, Americans began to consume more green than black teas. It is not entirely clear why this change transpired, but available trade statistics show U.S. ships began carrying more greens than blacks beginning in the 1805–1806 season.[45] U.S. traders were no doubt motivated to bring green teas because even with steeper tariffs placed on them, green teas fetched significantly higher retail and thus presumably wholesale prices. In 1804 in Philadelphia, imperial sold for $1.76, hyson for $1.40, but bohea for only 30 cents a pound.[46] Because of disruptions caused by the War of 1812, hyson later commanded even higher market prices, in August 1813 selling for $1.95 in Baltimore and a whopping $3.00 per pound in Savannah, Georgia.[47] Throughout the country, tea retailers ran advertisements that listed green gunpowder and imperial as well the three varieties of hyson before black souchong and bohea teas.[48]

The price difference and order in advertisements probably reflected the growing reputation of green tea as a more exclusive and elite product. Americans of lesser means, such as those living in a Philadelphia poorhouse, drank inexpensive bohea but only a small amount of hyson.[49] A family living on a plantation on the James River in Virginia regularly consumed bohea but reserved hyson and young hyson for special occasions.[50]

Newspapers also carried references to green tea's prestigious image. In a blistering condemnation of the first two years of Thomas Jefferson's presidency, in May 1803 the *Trenton Federalist* printed an editorial packaged as a letter to the president from a "Friend of Christianity." The editorial lambasted Jefferson for raising taxes and apparently increasing the salaries of government officials:

Instead of relieving us of our taxes, you have only taken the taxes off *whiskey, loafsugar, coaches,* &c while they still remain on *salt* and other necessaries of life which the common people use and cannot live without. Think, great sir, how the indignation of the poor must be raised to see you, and all the rich and luxurious, riding in your coaches, drinking your wine, your *hyson* and *green tea,* sweetened with *loafsugar,* while we *farmers* and poor people, that labor hard to raise your bread and your beef and pork to maintain you, can't get one bushel of salt, one gallon of molasses, nor a pound of tea or sugar.[51]

YANKEE TEA PARTIES

Like their colonial predecessors, Americans continued to embrace the social ritual of the tea party, which according to some accounts would now include a vast array of products from around the world. A writer mused that the tea he or she imbibed at one gathering was "a specimen of the soil and workmanship of a land and people on the other side of the globe" sweetened with West Indies sugar that "had cost many a day of toil to the poor slave, dragged from beyond the equator, from his own date tree and hut, amid the wastes of Africa, to spend his life in thankless servitude, that this luxury might pamper our tastes." The author also noted the nuts from Jamaica, the oranges from Havana, and the Sumatra pepper sprinkled on his or her oysters, remarking that "in truth with the exception of bread and butter and a slice of beef steak, very little of American growth was consumed that night."[52]

Americans also developed new styles of tea parties, replete with popular elements that distinguished them from the largely upper-class affairs of colonial times. In 1819, a town on Massachusetts's South Shore held a "country tea party," an event organized and attended exclusively by women. Earning extra money by knitting stockings, groups of women would pool their funds to make cakes and other sweets for such regularly convened events.[53] The *Saturday Evening Post* proclaimed that such tea parties embodied the democratic essence of the young republic. The magazine gushed that "no royal gala, levee, or formal rout, where the gilded insects of fashion vainly sip the sweets of enjoyment . . . can compare to the wholesome joy, the gabbling music, the pies, nutcakes, slapjacks, and cookies of a yankee tea-party." Its participants prepared by first charging the "smartest urchin among the household" with delivering invitations. Mothers and daughters threw themselves into a flurry of baking, and another family member was "despatched to the grocers for some of the very best green tea with the useless but unfailing injunction to ask him first 'how much it is a pound.'"[54]

In Southern states as well, gatherings over tea remained popular, especially in Virginia, Georgia, and the Carolinas. Members of the plantation aristocracy often held women-only tea parties at which green tea was apparently often served. A wealthy South Carolina family recorded regularly purchasing green tea and possessed silver tea services and porcelain ware for tea gatherings. At some parties, hosts served punches made with a green tea base and enhanced with fruit juice and liquor. A

Kentucky housewife shared her recipe for another punch that could be served hot or cold: bring to a boil a pint and a half of "very strong tea" and pour it on a pound and a quarter of loaf sugar. Next add a pint of "rich sweet cream" and finish by stirring in a bottle of claret or champagne.[55]

Such recipes notwithstanding, there is little indication of a standard American style of consuming tea, either green or black, that would as a matter of course include milk and sugar, as is the case with, for example, chai consumed in India since the 1960s (and, in recent years, a type of tea popular throughout the United States).[56] Neither have I found any early-nineteenth-century reference suggesting that a cup of green tea—today often considered spoiled by the addition of milk and sugar—was to be consumed straight. At tea parties and in private, Americans made individual choices about what to add to their tea. Many probably chose to include milk and sugar because long steeping made their teas bitter; housewives were counseled to let a pot of tea steep for ten or fifteen minutes.[57]

When weighing the addition of milk and sugar, Americans appear to have been concerned about the possible positive or negative health benefits—a question raised in numerous periodicals. The *Boston Medical Intelligencer* identified no difference in the effects of green and black teas on the body but concluded that green tea "is much more apt to affect the nerves of the stomach than [black tea] more especially when drank without cream, and likewise without bread and butter."[58] Another New England newspaper stressed that physicians had determined that "if good tea be drank in moderate quantities, with sufficient milk and sugar, it invigorates the system, and produces a temporary exhilaration, and a clearness of ideas."[59] Americans also debated the general health benefits of tea. An 1826 newspaper article summed up the broad range of ideas and opinions: "there is no subject which has occasioned a greater controversy amongst dietetic writers than the subject of tea. By one party it is decreed a poison; by another it is extolled as a medicine, and a valuable addition to our food."[60]

Green tea often received special attention given that—according to one widely cited rumor—it allegedly contained prussic acid, "the most dangerous of all poisons."[61] By contrast, the *Boston Medical Intelligencer* summarized a positive appraisal by W. Newnham, a British author, who believed green tea to hold medicinal benefits. Based upon uncontrolled experiments, Newnham concluded it helped with headaches and even trauma. He administered a strong dose of green tea to a woman with a concussion and asserted it had aided her recovery. Newnham also found that "swallowing a strong infusion, one ounce of gunpowder tea to a pint of boiling water," alleviated his own severe headache. The Briton concluded that green tea produced such effects because it was a sedative. (The Boston reporter demurred, noting that "many persons in health cannot drink a cupful of hyson tea in the evening without losing some hours of sleep.")[62]

AMERICAN KNOWLEDGE OF
TEA PRODUCTION

Culinary guides counseled Americans to strive to purchase teas of the best quality, which would look "firm and glossy" and have a "strong fragrant smell." "The best of green tea will look smartly green in the cup, after it is drawn, and good black tea will look dark," although black teas were said to produce "considerably weaker" brews than greens.[63]

Although definitions of quality teas were emerging, Americans appear to have possessed limited knowledge of the refining techniques that made greens distinct from black teas. Newspapers and periodicals were not helpful, offering contrasting and sometimes alarming descriptions. One periodical reported that a traveler who had visited China concluded that green teas were "unwholesome" because Chinese producers used copper sheets or plates to dry them and enhance their green color.[64] An agricultural monthly debunked such reports. It more accurately advised readers that a study recently published in London by "a member of the royal institution" had shown that Chinese tea men actually dried their tea on porcelain, and thus green tea was free of poisons and safe to consume.[65]

American tea drinkers were not unaware that Chinese producers added minerals and pigments to give a richer, green color to some exported teas. One writer advised that green teas are "unwholesome from being often coloured with Prussian blue or smalts [cobalt glass], and are likewise extremely astringent and corrosive. The Chinese, I observed, very seldom drink of them."[66]

In the late eighteenth century, Chinese tea refining operations in Canton first began adding Prussian blue to teas destined for Western markets. Developed in Western Europe earlier that century, the pigment gained its name because of its use as a blue dye for Prussian military uniforms. Canton-area producers initially relied on the English East India Company to import Prussian blue from Europe. Kate Bailey, an art conservator, has uncovered evidence that in the 1820s Chinese entrepreneurs, in response to increased demand, built a factory in Canton to manufacture Prussian blue, thereby effectively ending the company's imports and assuring a steady supply for use in the tea export trade.[67]

William Alcott, an author of numerous books on health matters and a critic of tea (which he termed a poison) found little fault with Chinese adding Prussian blue—instead placing blame on U.S. consumers. "We have reason, at the least, to *suspect* that a large share of the teas imported, are damaged or worthless teas, *manufactured to suit the market. The Americans must have tea, and the Chinese, an accommodating people, are ready to furnish them with it!*"[68] If concerned about possible coloring, a consumer could consult a manual providing specific tests to detect coloring in black and green teas alike: Japan earth (*catechu,* a brown dye made from tree bark) added to black tea and green vitriol (sulfate of iron) to green tea.[69] Americans also read reports of their coffees and teas being adulterated, coffee with peas and beans and tea with leaves from willow and sloe (blackthorn) trees.[70]

However, commentators claiming to have studied tea in depth found little evidence that such practices were widespread.[71] Reports from Canton stressed that despite the prodigious volume of tea produced in China for domestic consumption and export, "there is proportionably but little garbling or deception practiced in this article."[72] In later chapters, I will explore issues of coloring and adulteration in depth. Suffice it to say here that colored varieties had become part of the panoply of green teas marketed in the United States, increasingly noted in price lists along with hyson, imperial, and other grades.

Despite naysayers like Alcott, Americans continued to consume increasing amounts of tea, with imports nearly doubling from 8.6 million pounds in 1830 to 16.3 million pounds in 1836. Alcott noted that green teas composed nearly three-quarters of all the teas brought to the United States and lamented that imports overall would continue to increase. The American preference for green tea contrasted from that of Britain, where in 1836 black tea composed the vast majority—close to 80 percent—of all teas imported.[73]

In 1833, the federal government encouraged the nation's tea habit by eliminating duties on all teas imported by U.S. vessels.[74] The year before— apparently prompted by Secretary of War Lewis Cass, an adherent of the temperance movement—the secretary of the navy encouraged the consumption of tea on naval vessels by directing that it be offered, along with coffee, sugar, and even cash, as a substitute for the liquor ration. The change seems also to have been implemented at the U.S. Naval Asylum in Philadelphia. During the 1840s and 1850s, retired sailors living at the asylum received weekly allotments of green (unroasted) coffee along with young hyson, which they preferred over black teas. The pensioners would drink coffee with breakfast, ice water for dinner, and tea for supper.[75]

Yet while ice water was a part of meals, iced tea does not appear to have been widely consumed.[76] An article reprinted in newspapers throughout the country presented it as a beverage discovered by a man traveling to Russia. During the hot summer days, he had enjoyed it with a slice of lemon and recommended it be served "well sweetened, with good milk, or better, cream in it . . . with the whole mixture cooled in an ice chest to the temperature of ice water."[77]

Although difficult to determine definitely, the American thirst for tea seems to have kept pace and at times even surpassed that of coffee. Based on analysis of U.S. trade statistics, the historian Dan Du argues that assuming many people reused leaves of both green and black teas to brew multiple pots, on average Americans drank more cups of tea than coffee throughout much of the nineteenth century.[78]

AMERICAN TEAWAYS MOVE
WEST—AND DIVERSIFY

As the United States expanded westward, newcomers to the frontier states brought the tea habit with them. In 1831, John M. Roberts moved his family from New York State to a farm near Peoria in central Illinois. In diary entries for 1835, Roberts records purchasing a pound of tea for a dollar, along with five pounds of coffee for the same price. We can gauge the price of tea relative to other goods by noting that on the same shopping trip, he purchased a clock for $15, postage of 37 cents for two letters, and nails for two dollars. Three years later, he bought one half-pound of tea (green or black was not specified) for 50 cents, along with (presumably a pound of) loaf sugar for 68 cents—items that the "Friend of Christianity" in his diatribe against President Jefferson in 1803 claimed were beyond the means of a farmer.[79]

Further south in Illinois, a young Abraham Lincoln and his wife, Mary, also regularly bought tea at a Springfield store. The Lincolns proved inveterate green tea drinkers, apparently consuming one half-pound of gunpowder each month. One day in April 1845, the family purchased a half-pound of gunpowder for 75 cents and for 31 cents bought whalebones and hooks and eyes, items used in sewing garments.[80]

After 1850, Americans also began to consume oolongs, teas oxidized to a level roughly between greens and blacks. It is unclear why oolong, produced mainly in Fujian Province in southern China, began to appear on the U.S. market during the 1850s, but it soon became a mainstay in tea shops in New York and other East Coast cities.[81] At their local grocers, Americans also increasingly encountered a new black tea brand called "English breakfast." Some accounts ascribe it as a blend created by a New York merchant in 1843; others contend it was simply a new moniker to enhance the image of low grades of Congou tea.[82] In any case, English breakfast appears to have been a decidedly American invention. In 1852, a New York retailer advertised grades of young hyson for 50 and 75 cents a pound, "curious oolong tea" for 50 cents, and English breakfast for 37 cents.[83]

The appearance of English breakfast and oolong illustrate how, over roughly the first half-century of the republic, American tea consumption had moved beyond the British-laid foundations of the colonial era. Gatherings for tea also included particular American flairs, whether they were the women-only affairs of New England or Southern parties at which green tea punch was served. Most of all, Americans continued to affirm the national preference for green teas, which included new varieties, notably those with additives to enhance their green color.

THE U.S. TEA TRADE EXPANDS

Beginning in the 1820s, the English East India Company brought increasing amounts of Indian opium to Canton to meet burgeoning Chinese demand. As a result, British merchants could use less silver to obtain tea and, in fact, began to carry silver away from Canton. Britain's military victory over China in the Opium War (1839–1842) and the treaties signed thereafter allowed the Western European sea power to codify its commercial advantage. Britain gained the island of Hong Kong as a colony, and five Chinese coastal cities were designated as "treaty ports," with Shanghai emerging as the most prominent.

Under the new treaty port system, commerce was now conducted under the auspices of Western-style "free trade," eliminating the guidelines and restrictions set by Qing officials. For example, Western merchants could now bring their families and live year round at foreign concessions—autonomous urban zones—directly administered by their home governments. In what increasingly came to be seen as an infringement of national sovereignty, the treaties forbade the Chinese government from altering the newly established tariff rates. Overall, China now held a weaker commercial position vis-à-vis Britain and, later, the United States and other Western European nations that signed similar treaties with the Qing regime.

To acquire more sustained revenues from maritime commerce, the Qing, with the backing of Western diplomats, established the Imperial

Maritime Customs Service in 1854. Although an official organ of the Qing regime, it was staffed largely by Westerners. In 1858, Horatio Nelson Lay, the son of an early British consul in China, became its first inspector general. He thereafter drafted plans to quickly expand the Customs Service's reach to other treaty ports (plans we will explore in the next chapter).[84]

Despite the concessions it made following the Opium War, China continued to hold a commercial advantage as the sole exporter of tea to the world market—a position that shaped the immediate impact of the new treaty port system on Anglo-American trade. In 1844, Robert Forbes, a prominent Boston merchant, cautioned that "the prospective extension of the China trade, in consequence of the opening of four new ports, is very much over-estimated." He advised that "we must materially increase the consumption of tea and silks in this country, before we can expect to enlarge materially our trade with China; and the same remark applies to Great Britain." Forbes concluded that "therefore it is clear, that we can only sell in China, profitably, just as many goods as will pay for the articles of export from China, which we respectively want."[85]

Forbes proved prophetic. When, several years later, Anglo-American trade with China did expand, it was largely driven by a surge in U.S. and British tea consumption. In 1849, the United States imported just over 18 million pounds of tea, a figure that soared to 40.2 million by 1856. Over the same period, Britain's tea imports nearly doubled, swelling from 47.2 million to just over 91 million pounds.[86] As Forbes predicted, the Anglo-American demand for tea (and to a smaller degree, silk) enabled China to import more opium and British-manufactured cloth. Nonetheless Anglo-American imports to China failed to offset completely their increased purchases of tea, requiring British and U.S. ships to again bring large cargoes of silver.[87]

During the 1840s and 1850s, the U.S. merchant fleet began to include the iconic clipper ships, which had less cargo space but a larger total sail area than other ships of the era. Thanks to these enhancements, clipper ships became renowned for their speed in traversing the globe. They fed the growing U.S. demand for tea, which continued to be purchased from China mainly with silver. Departing New York, Boston, or another East

Coast port, a clipper would sail around Cape Horn, often stopping in a South American port, such as Valparaiso or Lima, to take on silver.

The journeys of two vessels give a sense of the scale of the transpacific silver trade. In October 1848, the clipper ship *Sea Witch* loaded just over $126,000 in silver bars and coins at Lima, Peru, before making its way to Canton. Two years later, another U.S. vessel, *Congress*, stopped at Valparaiso, Chile, where it took on silver and copper (and some gold) valued at over $120,000, which it transported to Canton.[88] A British or U.S. company with offices in Canton would use the silver to obtain tea, often sending representatives into tea producing regions.

A clipper loaded tea as its return cargo, sailing via the Indian Ocean and around the Cape of Good Hope. In the Atlantic at a point just south of the Equator, ships would diverge for either New York or London. In 1849, the British government reformed its navigation laws, allowing ships sailing under any national flag to offload tea at British ports. The move prompted many U.S. ships to transport tea to London, and U.S. clippers became famous for their speed, carrying cargoes of tea from Canton to London in around one hundred days.[89]

U.S. clipper ships also set records transporting tea to New York. *Sea Witch* reached New York just seventy-four days after leaving Canton. Another clipper that wrecked off Long Island in 1856 was laden with $300,000 worth of teas and silks, giving another indication of the value of cargoes carried by vessels sailing from China.[90]

INCREASING U.S. INTERACTION WITH JAPAN

The 1840s and 1850s also marked the expansion of the United States across the continent to the Pacific coast. The resolution of the Oregon dispute with Britain in 1848 confirmed U.S. political control of the territories that would become the states of Oregon and Washington. Two years later, California entered the Union. Many in the United States hailed this expansion as confirming Manifest Destiny—a divinely anointed right to control much of North America from coast to coast.

The 1840s also witnessed a growing U.S. presence in Hawai'i, precipitated by rising demand for whale oil, which was used to lubricate machinery and keep lamps burning. The whaling boom continued throughout
the 1850s and made Honolulu a provisioning and exchange center for
U.S. Pacific trade.[91]

In pursuit of whales, U.S. whaling ships also began to sail in waters
around Japan. Imperiled by a storm or an incident at sea, members of
whaling crews might find themselves shipwrecked on a Japanese shore.
In his 1851 novel, *Moby-Dick*, Herman Melville presented whalers as a
force that would reshape Japan's interactions with the outside world. He
proclaimed that "if that double-bolted land, Japan, is ever going to
become hospitable, it is the whale-ship alone to whom the credit will be
due; for she is already on the threshold."[92] Melville's quote has often been
used to present a case of national extremes: a "closed," traditional, and
unchanging Japan versus a vigorous, dynamic, and modern United
States.

Such contrasts seem less persuasive when we when compare demo-
graphic, political, and economic aspects of the two states. In 1850,
the United States and Japan were certainly not comparable in territory; the United States encompassed over 2.9 million square miles,
dwarfing Japan's roughly 142,000 square miles. Yet in overall population and level of urbanization, the differences may be surprising: the
U.S. population had reached just over 23 million, with New York being
the largest city, with approximately 500,000 people. By contrast, the
islands of Japan held 35 million souls, with one million living in the
metropolis of Edo (today's Tokyo).[93]

Nonetheless, early-nineteenth-century Japan's population was static,
in part because of the persistence of famine, which other Eurasian states
had largely avoided since the early eighteenth century.[94] Famine contributed to peasant uprisings and political tensions throughout the
realm. The U.S. population, by contrast, fueled in part by immigration, expanded by 35 percent from 1850 to 1860.[95] The burgeoning population was one factor in the growing U.S. demand for tea during that
decade and, as we shall see in later chapters, would help make the
United States the prime market for Japanese tea.

U.S.-JAPANESE TIES FORMALIZED IN THE 1850s

The most well-known encounter between the United States and Japan in the nineteenth century came with Commodore Matthew C. Perry's mission. Departing in 1852, Perry sought to secure permission for U.S. whaling and commercial ships to visit Japanese ports to obtain provisions and make repairs. He also hoped to establish repatriation protocols for U.S. castaways (often from whaling ships that wrecked in waters near Japan) and create avenues for U.S. commerce.

Calling at a port near Edo in the summer of 1853, Perry delivered a letter addressed to the Japanese emperor penned by President Millard Fillmore. In it, Fillmore noted that "our Territory of Oregon and State of California lie directly opposite to the dominions of your imperial majesty. Our steamships can go from California to Japan in eighteen days." He also speculated (correctly, as it would turn out) that Japan had coal in "great abundance," which he envisioned would supply U.S. steamships increasingly plying Pacific routes. Fillmore cleverly painted an image of U.S. commercial energy surging across the Pacific, one bolstered by the presence of well-armed steamships in Perry's naval squadron. The U.S. side hoped that the display of military power might push Japanese leaders to establish commercial and diplomatic ties.[96]

Despite internal dissent, Tokugawa leaders signed with Perry the 1854 Treaty of Kanagawa, which allowed for limited trade at a port south of Edo as well as at Hakodate on the southern coast of Hokkaido, then the northern frontier of the Japanese state. In 1858, another U.S. envoy, Townsend Harris, negotiated a more expansive commercial agreement, the U.S.-Japan Treaty of Amity and Commerce. Modeled on the bilateral pacts imposed by Western nations on China a decade before, the treaty also afforded U.S. citizens extraterritorial rights, meaning that if charged with a crime in Japan, the accused American would be held and tried according to U.S. law. The agreement allowed Americans to reside in the treaty ports of Hakodate, Yokohama (near Edo), and Nagasaki, a port in Kyushu. The treaty also directed that tariffs for almost all imports be fixed—in 1866 the rate became 5 percent—without clear stipulations for when duties might be revised. Tokugawa officials later signed similar agreements with Britain and other Western European states.[97]

Of the three ports "opened" in 1859, Nagasaki had by far the longest history as a center for foreign trade. The Tokugawa regime directly administered the port and in the 1640s had ordered that only ships of the Dutch East India Company and Chinese merchants be permitted to call and to maintain trading outposts. Throughout the seventeenth century, Nagasaki served as a center of Japan's silver-for-silk trade with China, which because of a diminishing supply of silver, the shogunate at first curtailed and then eliminated during the mid-eighteenth century. Nagasaki merchants thereafter exported copper and select marine products—sea cucumbers, shark fins, kelp, and abalone—which were in demand for their culinary and medicinal uses in China. In return, Japan imported medicinal products made from various plants and animal parts, valued because they came from China, the trusted source of medical knowledge. This trade with China remained the mainstay of commerce at Nagasaki and initially offered the most lucrative trading options for British and U.S. merchants arriving in Nagasaki in 1859 (to be explored in the following chapter).

The importance of trade with China explains why Japan—despite its extensive cultivation of tea—did not focus on exporting the leaf during the Edo period. Like their forebears had for centuries, Japanese traders looked primarily to the wealthy and powerful Qing empire as a commercial partner. This stance displayed neither a lack of vision nor a closed mindset. Rather it was born of Japan's long and valuable connections with China and the economic realities of the age. Japanese producers had little incentive to pursue tea exports and compete with their East Asian neighbor, then the world's dominant tea producing and exporting state.

That calculus changed in the 1860s with the convergence of two major developments: rising demand for tea in the United States and, in Japan, the recently inaugurated trading regime with Western nations. These events helped open a new era in the global history of tea—a story to which we will now turn.

2

TEA AMID CIVIL WARS

n February 1863, the *Chicago Tribune* reported that a ship from Yokohama had docked in New York City, bringing the first direct shipment of Japanese tea to the United States. The newspaper described the new arrival as bearing a "close resemblance to the finest green tea of China, known as Moyune, differing chiefly in this, that it is perfectly pure and free from coloring matter. While the Japan tea is not deficient in strength, it possesses a great delicacy and softness of flavor which has already made it very popular with the nicest judges."[1]

Within a few years of this auspicious debut, enterprising New York tea merchants had made Japanese green tea a popular part of American teaways, as well as the only variety of tea named for its nation of origin. As this chapter will show, growing U.S. demand stimulated the development of a Japanese tea industry that included an international mix of British, American, Japanese, and Chinese participants. That Japanese industry emerged even amid domestic turmoil, as the Tokugawa shogunate and powerful domains jockeyed for the upper hand. During the 1860s, their competition turned increasingly violent, leading to a series of armed conflicts and eventually a short but bitter civil war. Such divisions, and the treaties Japan had signed with Western nations a few years earlier, created openings for enterprising Westerners to come to Japan and help create the new tea industry.

A YOUNG BRITON'S PATH TO A TEA TRADER

One such Westerner was William Alt, who in 1853 at the age of thirteen decided to make a life on the seas. His father, an officer in the British army, had died, and young William needed to help support his mother and three younger siblings. He probably made his way to the London docks, with its extensive array of warehouses containing a wealth of imported goods, including large amounts of Chinese tea. Alt would have found in the docks one of the "few places in the metropolis where men can get employment without either character or recommendation."[2] His search was aided by members of the Hellyer family, into which his half-sister, Barbara, had married in 1845. The Hellyers had long worked as carvers and craftsmen, supplying specialized equipment and parts to shipyards in southern England. They were therefore likely acquainted with many ship captains and others who made their lives on the sea.[3]

Young Alt eventually secured a position as an apprentice on the *Charlotte Jane*, a ship that transported goods and people around the globe.[4] Like the clipper ships crossing the Pacific, the *Charlotte Jane* also moved silver and tea. In April 1852, she carried £30,000 in coins from London to Adelaide. For the return trip that July, the ship loaded what an Adelaide newspaper called "one of the most valuable cargoes ever despatched from the province": gold and copper worth "no less a sum than £238,000," including a significant amount of gold dust from Australia's burgeoning goldfields.[5]

Alt grew up aboard the *Charlotte Jane*. On stopovers in Britain, he brought his family tales of his travels and mementos from various lands, such as coral collected on the island of St. Helena.[6] In October 1857, the *Charlotte Jane* arrived in Shanghai, from where Alt posted a letter home, updating his family about his most recent voyage. The now seasoned sailor speculated that his ship would load tea for its return voyage to Britain.[7]

While in the Chinese port, William, then seventeen, made the acquaintance of a Portuguese merchant who had become wealthy from the tea trade. Looking for help with his commercial enterprises, he

FIGURE 2.1 William J. Alt, circa 1865.

Source: Collection of Glover Garden, Nagasaki, Japan.

proposed that Alt remain in Shanghai under his employ. After much vacillation, Alt decided to leave the *Charlotte Jane* and become a merchant involved in Shanghai's burgeoning commerce with the outside world.[8] The decision changed the course of his life; he would spend the next fifteen years in East Asia. He worked two years in Shanghai, briefly for the Portuguese merchant, then as a clerk in a British firm, and eventually landed a job in the Imperial Maritime Customs Service. The service's inspector general, Horatio Nelson Lay, was then ambitiously adding personnel, with the aim of establishing branch offices in other Chinese treaty ports. Yet after only a few months, Lay failed to realize his expansion plans, making Alt redundant. He received a letter of reference from Lay, which praised the work ethic of the young Briton, and severance pay totaling roughly $400.

Alt explained in a letter to his mother that—"having nothing to do in Shanghai" and "not being able to lead an idle life"—he had decided to seek new opportunities in Japan. His destination, Nagasaki, was then opening as a treaty port and thus was an apt choice for a young man filled with ambition. Alt prepared well, securing a position as the Nagasaki agent for Shanghai's *North-China Herald* newspaper and obtaining a letter of recommendation from the Shanghai office of the prominent British trading firm Jardine, Matheson and Company.[9] The captain of the ship that carried him to Japan was so impressed with the young man's enterprise that he invested $1,500 in Alt's planned business ventures. Shortly after his arrival, Alt ran an advertisement in the *Herald* announcing that from early January 1860 he would serve as "a *General Commission Agency* at this port [Nagasaki]" and soon thereafter established his own trading firm, Alt and Company.[10]

DEVELOPING A TEA EXPORT TRADE

Alt and other British and U.S. merchants, eyeing ways to build commercial links with their home countries, took the lead in developing Japan's tea export trade. British and U.S. merchants anticipated that Japanese green tea would be well suited for the green tea–dominated U.S. market. They also calculated that supplies from Japan could help overcome expected shortfalls in Chinese production caused by the Taiping Rebellion, a civil war that raged from 1850 to 1864, taking the lives of millions.[11]

In Nagasaki, Thomas Glover, a Scottish merchant, emerged along with Alt as a prominent tea trader. Glover founded his company while working as an agent for Jardine, Matheson and Company. Although competitors, Glover and Alt worked together on issues concerning the Nagasaki foreign community and built adjacent Western-style homes on a bluff in Nagasaki. Today both are part of Glover Garden, a famous tourist attraction.

The treaties signed in the 1850s between the shogunate and Western nations afforded Western merchants many commercial rights but prohibited them from traveling outside the small foreign concessions created in the treaty ports. They therefore worked with native brokers, who purchased teas and arranged for their shipment to Nagasaki or Yokohama, the other main port for export. Although some brokers worked independently, many were often associated with larger wholesale houses based in Edo or Osaka, which operated branch offices in the treaty ports.

In Nagasaki, Alt probably purchased tea from Ōura Kei, a broker who had sold the leaf to Dutch merchants several years earlier. Ōura is a remarkable historical figure: a woman who by selling Nagasaki-area teas to Westerners achieved financial success in a male-dominated, Nagasaki commercial scene. In a memoir written late in life, Ōura counts Alt as one of her earliest customers, coming to Nagasaki in 1856 to purchase tea. This is unlikely, given that the *Charlotte Jane*, the British ship on which the then sixteen-year-old Alt served, would have been prohibited by Tokugawa regulations from calling at Nagasaki. Nonetheless, more detailed accounts from the early 1870s indicate that Ōura often sold tea and other products to Alt and Company, suggesting that a business relationship had blossomed in preceding years.[12]

Further north in Yokohama, Ōtani Kahei emerged as a prominent tea broker and eventually a wholesaler. He hailed from a town famous for its teas, located in a mountainous area of Ise Province not far from Kyoto. The youngest son of a peasant family, Ōtani received a rudimentary education in a Buddhist temple, a common practice of the time. In his youth, he witnessed other young men pursue opportunities as merchants in Edo and, after 1859, in the newly created Yokohama treaty port. He yearned to leave life in his small village and, much like Alt, used family connections to secure in 1862, at the age of nineteen, a position with an Ise wholesaler trading in tea and other local products in Edo and Yokohama.[13]

Ōtani later gained employment in a U.S. trading firm, Smith, Baker and Company. In 1867, the company tasked him with overcoming unexpected shortages in tea available for export. Using personal connections and working with his former wholesale firm, in just three months

Ōtani acquired an estimated 92,000 pounds of tea, mostly in the area around Ise and Kyoto. He arranged for its shipment by boat from Osaka to Yokohama, thereby saving the day for Smith, Baker and Company. Garnering a large financial reward for his efforts, Ōtani opened his own tea wholesale house and established himself as a key figure in the Yokohama export trade, where he became renowned for his ability to locate quality teas and deliver them to foreign export firms.[14]

CHINESE-STYLE JAPANESE
GREEN TEA—FOR AMERICANS

When tea from Kyoto and other parts of Japan reached Nagasaki or Yokohama, Western exporters supervised the necessary additional refining, as well as packing and shipment. Alt and Glover displayed their business acumen in raising the necessary capital to start their respective firms in Nagasaki. Nonetheless, in achieving success the Britons depended on the knowledge and experience of Chinese experts in the processing and packing of tea for export.

Tea flowing into Nagasaki or Yokohama was harvested from late April to early September. Farmers would make at least two but sometimes three pickings, although new-growth leaves picked in the first harvest were considered the most tender and desirable (as is the case today). Farmers would quickly expose the harvested leaves to heat (either by steaming them or placing them briefly in a heated pan), which stopped the oxidation process and allowed the leaves to remain fresh for several months for transport and sale on the domestic market.[15] Brokers and wholesalers, like Ōura and Ōtani, would purchase that lightly refined tea from farmers, sorting it into different grades. They would offer samples of various teas for representatives of Western firms to judge and purchase according to their estimates of U.S. market demands.

The first direct shipments of Japanese tea to the United States seem to have been of tea that had undergone little additional refining and thus generally free of coloring agents. Yet Chinese experts guiding the

FIGURE 2.2 In the first stage of what Westerners dubbed "country tea processing," a Japanese farm family steams a batch of freshly picked tea leaves (on the right) and then dries them to stop the oxidation process.

Source: Yokohama Archives of History, Yokohama, Japan.

process no doubt impressed upon their Western and Japanese colleagues that to successfully export tea on a large scale, additional "firing" was necessary so that, after storage and transit by sea, Americans would not open a moldy chest of tea. Under Chinese supervision, two methods came to be widely used. The first was "pan firing," which involved placing the tea into an iron pan inlaid into brick stands and heated by a charcoal brazier underneath. Another method, "basket firing," entailed placing a tray on top of a sturdy bamboo basket that rested over a charcoal brazier. The basket would conduct heat and steam up to the tray. In both styles, a standing worker would gradually stir the tea until the requisite amount of moisture was removed. Chinese experts often oversaw the capstone stage of adding Prussian blue or other coloring agents to make the fired tea, which often turned yellow or gray under the intense heat, green and palatable for British and U.S. consumers. The importance of Chinese experts to the tea export trade and, indeed, all commerce through Nagasaki is underscored by the fact that during the 1860s, Chinese always outnumbered Westerners in the port city.[16]

Alt had wisely hired several Chinese.[17] Glover initially resisted this path. In a missive sent to Jardine, Matheson and Company offices in Shanghai, the Scot lamented having to pay higher wages to Chinese workers. He tried employing less expensive Japanese laborers but found them lacking the necessary expertise, forcing him to pay skilled Chinese to teach their Japanese counterparts the refining processes.[18]

Glover and Alt each built factories in Nagasaki, employing hundreds during day and night shifts that refined and packaged tea as it flowed into the port. Chinese experts oversaw the layout and construction of these industrial facilities, taking refining practices usually conducted outdoors in China and placing them inside high-ceilinged buildings within the Nagasaki foreign concession.[19] In late 1860, Alt invested £2,000 to build his first factory, which apparently began operation the following year.[20] In the summer of 1862, he boasted that in a few months his factory would expand to "employ about 1000 men, women and children on our premises picking and packing teas." He explained that "we are of course obliged to build several more large warehouses to do this [process teas]—one 110 feet x 45 feet and two stories high—all this walks away with lots of money but it will all come again by and by. Business as you can imagine is therefore better than it was."[21]

In 1864, Alt married Elisabeth Earl, the daughter of George Windsor Earl, a former English India Company official and scholar of Southeast Asia, whom he had met on board a ship. Elisabeth joined him in Nagasaki, where they would start a family.[22] She later recalled visiting Alt and Company's tea refining factory, humming with activity late into the night. Relating her observations of an apparent combination of the pan and basket firing methods, she noted that

there were hundreds of copper pans of red hot charcoal and over these were being dried the raw green leaves of tea, jerked from side to side of large flat baskets—never still for a moment. The large high building lighted by flares of some kind, the burning charcoal, the misty dust or steam from the leaves, the perspiring men and women, the former almost quite naked, the latter naked to the waist—it was an inferno! Then added to these sights there was a din of indescribable noise— packing of the tea seemed to be going on in the same great hall or shed, packing seemed mostly to consist of the wooden chests into which men were pouring the already "fired" tea being shaken violently from one side to the other to make the tea settle down.[23]

Imitating Chinese practices, workers like those seen by Elisabeth Alt placed refined tea, either loose or in one-pound packages, in lead-lined wooden chests. The chests weighed up to eighty pounds and were wrapped in woven rattan for extra support. Over the rattan were attached labels, often illustrated with flower motifs mimicking Chinese patterns.[24]

By the mid-1860s, Alt and other Western traders, working with brokers and wholesalers like Ōtani and Ōura, had laid the foundations of a new tea export industry. Under the guidance of skilled Chinese, Alt and Company and other Western export firms sent to the United States what is best classified as "Chinese-style, Japanese green tea." This type of tea would remain a mainstay of Japanese exports for several decades.

With shipments dispatched from Nagasaki, Alt would sometimes include boxes addressed to his mother in London. Seeming to allude to the British preference for black teas, on one occasion he told her to expect "two or three more boxes, same as before. We don't make *Black Tea* but I suppose *Green* and *uncolored* is welcome enough."[25] Alt was, after all, focusing his business on the green tea–dominated U.S. market.

TEA TAKES A BACKSEAT: NAGASAKI BECOMES AN ARMS-TRADING CENTER

The creation of Japan's export business took place during—and was inevitably affected by—the domestic unrest building throughout the

Japanese archipelago. On a snowy night in early 1860, the shogunate looked suddenly vulnerable when Ii Naosuke, who had recently assumed a top leadership role just below that of the shogun, was assassinated outside a gate of Edo Castle, the bastion and symbol of Tokugawa power. The samurai band who executed the bold attack—akin to assassinating the vice president on Pennsylvania Avenue outside the White House—was composed of men from several domains. They had bonded in their disgust with Ii and other Tokugawa leaders, who they believed had overstepped their authority by signing treaties with Western nations without the approval of Emperor Kōmei. The band, representing a growing number of samurai throughout Japan, sought a larger governing role for the emperor, who, like his predecessors since the early seventeenth century, wielded only limited power in the realm's political system. These "loyalist" samurai, so called because of their commitment to the emperor, also opposed the presence of Westerners on Japanese soil, leading to the rallying cry: "Revere the emperor and expel the foreigner."

In Edo and the treaty ports, loyalists began to attack Westerners. Bands struck against diplomatic legations, and in September 1862 near Yokohama, samurai from Satsuma killed a British merchant, Charles Richardson. In response, the British government pressured the shogunate to force Satsuma to pay a sizeable cash indemnity for the incident. Britain also dispatched naval vessels to Yokohama. To prevent further attacks, the shogunate assigned men to guard Western commercial establishments and legations in the treaty ports.

Among those Yokohama sentries was Tada Motokichi, a low-ranking samurai whose family served as a direct vassal to the Tokugawa house. Growing up in what is now Chiba Prefecture, Tada studied fencing in Edo as a teenager. We know little about his life until 1860, when, at the age of thirty-one, he joined the guard detail, a position he would hold for five years.[26] We can only speculate what interactions, if any, Tada and others on guard detail had with the Westerners ostensibly under their protection.

Alarmed by the presence of Western gunboats in Japanese waters, the leaders of the shogunate also took measures to improve Japanese maritime defenses. To help lords have more funds for defense, in 1862 the shogunate reduced the frequency with which they were expected to travel to Edo in the system of alternate attendance; the number of days required to stay in the capital was also lowered.[27] Reflecting the gravity of the internal situation, Tokugawa leaders made similar reductions in the ceremony of transporting Uji tea to Edo.[28]

In addition, the leaders of the shogunate in Edo no longer required domain lords to receive permission from them to acquire warships and large sailing vessels; thereafter lords could freely purchase ships from Westerners through the mediation of shogunal magistrates at the three treaty ports.[29] The policy change proved a tremendous boon for Alt, Glover, and other Western merchants. Nagasaki became a ship emporium; between 1863 and 1870, 106 ships were sold there, compared to just fourteen at Yokohama.[30] The trade in ships, and later arms, occupied just under half of all imports by value in Nagasaki from 1864 to 1868, well exceeding another key import sector: manufactured cotton cloth and clothing. Tea, though still a steady export, failed to match the value of imported ships and arms. For example in 1865, over $157,000 worth of tea was exported, while imports of ships, arms, and ammunition that year totaled close to $915,000.[31]

Alt profited handsomely from the sale of ships and subsequently branched out to sell arms. Glover became especially active, selling ships and—against the wishes of leaders of the shogunate—arms to the Chōshū domain. He also established a trading relationship with Satsuma, which in 1866 made a secret pact with Chōshū to challenge Tokugawa rule.[32] The Chōshū leadership, dominated by men discontented with the shogunate, hurried to strengthen their domain's defensive posture as the shogunate prepared to launch a punitive expedition. The leaders of the shogunate sought to rebuke Chōshū for its continued military and political forays and to ensure that the domain would no longer pose a threat to Tokugawa dominance over the Japanese realm.

Since the beginning of the Edo period, the shogunate, although the central authority, had not maintained a national army, as was the case in Western European nations. During times of internal disturbance, the shogunate had ordered lords to mobilize men from their domains to quash an uprising or threat. Yet because of the gravity of the external and internal threats that emerged in the 1860s, the leaders of the shogunate began to form dedicated shogunal units, organized along structures employed by Western armies. The shogunate directed these units, as well as forces mustered by lords, to move against Chōshū.

Early in 1866, Tada Motokichi became a foot soldier in one of the shogunate's new infantry platoons and was dispatched to Osaka, Kobe, and to the front on Chōshū's eastern border. Tada was involved in battles around the city of Hiroshima. He kept a memento—a battle plan of that campaign—which remains in his family's possession.[33]

The Chōshū forces, outnumbered but enjoying better weaponry and superior élan, repulsed the shogunal land and naval forces sent against them in June and July 1866. Tokugawa leaders, reeling from their battlefield losses, used the death from illness of Shogun Iemochi in August as an excuse to halt their failed military expedition. Tokugawa Yoshinobu, a key figure in attempts to revitalize Tokugawa rule in previous years, became the new shogun.[34]

As internal divisions brewed, leaders of domains like Tosa sought to bring more funds into their treasuries to help gain stronger positions in the competitive political and military environment. Tosa leaders established the Kaiseikan, a multipronged program designed to increase the domain's profits from commerce. Opened in the castle town of Kōchi, the Kaiseikan included a school where students would learn English and French, offices to expand whaling and mining, and an industrial department to promote the production of camphor, paper, sugar, and tea. Tosa leaders aimed to expand sales of those goods within the Japanese state and hoped to develop overseas markets as well. To facilitate such plans, they sought to acquire ships to transport goods. Like their counterparts in Chōshū, the Tosa leadership anticipated that such vessels would also prove valuable for military uses, given the turbulent internal situation.[35]

In 1866, Gotō Shōjirō, a high-ranking samurai, led a Tosa contingent to Nagasaki and met with Alt and other Western merchants.[36] Gotō established a domain office in Nagasaki and delegated a lower-ranking samurai, Iwasaki Yatarō, to handle future business deals. During the summer of 1867, Iwasaki oversaw Tosa purchases, often on installments spread over a few months, of several steam and sailing ships from Alt and Company.[37] In lieu of cash payments, Iwasaki often provided Alt with domain goods, especially camphor, Tosa's most lucrative product at the time. Alt most likely also received tea as payment.[38]

Meanwhile, during the summer and fall of 1867 leaders from powerful domains increasingly put pressure on Shogun Yoshinobu to return some power to the imperial court, which he did in November, along the lines of a plan drafted by Gotō. Concerned that the move might lead to disorder, Yoshinobu recalled shogunal military units to the capital, including one stationed at Hakodate, of which Tada Motokichi was a member.[39]

On January 3, 1868, samurai from Chōshū and Satsuma staged a coup at the Kyoto Imperial Palace, "restoring" the Emperor Meiji, then only fifteen years old, to a dominant political position (his father, Emperor Kōmei, had died suddenly in 1866). The men behind the coup described their act as a revival of the ancient order, in which the emperor would thereafter rule as his predecessors had done during the days of the Yamato court in the seventh century. The coup, although commencing what was unquestionably a revolutionary period in Japanese history, therefore came to be known as the Meiji Restoration.

Chōshū-Satsuma leaders presented themselves as establishing an imperial government and dubbed their military units "imperial forces" to enhance their prestige. Not accepting the power grab, Yoshinobu mobilized shogunal troops as well as loyal lords. Together they moved against Chōshū-Satsuma contingents near Kyoto, commencing the Boshin War (1868–1869). The Tokugawa force lost decisively in a three-day engagement around Kyoto. Yet pro-Tokugawa groups and domains in northern Honshu continued to resist. Some aimed to restore Tokugawa rule, while others feared that the Chōshū-Satsuma alliance would establish an unfriendly military regime along the lines of the toppled shogunate. To prepare for anticipated deployments, Tada Motokichi and his unit received training in the use of cannon, although he did not see further combat.[40]

In July 1868, Chōshū and Satsuma samurai, supported by comrades from Tosa, defeated a pro-Tokugawa group, the Shōgitai, during a one-day battle in Edo, effectively ending armed opposition to the alliance's

FIGURE 2.3 Tada Motokichi circa 1880.

Source: Kawaguchi Kuniaki, *Chagyō kaika: Meiji hatten shi to Tada Motokichi*
[The Creation of the Tea Industry: Tada Motokichi and the History
of Meiji Era Expansion], (Tokyo: Zenbō-sha, 1989), 19.

control of the capital. Nonetheless, throughout the fall of 1868, battles
raged in areas along the Japan Sea coast. In the castle town of Aizuwakamatsu in northern Honshu, samurai of the Aizu domain fought along
with commoners in a desperate and ultimately futile attempt to hold off
Chōshū and Satsuma units. In the spring of 1869, Chōshū, Satsuma, and
aligned divisions vanquished the remaining Tokugawa stalwarts, who
made their last stand in a Hokkaido fortress. Following that victory, the
new central government could begin to assert a more definitive control
over Japan.

This history underscores how the tea industry emerged despite Japan
facing grave, internal divisions that culminated in the Boshin War. The
next chapter will follow the "postwar" lives of Tada Motokichi and members of pro-Tokugawa groups, such as the Shōgitai. These samurai and
their families would become farmers, producing tea for the American
market.

TEA IN A UNITED STATES AT WAR

From 1861 to 1865, the United States was also in the throes of a civil war. Unlike Japan, long a patchwork of feudal domains, the United States had existed as a unified nation for some eighty years. In the U.S. Civil War, two regions battled over the future of the nation: would the southern Confederate states achieve independence and preserve slavery, or would the northern Union be able to restore national integrity and move to eliminate America's "peculiar institution"? Historians have detailed and analyzed the conflict in countless studies, accounts that need not be revisited here. Instead, I will focus on how events in the war shaped trends in tea consumption and established new distribution channels for the movement of tea throughout the United States.

Soon after hostilities commenced, the Union imposed a naval blockade to choke off imports of food and military supplies into the Confederacy, as well as exports of cotton, the South's most lucrative product. Because of the blockade, those in Confederate states quickly found tea scarce and expensive. In mid-October 1861, grocers in Winchester, a town in northern Virginia, charged two dollars a pound; by late November, the price had climbed to three dollars.[41] As tea grew harder to obtain, newspapers advised readers to use blackberry leaves to make a "sweeter flavored brew than the best quality China green" and suggested raspberry leaves as a substitute for hyson tea.[42] Another publication suggested that tea drinkers should gather and dry sassafras blossoms because "by many who have tried it, it is pronounced to be a most delicious and palatable beverage."[43]

The Union blockade extended up the Mississippi and its tributaries, severing established flows of agricultural products down the river to New Orleans. In response, merchants in the North began to ship products via expanding rail networks fanning out across the Northeast and Midwest. Chicago emerged as a rail hub, becoming an emporium for agricultural goods. Emblematic of its growth, the city soon eclipsed Cincinnati and St. Louis as a center of the meatpacking industry.[44]

On Christmas Day, 1863, the *Chicago Tribune* boasted that Chicago had not only overtaken the aforementioned "elder sister" cities but had been "progressing as a Market for the great staples of the world, to an extent far surpassing the brightest dreams of the wildest enthusiast among us." In fact, "there has been steadily growing up in our midst a branch of Commerce which, large as it is at present, so far as the Western states are concerned is only just in its infancy. We mean none other than the Tea Trade." The article stated that the residents of Illinois consumed 1.5 million pounds of tea each year, "by which the far larger portion is that commonly known as green." The *Tribune* noted that the Chicago Tea Warehouse, recently established by a group of prominent grocers, was poised to take advantage of emerging markets to Chicago's west.[45] With such plans, Chicago merchants could draw upon an already strong base of consumption in the city. Chicagoans enjoyed wide access to various green teas, and diners at hotel restaurants could choose between black or green teas at breakfast.[46]

Union soldiers also appear to have consumed a fair amount of tea. A manual published just before the war provided detailed instructions to army cooks for brewing batches to serve twenty-five men. It directs a cook to use

> 12 quarts of water, [and] put the rations of tea—a large teaspoon full to each—in a cloth tied up very loosely, throw it into the boiler while it is boiling hard for a moment, then take off the boiler, cover it, and let it stand [a] full ten minutes, when it will be ready to use; first add sugar and milk if to be had at the rate of 3 pints to 2 quarts, a pound or a pound and a half of sugar.[47]

Another handbook advised that oolong was best for "general army use" because it was not as astringent as black teas and less stimulating than greens.[48] Military hospitals provided green tea to patients.[49]

As tea continued to flow into Union ports, federal leaders levied duties to help finance the war. In 1861, they twice raised tariffs on tea, followed by an increase to 25 cents per pound in 1864, which garnered approximately $6.6 million in revenue that year.[50]

THE BIRTH OF THE JAPAN TEA BRAND

Like other New York retail tea vendors, the Great American Tea Company, founded in 1859, began to sell Japanese teas. An 1864 company price list offered customers Japanese teas of "every description, colored and uncolored," along with numerous varieties of Chinese green and black teas.[51] The Great American Tea Company revolutionized the U.S. retail trade, especially by spending lavishly to promote its brand of teas and coffees. In large newspaper advertisements, Great American boasted of selling teas at lower prices by bypassing wholesalers and providing teas directly to consumers. This was an exaggeration: the company was not an importing house and had no agents in China or Japan. Yet it proved a powerful promotional device that ignited sales. The company also advanced the practice of mail-order buying clubs, where a group would submit a combined order, thus saving on shipping costs. Great American strategically promoted club buying in religious weeklies, farm journals, and professional publications. Overall, the company demonstrated the power of brand marketing, quickly gaining a national profile as its profits soared.[52]

Following the lead of newspapers, Great American, along with other New York tea retailers, titled Japanese green tea "Japan Tea," thereby christening a distinct new market category. Since colonial times, Americans had chosen among categories defined by Chinese producers and Western merchants trading in Canton: imperial, hyson, gunpowder, and bohea being the most prominent. Seeing a retail opportunity, New York tea sellers created in Japan Tea the first "national" tea brand on the U.S. market. American tea sellers and Japanese producers alike would use the Japan Tea brand for nearly a century. Its wide adoption and longevity resulted from yet another convergence of events unfolding in the United States and Japan in the 1870s and 1880s, events explored in the coming chapters.

3

MAKING JAPAN TEA

At length, this "cruel war" is over; but for what space of time Japan is destined to enjoy the blessings of peace is exceedingly problematical.

—DISPATCH FROM YOKOHAMA TO THE *NEW YORK HERALD*,
JULY 28, 1869

Such was the conclusion of a U.S. newspaper reporter upon learning of the victory of the Chōshū-Satsuma alliance at the Battle of Hakodate, which ended the Boshin War. The reporter explained that "so far the revolution has succeeded. In the space of eighteen months, the whole form of the government has been changed." He or she described the Tokugawa house as "entirely demoralized" and its leaders confronting the fact that "glory has departed from their house." Nonetheless, the reporter speculated that rivalries within the Chōshū-Satsuma alliance, and especially dissatisfaction among lords over central government reforms, would soon renew armed clashes.[1]

Disputes within the Chōshū-Satsuma leadership would in fact contribute to unrest—but not for close to a decade. Building upon their victory, the Satsuma and Chōshū men leading Japan's new central regime, dubbed the Meiji government by historians, were able to solidify their political position in part by appeasing displaced lords. Ruling as oligarchs, they moved quickly, implementing a series of expansive economic, political, and social reforms that brought to fruition the revolution begun with the palace coup in January 1868 and set Japan on a path to become a more unified nation.

This chapter will detail how the emerging tea export industry contributed to the success of those reforms and thus the formation of the modern Japanese nation. In the years immediately following the Boshin War, more fields were planted, and transportation networks grew to bring increasing volumes of tea to major ports. New refining facilities were built to process and pack the tea for shipment. These sectors of the Japan-U.S. tea commodity chain—the first phase in the actual making of the product that would be sold as Japan Tea in the United States—brought fresh employment opportunities and thus avenues for personal reinvention across Japanese society, helping salve the socioeconomic and political wounds of the war and the dislocations brought by Meiji government reforms.

Meanwhile in the United States, advancements in advertising, prejudice against Chinese tea and Chinese in the country, and a comparatively more positive view of Japanese and "things Japanese" paved the way for Japanese teas to gain popularity among U.S. consumers. Japan Tea, the moniker created by New York retailers, was made into a distinct and durable category on the U.S. tea market, a brand adopted and promoted on the American and Japanese sides of the transpacific trade.

TEA IN A POST-CIVIL WAR UNITED STATES

At the end of the Civil War, the victorious Union leadership sought to reunite the nation and ambitiously create a more equal American society, one in which freed slaves could participate fully as citizens. The Reconstruction amendments to the U.S. Constitution (the Thirteenth, Fourteenth, and Fifteenth) abolished slavery and expanded rights of citizenship and equal protection under the law. In addition, the amendments

offered provisions intended to prevent future central and state governments from denying citizens the right to vote. Federal leaders in Washington sent troops to Southern state capitals to ensure that local officials
would not subvert reforms. They also sought to foster the participation
of freedmen in the political process.

While implementing those social agendas, leaders in Washington also
faced the task of literal reconstruction: a four-year conflict had taken the
lives of over seven hundred thousand souls and left in ruin major Confederate cities such as Richmond, Fredericksburg, and Atlanta.[2] Aware
also of the federal government's debt incurred from the war, in
March 1865, a month before General Robert E. Lee's surrender at Appo-
mattox, the U.S. Treasury Department formed a three-man commission
to assess the revenue system, including tariffs on tea, which had been
increased during the war. The commission's report, issued six months
later, concluded that retaining a levy would not dampen consumption
because "tea is probably less affected in price to the consumer, by any
increase or decrease in duty, than any other article that enters into consumption by civilized peoples." The report's authors noted that in Britain during the previous fifteen years, importers and middlemen had kept
prices constant even when duties were slashed. Believing that the U.S.
market held the same price dynamics, they advised that a lower tariff of
10 cents per pound remain on all imported tea. Aiming to maintain a
consistent revenue stream, federal government leaders ignored the suggestion, leaving in place the existing 25-cents-per-pound rate.

The three commissioners highlighted contrasting British and U.S.
consumption patterns, emphasizing that working-class Britons consumed tea three times a day, replete with ample helpings of sugar, as a
"substitute for other and more concrete food," while Americans drank
it less frequently and more as an accompaniment to food.[3] They also
noted the rise in consumption of Japanese teas during the Civil War and
anticipated their continued growth.

In addition, the report's authors stressed the profits of jobbers, which
often were small-scale operations with limited capital who purchased
teas from importers and sold it to retailers, at times on an ad hoc basis.
Jobbers thus competed with larger, better-capitalized wholesalers who

cultivated longer-term relationships with retailers.[4] In their report, the commissioners asserted that profits taken by jobbers and retailers "by far [made up] the largest proportion of the cost of tea to the American consumer."[5]

The Great American Tea Company, which as we noted in the previous chapter had increased mail-order sales and used creative marketing slogans, continued to take advantage of the significant profits available in the tea retail trade. In 1869, the Great American expanded under the name of a twin firm, the Great Atlantic and Pacific Tea Company. Popularly known as the A&P, the company soon opened stores in sixteen U.S. cities, including the growing metropolis of Chicago. Around 1870, the A&P began marketing its own tea brand, Thea-Nectar, described as "a pure black tea with green tea flavor" sold in half- and one-pound packages.[6]

A&P's advertising of Thea-Nectar and price lists from the decade after 1865 affirm that U.S. consumers continued to favor green over black teas. At prices ranging from 50 cents to $1.40 per pound, Great American offered the standard green tea categories of imperial, hyson, and gunpowder, along with oolong and a mixed black and green tea. The company classified oolong as a black tea but marketed only one true black tea, English breakfast, which included an asterisked warning: "we do not recommend the purchase of English Breakfast Tea, unless the party ordering it is accustomed to its use. Its peculiar flavor will not please those unaccustomed to using it."[7]

No such provisos were offered concerning Japan Tea. Great American sold four grades of it, ranging from 80 cents to $1.10 per pound. The American and China Tea Company, a competitor located on the same New York street, offered several grades of Japan Tea, priced from a dollar to $1.50 per pound. (Neither store stated what differentiated the various grades of Japan Tea or other varieties.) The American and China Tea Company proclaimed its natural-leaf Japan Tea "very fresh" and shipped "overland from Yokohama," which indicated that it was transported by rail from San Francisco instead of arriving by ship in New York.[8]

As the market expanded, U.S. retailers came to sell Japan Tea in three main categories: uncolored, basket fired, and pan fired. Despite its name, uncolored tea often included coloring agents, as did pan-fired teas. Only

The above is an engraving of a pound package of our Japan Tea. All our Teas are packed in a similar style. AMERICAN AND CHINA TEA COMPANY.

The American & China Tea Company,

No. 39 VESEY STREET,

P. O. Box 4263.   *NEW YORK.*

All Orders are Sent off by this Company on the Day of their Receipt.

Examine with care the following

LIST OF PRICES.

They will be found to be Pleasant and Profitable Reading.

OOLONG, a very good Tea	$ 80	HYSON, a good and strong Tea.....$ 90
" a good family Tea	90	" a fine-flavored Tea.........1 00
" a very choice Tea	1 00	" an excellant Tea.............1 25
" fine garden growth	1 25	" a very superior Tea........1 50
" very rich, finest in market	1 50	" very rich, handsome leaf...1 75
MIXED, good useful Tea	90	YOUNG HYSON, a good Tea......... 90
" fine family Tea	1 00	" a fine family green Tea......1 00
" Hyson and Oolong, very fine..1 25		" superior fine-flavored Tea.....1 25
IMPERIAL, a good Tea	90	" rich, strong, and pure flavor..1 50
" pure bold leaf	1 00	" very finest imported.........1 75
" very superior	1 25	ENG. BREAKFAST, good and strong..1 00
" finest imported	1 50	" strong and rich....1 20
GUNPOWDER, good useful Tea	1 00	" very finest imported.......1 50
" very fine flavored Tea....1 25		JAPAN, fine delicate flavor.........1 00
" strong and rich Tea....1 50		" rich, fine Japan flavor.......1 25
" best to be had at any price.1 80		" very finest imported.........1 50

SPECIALITIES.

The following are imported direct by us, and sold in the original One Pound Packages, having been grown and packed especially for our trade:

NATURAL LEAF JAPAN, very fresh, overland from Yokohama $1 40
KIANGSI OOLONG, very fresh.......1 30

COFFEE LIST

Whole, Roasted, or Ground, in one pound packages.

Rio..30 cts.
Breakfast and Dinner................30 cts.
Old Government Java...............40 cts.
Finest Old Mocha.....................50 cts.

All these Goods may be had of our Agents, who charge a small Commission of five cents for each Package, just enough to pay freight.

FIGURE 3.1 An 1870 Japan Tea package of the American & China Tea Company. The company's price list illustrates the predominance of green tea varieties on sale. Like the A&P, the company sold a good portion of its teas through club and mail orders.

natural leaf or basket fired was potentially free of coloring agents, the latter producing a tea with a pale olive color when infused.[9]

As these examples show, Japan Tea sold at prices comparable to Chinese varieties. And as we noted in the previous chapter, beginning in the early 1860s most Japanese teas were refined using Chinese practices, which included the addition of coloring agents. If price and distinction from Chinese varieties were not factors, why did U.S. consumers choose Japan Tea over established types of Chinese teas?

Prejudice against Chinese teas seems to have been the biggest factor. Writing in the 1880s, Joseph Walsh, a Philadelphia tea merchant, concluded that the rapid increase in demand for Japan Tea emerged because the "first receipts were of the choicest kinds, and [because there was] the strong prejudice then existing against Chinese green teas under the impression that coloring matter was used extensively in the preparation of all green teas."[10] Echoing other observers, Walsh stressed that Chinese tea merchants used coloring agents to mask the inclusion in export shipments of bogus leaves (those from non-tea plants) or exhausted leaves already used to make tea. By contrast, he gave Japanese producers the benefit of the doubt, asserting that their coloring agents were harmless and "only used in the preparation of poor teas, for the purpose of making these inferior sorts salable and pleasing to the eye."[11] In other words, Japanese producers used coloring agents to meet American preferences, but Chinese sought to hoodwink tea drinkers into purchasing teas of substandard quality.

Walsh identified a contradiction in the tastes of American consumers—their embrace of the first shipments of Japanese teas for being less refined and uncolored—and then in a turnabout, their acceptance of Japanese teas enhanced with coloring agents. Contemporary observers puzzled over the American taste for colored teas, which apparently emerged as something of a fad. The U.S. consul in Kobe concluded that around 1870 Americans began to demand colored varieties. He stressed that Japanese producers, respecting the delicacy and fragrance of their product, saw colored teas as an "abomination" but reluctantly provided them to U.S. consumers.[12] A reporter writing in the *Chicago Daily Tribune* reinforced that conclusion. He or she noted that "the United States is a nation of tea-drinkers" and that "in a great many families tea is on the table three times a day." The reporter concluded that especially women chose higher-priced, colored green tea over black teas. He or she mused:

> It is one of the curiosities of the trade, as well as of human nature, that people should deliberately prefer Prussian blue and gypsum in their tea at the high price to the pure article at a low price, and shows that people have so hardened and depraved their tastes, that, like confirmed whiskey-drinkers, it is only the adulterated article that gives them any satisfaction.[13]

Literature introducing Japan also made note of the American preference for colored teas, such as a book, directed to young readers, that followed two fictional American boys on an imagined study tour of Japan.

Upon visiting a Yokohama tea refining factory, the boys witness workers putting into firing pans "a teaspoonful of some coloring substance that they keep secret." When one boy inquires why such additions were necessary, a factory supervisor explains,

> it was to make the tea sell better in the American market. It looked so much better when it had been "doctored" that their customers in New York and other cities would pay more for it, though they knew perfectly well what had been done. Then he showed me some of the tea that had been fired and put side by side with some that had not. I must say that the fired tea had a polished appearance that the other had not, and I could readily understand why it sells better.[14]

At their tables, U.S. tea drinkers employed brewing techniques that may have made one oblivious to the presence of Prussian blue or other coloring agents when the tea was poured into a cup. A guidebook for young housewives published in 1870 suggested that when making tea, one should first "scald your teapot with boiling water, and allow a teaspoon of tea for each person and one over. Pour enough boiling water on the tea leaves to rather more than wet them. Let it stand fifteen minutes; pour on as much boiling water as will serve to each of the company." The guidebook also counseled that after it was brought to the table, the tea should be kept boiling by placing a spirit lamp (which burned alcohol or another liquid fuel) under the pot. Such practices probably diluted chemical additions or led them to collect as sediment in the bottom of the pot.[15]

TRADE CARDS, LABELS, AND PREMIUMS

We can see more fully the depth of sentiment against Chinese teas, as well as trace trends in the tea industry, by examining advertisements and promotional practices. In the early 1870s, the founder of Great American and the A&P, George Gilman, started including mass-produced chromolithograph prints in packages. Customers would collect the prints, placing them in albums or in frames hung on their walls. Gilman thereby advanced the idea of a premium, a small token or gift added to a purchase, a practice that thereafter became a key part of the retail tea trade.[16]

Around the same time, trade cards, which also tapped into a consumer desire to collect, began to be widely used by U.S. tea shops and wholesalers. In the first few decades after the Civil War, newspapers and magazines gave limited space for product advertisements. Therefore, many tea merchants and grocers used trade cards to deliver information to consumers. Originally developed in Britain, a trade card included an image, often a lithograph print on one side, and information about the product and the retailer on the other.[17] Great American and the A&P distributed a wide range of trade cards, many times in the form of multicard series, which sported images of natural landscapes, humorous situations, or famous individuals such as U.S. presidents. On the card's flip side, the A&P would offer information about its stores, prices, and ordering information.

Images on A&P trade cards defy easy thematic categorization. One includes a grandmother in her parlor about to drink tea or coffee from a saucer. Next to the image a caption reads, "The Great Atlantic and Pacific Tea Company's Teas and Coffees have been my solace throughout my life. Grandmother." The card's opposite side gives information about A&P stores and states that teas, including "Japans," sell for 50 cents per pound. Another six-card series depicts a dog and a monkey drinking alcohol and playing cards before descending into a fight that leads to their arrests. The reverse sides of the cards list A&P stores throughout the United States.[18]

The dog-and-monkey series may have been an attempt to appeal to customers embracing temperance. The A&P produced another series of six trade cards illustrating a bar patron ordering various drinks, growing intoxicated, and engaging in a brawl with the bartender and other patrons before being arrested and ending up remorseful in a jail cell, with only bread and water as solace. Under each image, the card advises that such lamentable incidents are "the result of not using the Great Atlantic and Pacific Tea Company's celebrated teas & coffees." Nonetheless, it is challenging to see the temperance movement as a driving factor in expanding post–Civil War tea consumption. Temperance literature, while detailing similar tales of woe that resulted from alcohol, emphasized the benefits of "pure sparkling water" over tea and coffee, and the virtues of water formed a consistent refrain in songs sung at the movement's gatherings.[19]

Temperance literature also included illustrations showing prejudice against Chinese. A flier advertising a temperance picnic, probably from the 1870s, has in one corner a seemingly random image of a Chinese man brewing tea over a campfire and lists as one of the picnic's songs "The Heathen Chinee."[20] Drawn from a poem published in 1871, the ballad, which includes a line referencing the fear of being "ruined by cheap Chinese labor," tells of a card game between two men, one American and one Chinese. The poem casts particular ridicule on the Chinese man, whose trickery of hiding cards while feigning a lack of knowledge of the game is eventually uncovered.[21]

Trade cards distributed by U.S. tea and coffee sellers drew on similar racial stereotypes with images that mocked Chinese for their appearance and English-speaking skills. The Union Pacific Tea Company, based in New York and with outlets throughout the Eastern Seaboard and Midwest, issued a card with a crudely sketched Chinese man, identified by his queue, stumbling on a cat's tail. The text reads, "Chinaman stepee on cat's tailee and break Melican man's plate." Another card shows an overweight Chinese man, sitting on a tea chest, holding a steaming cup of tea and telling a distressed, Uncle Sam–like white man: "Melican Man he mus dlink Tea an den he get so Fat like me."[22]

The historian Robert Jay notes that images of Chinese, while less prevalent than the racial stereotypes of Black and Native Americans used in post–Civil War trade cards, often had a sharper edge, reflecting racial anxieties and prejudices of the period. In 1875, Congress passed the Page Act, a law named for a California congressman that restricted entrance into the United States by Chinese men, who often came as contract "coolie" laborers, and Chinese women, who were suspected of seeking to enter the country for "lewd and immoral purposes," namely,

FIGURE 3.2 Distributed by the New York–based Union Pacific Tea Company, this trade card, probably from the 1870s, exemplifies the often racist portrayals of Chinese in tea advertisements.

Source: Warshaw Collection of Business Americana—Tea, Archives Center, National Museum of American History, Smithsonian Institution, Washington, DC.

to engage in prostitution. Jay points out that anti-Chinese sentiment, while strongest on the West Coast, was then gaining adherents in Eastern cities, where lithographic printers and large tea retailers were concentrated.[23]

The use of such mocking images by merchants selling Chinese teas is puzzling—why deprecate the people of the producing country? We can speculate that U.S. consumers may have viewed such images, with their emphasis on the use of broken English, as directed at Chinese in the United States and not specifically at Chinese in China producing the teas sold on the U.S. market.

PORTRAYALS OF JAPANESE IN TEA ADVERTISING

Robert Jay notes that trade cards generally presented Japanese more generously, a trend evident in those distributed by tea retailers.[24] Remer's Japan and China Tea Store in Syracuse, New York, printed a card with an image of a Japanese man and woman, in traditional garb, drinking tea next to a drawing of a port with a mountain on the horizon, described as "Holy Mountain—Japan" (evidently Mt. Fuji). The shop also issued cards with a Japanese courtesan holding a teapot, another with a man making tea, and still another with a Japanese couple in kimonos heading to a tea gathering.[25] For its part, the A&P employed Japanese-style scenes of a woman in a kimono holding a fan and another of a kimono-clad woman pouring tea for a woman in Western dress.[26]

We can also glean information about perceptions of Japan Tea, as well as its marketing, through the labels affixed to chests (holding up to eighty pounds of loose tea) and to small packages (usually weighing one-half or one pound). In contrast to U.S. shops that used the newest lithograph technology, printers in Japan had initially designed and produced these labels in the treaty ports using woodblock printing methods perfected during the Edo period. Most of the labels include "Japan Tea"

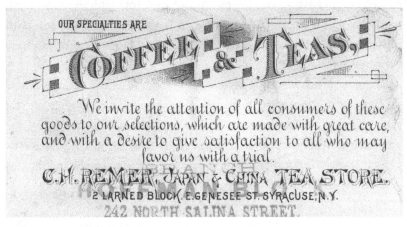

FIGURE 3.3 Likely printed in the 1870s, this trade card of the C. H. Remer Tea Store in Syracuse, New York, illustrates the comparatively more positive presentation of Japanese and Japanese tea during that decade.

emblazoned prominently, along with information about the refining method, such as "natural leaf" as well as "pan" or "basket fired."

An intriguing array of Japanese images adorned some labels, including a woman eating soba noodles and a sketch of an "Aborigine," an Ainu, the native people of the northern island of Hokkaido, an area then being politically and economically incorporated into Japan. As with trade cards, it is challenging to find overarching messages about Japan Tea conveyed through these labels. In fact, perhaps the only consistent "Japan theme" may be the prevalence of Japanese women in kimonos picking or drinking tea as well as undertaking various household and farming tasks.[27]

In using such images, Western export firms may have sought to take advantage of U.S. cultural trends that emerged with Japan's expanded intercourse with the outside world. Many U.S. and Western European artists were influenced by Japonisme, the fascination with Japanese works of art. Wealthy Americans eagerly purchased Japanese or Japanese-inspired costumes, décor, and crafts. They also acquired Japonaiserie objects—decorative swords, fans, and vases. Moreover the idea of "playing Japanese" gained popularity as the comic opera *The Mikado* was staged throughout the United States following its London debut in 1885.[28] Soon the A&P and other companies issued trade cards inspired by *The Mikado*, with images of white women dressed in kimonos, as they were in performances of the opera.

Some U.S. households, swept up in the fascination for things Japanese or *The Mikado*, may have purchased Japan Tea because of the images of Japan on the included trade cards or because of a colorful image of Japan seen on packaging at their local grocer. The addition of Japan Tea apparently added an "oriental" flair to some events. At a "Chrysanthemum Fair" in Sacramento, California, visitors to the tea booth "not only received a cup of delicious Japan Tea, but were also given the elegant little Oriental cup and saucer in which the tea is served."[29]

Yet overall, cultural interest in Japan and in Japanese-made wares seems to have played a limited role in spurring U.S. consumption of Japanese teas. This is evident in the fact that a good portion of the labels placed on chests and packages of Japan Tea included distinctly Western-style images—crowns, bells, and harps, as well as butterflies, flowers, and landscapes—none with any obvious connection to Japan.[30]

Other clues can be found at venues that peddled Japanese decorative objects and novelties, often with links to *The Mikado*. In 1886, a U.S.

FIGURE 3.4 A retailer, in this case F. W. Wollitz of Ripon, Wisconsin, used this type of bag to hold half- to one-pound packages of Japan Tea. The inclusion of both Japanese and English text of the Red Cross brand name suggests the label was printed in Japan, probably in the 1870s, by Renfro Bros., a Chicago-based import firm with offices in Yokohama and Kobe. The label also states the area of Shizuoka Prefecture—the Kawane District—where the tea was grown, a marketing strategy that grew less prominent in subsequent decades.

entrepreneur opened a "veritable Japanese village" in Boston, where visitors took in the "domestic drama of Japanese life." Strolling down a recreated Japanese street, patrons could view Japanese craftsmen making cabinets, cloisonné, and silk embroidery as well as visit a teahouse staffed by young Japanese women offering small cups of tea to visitors. A guidebook for the village gives no indication of the type of tea served or if packages of Japan Tea were on sale at the teahouse or anywhere else in the village. In fact, there is only one advertisement for Japan Tea among the guidebook's fifty-plus advertisements for Japanese curios and decorative goods as well as for objects with no relation to Japan: beds, sewing machines, flour, and glue. In its short description of the teahouse, the guidebook urges readers to focus their attention not on tea but on the "satin-skinned little women who make this bamboo bower an attractive place." It explains that the women's "most picturesque attitudes" would allow them to become realistic additions to a performance of *The Mikado*.[31]

As the aforementioned suggests, because of its growing place in U.S. homes over the previous quarter-century, Americans probably only loosely associated Japan Tea with the stereotypical, fantasy worlds of *The Mikado* and Japanese villages like the one installed in Boston. In general, there is also little indication that Americans would purchase Japanese tea ware to use specifically to brew and serve Japanese teas. The comparatively more positive image of Japan, or at least that of the Japan presented in *The Mikado*, is also evident in how retailers used images of Japan to peddle other products beyond Japanese teas. Pictures of women dressed in kimonos, many that customers would recognize as connected to *The Mikado*, also graced trade cards distributed by stores selling chocolate and cocoa.[32] All told, trade cards for Japan Tea, while varying in their illustrative content, were largely free of degrading images of Japanese people, in contrast to those of Chinese placed on other trade cards of the era. The advertisements therefore indicate that prejudice against Chinese teas, when combined with anti-Chinese sentiments, were factors in Japan Tea's success in challenging the dominance of Chinese varieties in the United States.

THE ROLE OF TARIFF REPEALS

The Japan Tea brand also benefited from a repeal of tariffs on tea and coffee in 1872. In the years following the end of the Civil War, newspapers offered articles debating the value of existing duties on tea (25 cents per pound) and coffee (5 cents per pound). On one hand, the tariffs annually added millions to the national treasury. On the other, a repeal was presented as beneficial to rural America. In 1867, next to an article detailing rumblings about impeaching President Andrew Johnson (which would occur the following year), an Indiana newspaper described how high taxes and tariffs swelled the cost of staple commodities, including tea.[33] In an 1870 speech, Vice President Schuyler Colfax pushed for the repeal of duties on tea and coffee. Colfax emphasized the benefits to rural households, urging that a "free breakfast" be brought to "every man's cabin."[34]

In pressing for a repeal two years later, Senator Simon Cameron of Pennsylvania offered testimonials from his constituents stressing the "necessity" of the two beverages in daily life. He presented a letter signed by a group of constituents remonstrating "against a change of the existing tariff laws abating or abolishing duties upon such articles as are produced in the country." Yet the group "pray[ed] for the repeal of all duties upon, tea, coffee, and such other articles of necessity as cannot be produced in the United States." Such appeals apparently motivated members of Congress and President Ulysses S. Grant to pass legislation that repealed the tariffs on July 1, 1872.[35]

In 1880, the *New York Times* analyzed trade data to consider how the elimination of duties had affected tea and coffee prices. The average declared import price for tea was 33 cents from 1870 to 1872 and rose slightly to an average of 36.6 cents in the period from 1873 to 1875. Between 1876 and 1879, however, the price declined to 26.5 cents. Although stressing the difficulty in determining average retail prices for the previous years, the *Times* concluded, "We may say that the consumer of tea appears to have derived some benefit from the abolition of duty, but that no decline in price is visible in coffee, the more important article of the two." Here the newspaper referred to the greater volume of coffee imported; for example, in 1879, 363 million pounds of coffee entered the United States, compared to only 59 million pounds of tea.[36]

Between 1866—the first full year of peace in the United States—and 1880, Japanese tea imports moved from occupying just under 20 percent to eventually holding 44 percent of the overall market share, the majority still being held by Chinese tea. Japanese teas would retain roughly that market share for the remainder of the nineteenth century.[37]

TEA AND NEW LIVES IN POST-CIVIL WAR JAPAN

The internal conflicts within the Japanese state in 1860s, including the Boshin War, left a far lower death toll than the U.S. Civil War—only about thirty thousand perished.[38] Large parts of Kyoto had burned following Chōshū's aborted coup in 1864, and some castle towns, notably Aizuwakamatsu in northern Honshu, bore the scars of war. Yet in comparison to the United States, damage to buildings and infrastructure was minimal. Tokugawa leaders and their Satsuma and Chōshū counterparts negotiated a settlement that spared the Edo metropolis the ravages of a final battle.

Nonetheless, beginning in late 1868 thousands of people, mostly Tokugawa retainers and their families, began to leave the city. Traveling by land and sea, they made their way to Sunpu, a castle town approximately 125 miles to the south. Some samurai families made the move out of loyalty to their lord, the ex-shogun Yoshinobu, who had retired to lands still held by the Tokugawa in and around Sunpu. Yet most left out of economic necessity. Because it now held fewer lands and thus income, the Tokugawa house could no longer provide annual stipends to support its retainers and their families. Sunpu, still nominally under "friendly" Tokugawa control, beckoned as a place for personal reinvention. Many families lodged in samurai and commoner homes in the castle town; others lived in farmhouses and temples in the surrounding countryside, where some remained for several years.[39]

The samurai relocating to Sunpu soon faced another challenge: the gradual dissolution of their class. Starting in 1869, the Meiji government created two ranks, upper samurai (*shizoku*) and lower samurai (*sotsu*), an initial step in a process of recasting the Japanese status system.[40] Sensing the intentions of the new regime, some samurai aimed to become schoolteachers or gain positions in the new government. A number attempted to develop businesses; others contemplated new lives as farmers. Knowing only life in Edo, many demurred at the idea of trading their swords for hoes, despite the common portrayal of such a move as a noble return to a purer existence, one connected with the land.

Tada Motokichi joined those leaving Edo. At the age of forty, he started anew as a farmer, settling in a hamlet near Sunpu on a patch of land acquired possibly through a personal connection with Tokugawa Yoshinobu. He built a small house and set about planting tea fields, later calling his wife, Uta, and their children to join him. As tea plants take several years to mature enough to harvest, the Tada family must have struggled through this period. Nonetheless, the family eventually stabilized its financial position enough to acquire additional land, which was cleared and planted with tea. How "city folk" like the Tadas learned to farm remains a lingering question. They may have availed themselves of manuals outlining tea cultivation published in the Edo and early Meiji periods while seeking counsel from tea farmers and merchants from the Kyoto area.[41]

Meanwhile, Meiji leaders implemented additional reforms that would shape the lives of other samurai in Sunpu. In 1869, they forced lords to surrender sovereignty over their domains to the imperial government. In return, the lords received a golden handshake of financial support and elite positions in the new sociopolitical structure. Meiji leaders made lords governors of their former domains, the distinction being that they now served at the behest of the imperial government in Tokyo, the new name of Edo beginning in September 1868. Tokugawa Iesato, the six-year-old boy who had become the head of the Tokugawa house following Yoshinobu's retirement, was appointed governor of the Sunpu domain, which was subsequently renamed Shizuoka (which also became the name for the castle town of Sunpu).

With the head of the Tokugawa family now serving as an official answering to the imperial government, the remaining Tokugawa military units were deemed anachronistic, and pressure mounted to disband them. One such unit, the Shinbangumi, or New Guard Unit, had initially maintained relevance (and its members' stipends) by serving as Yoshinobu's personal guards and simultaneously protecting an important mountain shrine in Sunpu dedicated to Tokugawa Ieyasu, who had founded the Tokugawa regime in the early seventeenth century. In late 1869, unit leaders realized that their positions and income would soon disappear and searched for new options.

Shinbangumi leaders identified Makinohara, an uncultivated stretch of former Tokugawa lands west of Shizuoka City, as an area for settlement. Their group became part of an estimated 250 samurai families that moved to Makinohara, once again living as guests in farmhouses and temples, or in temporary shacks until they could build more permanent homes. Families received a small stipend as well as an allotment of land, often with stands of woods that needed clearing to make way for tea fields. On their respective plots, each family began to build a house, dig a well, and plant trees to serve as windbreaks for their new homes and tea fields. Many constructed a separate room or detached shack for processing tea after picking. The historian Ōishi Sadao explains that while scholars disagree about when and how much was distributed, most conclude that the Shinbangumi's initial funding came from the Tokugawa house, with additional support later provided by the Shizuoka domain.[42]

As they settled into their new lives, Shinbangumi leaders communicated with members of the Shōgitai, the group that had fought in the Battle of Ueno in Tokyo the previous year. Following their defeat, a Shōgitai unit commander, Ōtaniuchi Ryōgorō, had guided the move of around one hundred members and their families to a coastal town in Shizuoka, where they hoped to secure employment and begin new lives. Shizuoka domain officials, however, refused to aid the Shōgitai members on the grounds that the group's armed clash at Ueno with Satsuma and Chōshū troops, the latter fighting ostensibly under the flag of the emperor, had tarnished the name of the Tokugawa house (the battle occurred after Tokugawa Yoshinobu had acknowledged imperial authority by retiring to private life). After nearly two years of failed appeals to domain officials, in 1870 Ōtaniuchi urged his brethren to join the Shinbangumi in Makinohara. For many in the group, the decision was not an easy one, as few aspired to become tea farmers. Ōtaniuchi resisted in part because of his own physical condition: a bullet wound suffered during the Battle of Ueno had paralyzed his right arm. Eventually, fifty-three families of Shōgitai members chose to move to Makinohara, where with the assistance of Shinbangumi samurai, they transitioned to lives as tea farmers.[43]

Meanwhile, the oligarchs controlling the Meiji government continued to move on multiple fronts toward the goal of forming a more unified Japanese nation. In August 1871, they accomplished what some have termed a second coup: the abolition of the domains and the establishment of prefectures. Backed by an imperial decree, the oligarchs removed any remaining lords, including Tokugawa Iesato, from their domains, installing instead governors dispatched from Tokyo. The move created an administrative structure that grew into the one that exists today: forty-four prefectures, with three additional urban ones formed around Tokyo, Osaka, and Kyoto. The new leadership also eliminated the feudal practice whereby villages paid taxes in rice and other goods. Instead, the central government directed that individuals use the new national currency, the yen.

The Meiji oligarchs tapped into the new tax revenue stream to build modern infrastructure. They directed that Western-style streets, replete with gas lamps, be built in Tokyo, and construction began on a rail line connecting the city with Yokohama. The central regime also sought to expand the transport of goods and the flow of people along the Tōkaidō Road (running from Kyoto to Tokyo). To that end, it issued a plan to construct a bridge across the Ōi River, which empties into the Pacific Ocean near Makinohara. When completed, the new bridge would make redundant a guild of roughly 1,300 porters, who had for generations received wages based upon how high the water reached on their bodies when ferrying people and goods, as well as assisting horses, across the river.[44] In response, a guild leader submitted a series of petitions to the local government. In them, he professed support for the bridge and the overall benefits it would bring to the area but asked for assistance for the soon-to-be-unemployed porters and their families. After repeated appeals, local leaders granted the porters and their families plots of land in Makinohara to begin cultivating tea.[45]

Several wealthy commoners, including Maruo Bunroku, played key roles in assuring that this initiative came to fruition by helping families through the roughly five-year period until the newly cultivated tea plants matured. Unlike the samurai families, the transport workers received no stipend for living expenses. Funds from Maruo and others thus helped the families build homes as well as obtain farm tools and fodder for their livestock as they tended the new tea fields. With these donations, Maruo followed a custom, present in other parts of Japan at the time, of wealthy landowners making financial contributions for the betterment of the social welfare of their home district. In 1878, when an imperial procession stopped in Shizuoka, Iwakura Tomomi, a powerful noble in the central government who had led a government mission to the United States and Europe a few years earlier, recognized Maruo's help in allowing the former porters to settle into new lives while also advancing tea production for the greater good of the nation.[46]

The former porters and their families lived in distinct enclaves interacting only occasionally with the former Shinbangumi and Shōgitai members. Many samurai, although stripped of their official elite status, sought to maintain the separation of classes that had defined the Edo-period status system. Keen to show airs of elite refinement, they donned fencing gear when working in the fields and instructed their children to wear formal kimonos every day.

The samurai also showed little regard for farmers living in villages surrounding Makinohara. Throughout the Edo period, area farmers had used the unpopulated stretch of land in common as a source for wood and animal fodder, not demarking the borders abutting their villages. The new samurai neighbors staked out tea fields, often ignoring the wishes of farmers. One farmer notably prevailed in a legal battle over land, but most did not. Although a modern Japanese nation based on civil institutions and laws rather than feudal privilege was emerging, old class boundaries and privileges lingered.[47]

TEA PRODUCING AREAS TRANSITION
TO A NEW AGE

Back in Tokyo, municipal leaders also moved to foster tea production in the now less-populated city. In hopes of boosting the city's economy, they urged the planting of tea and mulberry fields (for sericulture) in the now largely neglected gardens of the lords' official residences, estates that occupied large swathes of the newly designated national capital.[48] In Kyoto, the former capital, leaders also promoted the cultivation of tea and mulberry. Kyoto merchants, eager for a share of the burgeoning trade, proposed guidelines to the municipal government for how brokers and wholesalers could purchase tea from regional farmers for sale to Western export firms.[49]

Kyoto merchants could anticipate a bright future given that in nearby Uji and its surrounding villages, farmers had already ramped up production to take advantage of the export market. During the 1840s, the region had experienced a series of droughts and floods that prompted many to abandon existing fields. Yet when U.S. demand pushed up the market price for tea—doubling it between 1865 and 1869—farmers moved quickly to replant those fields and clear additional land for cultivation.[50]

In Uji, plans circulated to raise capital to finance further expansion of fields and the construction of factories that could refine teas using firing methods tailored for Western consumers. Tea farmers also developed a type of *gyokuro*, considered the green tea of the highest quality, that proved popular on the domestic market. All told, production was robust enough for Kyoto Prefecture to lead Japan in overall production in 1874.[51] Eliza Ruhamah Scidmore, an American traveling through Uji two decades later, described the bustle of the May harvest when the fresh leaves were picked and processed. "Groups of bobbing hats beside the tea-bushes, carts loaded with sacks and baskets of tea-leaves; trays of toasting tea-leaves within every door-way, a delicate rose-like fragrance in the air; women and children sorting the crop in every village; this was the tea season in its height."[52]

Some of Uji's tea experts, respected for centuries for their knowledge of the tea ceremony and skill in producing high-grade teas, found work

FIGURE 3.5 Tea harvest in Uji. Stereoscope, Keystone View Company, circa 1910.

as consultants in other parts of Japan then ramping up production. Yet many tea experts fell into poverty as their former patrons, lords and members of the Tokugawa house, lost their revenue sources with the elimination of feudal estates. Facing mounting debts, a Kanbayashi house elder distributed advice on trimming expenses. He exhorted family members to knit their own mats to cover tea fields instead of purchasing them. In addition, he advised refraining from buying gifts when visiting

Kyoto and Osaka and suggested eating simple meals and limiting their consumption of rice wine (sake).[53]

In Tosa, renamed Kōchi Prefecture in 1871, leaders also mobilized to expand tea production. As in Shizuoka, they aimed to create employment for displaced samurai. The last lord of Tosa, Yamauchi Toyonori, initiated the effort by pooling domain resources to finance the construction of seventeen tea-refining factories. In 1873, the largest of these factories opened near the mountain hamlet of Ōtoyo, which had long produced green and black teas for sale outside the domain. Emphasizing green tea production for export, the prefecture hired tea specialists from Kyoto to oversee close to seven hundred laborers, many probably from samurai families, in the making of pan-fired teas. Despite the strong commitment of regional leaders, the Ōtoyo plant and others in Kōchi faced excessive labor costs. Failing to realize profits, the prefecture soon closed them, ending this effort to use tea production to assist destitute samurai.[54]

In the area around Kawagoe, northwest of Tokyo, producers and merchants also mobilized to expand production, shipping their teas to Yokohama. Eighty area farmers joined forces to create the Sayama Tea moniker still used for teas produced in the area today.[55] In Sashima, Nakayama Motonari (introduced in chapter 1), an early adopter of Uji refining methods, emerged as one of the larger producers and as a constant promoter of the area's tea.

Sashima farmers with less extensive land holdings who had long grown tea on small plots and in-between fields now looked to augment that production by creating fields in forests and along mountain slopes. In 1871, the Oshida family purchased high-quality seeds in Tokyo and used them to cultivate new fields. During the first spring picking, the family hired workers from nearby towns, at times offering them free lodging for the duration of the harvest. In the spring of 1890, a husband and wife working for the Oshidas picked around 330 pounds of tea over seventeen days, for which they earned 1.62 yen, a decent wage for a such a span of work, considering that a hired hand employed on a small family farm around that time typically earned just over twelve yen a year.[56]

Later in the Meiji period, area producers arranged for steamboats to pick up tea and transport it, via the Tone River, directly to Tokyo. Rail-cars then took the tea to Yokohama, meaning that if all the connections worked, within a single day it could reach the godowns, the term used to describe Western factories and offices in the treaty ports.[57]

Overall, local government and private groups at points throughout Japan fostered the expansion of tea production in the decade following the Meiji Restoration. Former feudal lords provided funds, as did domain and later prefectural authorities. Local men of wealth, such as Mauro Bunroku, offered significant financial support to assist those planting and nurturing the fields growing tea for export. It was thus locals, often motivated by a desire to promote a regional brand, who drove the expansion of tea production. This regional energy also helped keep production centered on small farms, limiting the development of large plantations.

REFINING AND PACKING AT KOBE AND YOKOHAMA

On the eve of the Meiji Restoration, Kobe, near the market city of Osaka, became a treaty port. As tea production increased in central and western Honshu, more tea flowed through Kobe.[58] Western export houses soon constructed firing plants in the city, and the amount of tea shipped from that port quickly eclipsed that of Nagasaki.[59]

Nonetheless, largely because of its proximity to Shizuoka, Yokohama emerged as Japan's main export platform. In the early Meiji period, porters carried much of the Shizuoka tea over a mountain pass and on to Yokohama. Small cargo ships also transported it, sailing directly from Shizuoka harbors.[60]

As early as 1862, William Alt had sensed that Nagasaki would soon be eclipsed by other Japanese port cities. He identified Osaka as a bigger commercial stage and anxiously awaited the result of negotiations between the British minister, Rutherford Alcock, and Tokugawa officials concerning its possible designation as a treaty port. He wrote home that "upon that event, dear mother, my fortune in a great reason depends. I may be able to make enough to satisfy me there in one or two years, but at this place [Nagasaki] only it will take me much longer."[61] In July 1868, foreigners were allowed to trade in Osaka, and following through on his earlier aspiration, Alt established an office there. He subsequently assigned supervision of his firm's Nagasaki branch to Henry Hunt and Frederick Hellyer, a nephew of Alt who had arrived from Britain the previous year. Frederick's brother, Thomas, also came to Nagasaki from Britain and at times worked in the firm. The Hellyer brothers probably left Britain for new opportunities in Japan because of their family's financial woes. The family business, carving and crafting parts and equipment, often for ships built in yards in southern England, had experienced financial challenges for decades before eventually going through bankruptcy proceedings in 1875 and 1876.[62] During his time at Nagasaki, Alt had also often voiced his desire to return to Britain upon achieving a level of commercial success.[63] Having amassed a sizable fortune but battling ill health, in 1872 he decided to retire in Britain. Just thirty-two years old, he settled into a comfortable life, purchasing a home near London and later a villa on the Italian coast.[64]

Henry Hunt and the Hellyer brothers thereafter ran Alt and Company until 1881, when they split the firm into two new entities: Hunt and Company and Hellyer and Company. Both specializing in tea, the two firms played significant roles in the export trade over the next few decades. Hellyer and Company eventually opened a firing factory in Kobe, closing its now less lucrative Nagasaki office.[65]

Kobe and Yokohama buzzed with activity during the harvesting season, which extended from April to September. Writing in 1883, a British merchant described how the volume of refining at Yokohama's factories overwhelmed one's senses:

> During the season, we have daily experience of the aroma issuing from the open windows of the tea-firing godowns, of the troops of tea-firing men, women and children who clatter past our windows at an unearthly hour in the morning, and who make day hideous with their noise,

singing and crying. Probably most of us have also been inside these godowns and seen these women at work, stirring the tea in iron pans with unceasing vigour and song, only interrupted by the occasional shouts of the overlookers or by the motherly attentions required by the children slung on their backs or tugging at their skirts.[66]

A contemporary account offers further insight into the workers, of which 70 percent were women. During the season, Western firms employed approximately 7,000 to 8,000 people, most being women from

FIGURE 3.6 Tea being pan fired in a Yokohama or Kobe factory to prepare for its shipment to the United States. This circa 1895 photograph, its crude retouching obscuring the faces of some of the workers, illustrates how women were primarily hired to fire tea, adding Prussian blue as necessary from the small trays located next to their pans. The male employees standing behind would maintain the fires to heat the pans and shuttle back and forth the fired and unfired teas. The stacked chests on the right are adorned with labels, with a representation of a chrysanthemum in the middle, which state they hold "The Royal Chop Japan Tea," imported by P. H. Kelly Mercantile of St. Paul, Minnesota.

surrounding agricultural and fishing villages but also wives and daughters of rickshaw men and laborers living in Yokohama. Instead of seasonal contracts, Western companies hired daily. Therefore, workers began the day at around three to four a.m. by lining up outside the godowns to learn the factory's daily wage. The majority of workers stood and stirred the tea in the firing pans or baskets on summer days; the temperature inside would often reach 110 degrees Fahrenheit. Over the course of a day, on average a worker could refine forty pounds of tea.

Skilled staff
Geo. H. Macy & Co., Yokohama.

FIGURE 3.7 This circa 1910 photograph indicates that Chinese with expertise in industrial tea refining continued to be important employees in the factories of American tea export firms. (George H. Macy & Company was a New York–based company.) We can conclude that most of the men in this photograph are Chinese, based on their clothing and hats.

Source: Geo. H. Macy, *Oblong Book with 30 pages of Black and White Photos of the Tea Industry in Formosa, China and Japan* (circa 1910), n.p. Yokohama Archives of History, Yokohama, Japan.

Other workers would sift the fired leaves to separate the tea dust, pick out unwanted large twigs or residue, and pack the refined leaves loose or in one- or 1.5-pound packages in tin-lined, wooden chests. Each firm employed a handful of male employees in more permanent positions, including men to attend to the heating of the pans and Chinese staff supervising the coloring.[67]

During the tea season, a passerby might have heard the following ballad emanating from a Yokohama tea factory.

> I drifted around and ended up in this place
> The Yokohama port. Ugh, what a drag.
> I see hundreds of ships in the harbor, their smoke scorches
>   the sky
> A hustle-bustle port. Ugh, what a drag.
> The Noge Mountain, the Noge Mountain
> When the bell rings, the gas lamp is extinguished.
> You'd better get there fast, otherwise the pan will make a noise.
>   Ugh, what a drag.
> I bring my box lunch at three a.m.
> Hurry up and open the gate, Mr. Gatekeeper. Set the fire,
>   Mr. Fire-attendant.
> Unless you pay me in Tenpō coins, I'll not work the pan.[68]
> The chopsticks and rice bowls will play hide and seek, and then
>   the rice scoop will retire.
> The ladle will jump into [a pan].
> Ugh, what a drag.
> The hard-earned money that I make here, my husband takes it
>   and where does it go?[69]

The lyrics underscore the challenges and monotony of the job. During breaks, workers would cook rice as well as purchase snacks from stands located within the factory building. Others could obtain savory and sweet foods from peddlers positioned strategically outside the factory windows. The song's lines about eating utensils are probably playful references to how workers might slow down the pace of their work or even quit if dissatisfied.[70] Although purchasing food was common, workers no doubt valued the option of bringing a box lunch, as pointed out in the song. By preparing their lunches, workers could resist purchasing additional food, a practice that foremen of contemporary textile mills encouraged in order to sap workers' excess funds, part of an effort to keep them from fleeing the challenging work common in such factories.[71]

Tragedies also occurred with women who brought their children to the factory, which seemed a common practice. One woman remained so intent on, or exhausted by, firing tea that she failed to notice that the child strapped to her back had died. In June 1879, a Yokohama newspaper published news of a three-year-old boy left to play by the shore while his mother worked at a tea plant. The boy strayed from his seven-year-old sister minding him and drowned in the harbor. Hearing such sad tales and daily seeing the unattended children in front of her home, an American missionary founded a school for these children in late 1879, later dubbed the "tea factory school."[72]

Near the refining plants, sawmills opened to sell wood for making tea chests. Many export firms also had their own art and printing departments to produce the labels affixed to tea chests and packages.[73] Ide Nobuko, a historian of graphic design, has recounted in detail how three groups of artisans, employed on a seasonal basis, created the colorful labels. Just before the season began, Japanese illustrators would offer potential illustrations to a Western export firm. After learning the firm's choices, an illustrator would meet with an engraver to decide what colors to use and the potential cost. An engraver would in turn create woodblocks to supply to the printer, whose team created the labels. Because of their rattan wrapping, the tea chests had an uneven surface onto which labels would not easily adhere. A printer therefore used thin paper and employed colors mixed with malt corn syrup, which proved more effective than standard oil- or water-based colors in keeping the labels affixed. Traders disdained machine-made labels, fearing that the unpleasant odor emitted by them might seep into the chest and spoil the tea. In fact, they started using machine-made labels only in the 1920s, when tea chest makers began to use plywood for the exterior of chests. Because of these conditions, printers produced tea labels in a labor-intensive process. The thin paper necessitated that they work in enclosed rooms, free from wind or breeze. Like the women employed in the firing factories, the printers therefore toiled in often stifling conditions throughout the summer tea season.[74]

Although challenging, jobs in a tea factory proved comparatively better than those held by women in spinning mills, another emerging industry of the period. Many of the women working in Yokohama's tea godowns commuted from their permanent homes. By contrast, women in the textile industry, most under twenty years old and single, were recruited from rural areas and housed in dormitories near isolated factories. Because they were hired daily, if dissatisfied with conditions or pay at one refining factory, workers in a tea plant could find employment at one of the other roughly seventeen foreign houses in the Yokohama concession. In fact, workers would actively seek the best daily wage, freely moving to another factory to earn a bit extra for their day's labors.[75] Women employed on contracts in textile mills often faced the stark choice of either continuing to work for a low wage at a dismal, dirty, and dangerous factory or, in desperation, breaking their contract and running away. Finally, workers at the tea refining factories received competitive wages (which were always higher for men): in 1903, men earned between 32 to 40 sen (each sen being a hundredth of a yen) and women from 21 to 26 sen per day; a textile worker earned 27 sen per day. Printers making tea labels garnered high wages for the period: between one and two yen per day, above that of plasterers (88 sen) and carpenters (85 sen).[76]

Unfortunately, few records exist about the lives of the artists that created the labels adorning the tea chests and individual packages. Nonetheless, the story of Kobayashi Kiyochika, who emerged as a prominent woodblock-print artist, offers another instructive example of Tokugawa retainers transitioning into new lives following the dislocation brought by the Boshin War and Meiji government reforms. The historian Henry D. Smith has detailed how Kiyochika grew up in a low-ranking samurai family that for generations had supervised an Edo granary. Following the death of his father in 1862, he became the head of his family and served the shogun in Kyoto for several years. In 1868, Kiyochika fought in the Battle of Toba-Fushimi and was a scout in the Battle of Ueno. He subsequently joined the thousands of refugees who traveled to Shizuoka, where he apparently worked as a fisher for several years.

In contrast to Tada, Kiyochika did not remain in Shizuoka but returned to Tokyo in 1874. Becoming an artist, Kiyochika created prints of scenes of Tokyo emblazoned with English captions, indicating they were tailored for sale to Western customers. He would subsequently produce a wide range of prints and work as an illustrator for newspapers and magazines. Kiyochika's early career suggests how artists could earn income from opportunities born of Japan's expanded commercial intercourse with Western nations, whether in the production of collectible prints or tea labels.[77]

EXPANSION PLANS: THE MEIJI GOVERNMENT AND BLACK TEA

Early Meiji leaders coined broad slogans aimed at engendering popular support for their policies and by implication the larger effort to create a modern Japanese nation. The Meiji oligarchs promoted an ideal of "learning from the West," which was exemplified by the aforementioned mission led by Iwakura Tomomi—an extended tour of the United States and European nations undertaken by a group of oligarchs between 1871 and 1873. To better understand the ascendant West, the delegation visited arsenals, factories, and foundries between meetings with senior government officials and heads of state. The Meiji oligarchs also presented the Emperor Meiji as the leader and symbol of the new nation, akin to heads of state in Western Europe. The emperor began to wear Western clothing and eat Western meals at public functions and spent a good part of his days interacting with foreign envoys and dignitaries.[78]

Government officials and prominent intellectuals championed Western learning in order to cultivate "civilization and enlightenment" (*bunmei kaika*), which they proclaimed would further enhance the new Japanese nation-state. As another unifying, national banner, Meiji leaders emphasized the twin goals of building a robust economy and strong military by advocating for a "rich country, strong military" (*fukoku kyōhei*). The Meiji oligarchs also moved to create a strong bureaucracy, which they envisioned would serve as a steady hand to guide economic growth and move the nation on the path to industrialization, which became a national objective.

It that spirit, in 1874 the Meiji government created an Industrial Promotion Bureau in the Ministry of Home Affairs, which was tasked with identifying and cultivating potential new industries. The preface of the bureau's inaugural publication stressed that its staff would assess the commercial potential of all products in Japan, beginning with flora and fauna. Bureau staff would compile the results and disseminate them via regular publications. With due attribution to the "rich country, strong army" slogan, the publication stressed that through cooperation between the government and the people, profits would increase and losses be minimized, thereby assuring the future wealth of the nation.[79]

The government established a Tea Office within the bureau, tasking it with developing black tea exports to allow Japan to diversify beyond selling merely green tea to the United States. As a first step, the office published a "Guide for Manufacturing Black Tea," which was distributed throughout the nation.[80] The office's bureaucrats, mirroring the actions of Alt and Glover in Nagasaki over a decade before, sought guidance from Chinese specialists. In 1875, Tea Office officials arranged for two Chinese experts to visit central Kyushu, where for three weeks they instructed interested farmers in tea cultivation and refining techniques. The pair next traveled to the northern part of the island, where they spent another three weeks with a group of aspiring black tea producers. The knowhow tour subsequently made shorter stops in other parts of Kyushu before visiting Shikoku and points in western Honshu.[81]

Late in 1875, the Tea Office expanded its staff by hiring Tada Motokichi as a low-ranking official. Tada's ability to move into such a position suggests he had gained a fair amount of knowledge about tea during his roughly seven-year span as a farmer. We can speculate that Tada could obtain that post because on top of his growing expertise of tea cultivation, his elite samurai background gave him the education and requisite skills to serve as a bureaucrat. Whatever the case, Tada's ascension into the Meiji government offers another example of the tea industry providing opportunity for personal advancement and reinvention for those who had once fought against the Satsuma-Chōshū alliance that had founded the Meiji regime.

Tea Office directors tapped Tada to escort the Chinese experts back to Shanghai and remain for several months to study tea cultivation and production practices. Tada learned firsthand of the international nature of China's tea trade by visiting British and Russian export firms as well as refining factories in Shanghai. Traveling up the Yangzi River, he met farmers and merchants, viewing how the latter used coloring agents to give fired green teas "sparkle" and increase their value. He also gathered information about labor practices, taxes levied on tea, and about how Chinese dealers sold their teas to Western export firms.[82]

Tada seems to have made an impression with his report, and the Tea Bureau soon chose him for another overseas assignment: a member of the Japanese contingent to the Centennial Exhibition held in Philadelphia.[83] The 1876 fair marked the United States joining the world exposition club. As it had with previous fairs held in Europe, the Japanese government sent a large contingent of representatives as well as items to display. The Philadelphia fair marked the start of promotions of Japan Tea at world fairs, a practice that would continue well into the twentieth century.

The Philadelphia organizers chose to place China and Japan in adjacent pavilions to the west of the host nation's central pavilion. The East Asian neighbors offered displays of national art, architecture, and agricultural products including tea. The Japanese section exhibited samples, most of them of green teas, from over thirty independent producers, many from Kyushu but some from Kōchi and Kyoto as well.[84]

For their part, the heads of the China section created an exhibit to allow visitors to discern the "features or peculiarities" of the Chinese green, black, and oolong teas on display. An American commentator emphasized the quality and fine taste of many Chinese varieties while noting the "rapidly-increasing addition to the world's tea supply contributed by the Empire of Japan," which he estimated at twenty-five million pounds annually. "This large quantity, coming as it does more and more into competition with the teas grown in China, has naturally had great influence upon the trade, and has caused those engaged in it here to note very carefully the changes that have arisen and that are likely to occur in the future of our tea-trade with China."[85]

During its eight-month run, the fair attracted nearly ten million visitors from the United States and overseas, including William Alt. Enjoying the chance to travel in his retirement, he penned a letter to his daughter from the fair. On a page sporting letterhead with drawings of prominent exposition buildings, Alt bubbles with affection for his daughter as he describes the doll's house he will bring back to Britain. Unfortunately for our purposes, he mentions little about the fair and does not specify if he viewed the exhibits related to Japan, including the Japanese tea that had helped him attain a life of leisure.[86]

THE END OF THE POSTWAR PERIODS IN JAPAN AND THE UNITED STATES

In 1876, the Meiji regime moved aggressively to complete a key step, initiated several years before, in its larger reform agenda: the complete dissolution of the samurai class. The government struck at a key tenet of samurai privilege—the wearing of swords—by decreeing that hereafter only police and soldiers could carry them. In an even bolder move, Meiji leaders made mandatory the previously optional policy that stipends be converted into thirty-year bonds. With an interest rate between 5 to 7 percent, the bonds translated into at least a 30 percent drop in income for most samurai. Disgruntled samurai instigated a series of uprisings in Kyushu and notably in Yamaguchi (the new name for Chōshū), the home province of many Meiji oligarchs. The central government garrisons attacked by the insurgents quickly regrouped and extinguished these brushfires of rebellion.[87]

The following year, a larger uprising erupted in southern Kyushu. Saigō Takamori, a founding member of the Meiji regime, had returned home to Kagoshima Prefecture, the new designation for the Satsuma domain, following a dispute within the oligarchy in 1873. The historian Mark Ravina concludes that Saigō held a strong desire to expand what he envisioned as virtuous rule. In addition to the loss of samurai privileges, Saigō disliked Meiji government reforms that had eliminated feudal practices allowing access to common lands. He believed that market-based land holding, such as that advanced by the Meiji leadership, would drive the poor further into poverty, eventually forcing them to sell their land to wealthy elites.

Assembling a force of nearly thirty thousand men and boldly proceeding north across Kyushu, Saigō anticipated picking up followers as his band marched toward Tokyo on what he believed was a just mission for reform. His army first laid siege to a castle in central Kyushu, a pause that allowed Meiji leaders to dispatch additional troops via steamship to the area and stall Saigō's momentum. Saigō hampered his cause by failing to articulate a clear vision of what he aimed to accomplish with the insurrection. Following a series of hard-fought battles with government troops, he eventually retreated to Kagoshima with a fragment of his army. Surrounded, the mercurial leader committed ritual suicide in the style of a samurai, ending his quest to challenge the leadership of his former comrades.[88]

The Satsuma Rebellion, as it came to be known in the West (in Japan, the Southwest War), and the string of other samurai-led rebellions illustrate that the Meiji oligarchs did not seamlessly establish control over the Japanese state in the years after the end of the Boshin War. Yet those who sought to turn back the clock and revive aspects of the Edo-period order came largely from areas that had led the Meiji Restoration. Former members of the deposed Tokugawa regime did not join them to mount an insurgency to restore the previous order.

One reason for this was the development of the tea export industry, which created opportunities for ex-Tokugawa samurai, including members of groups such as the Shōgitai, who had fought tenaciously against the Satsuma-Chōshū alliance during the Boshin War. Commoners displaced by the rapid, socioeconomic changes of the early Meiji period were also assuaged with new vocations. Former transport workers became tea farmers, and artists skilled in woodblock printing could transition into Japan's new media age by producing labels for the chests shipped to the United States. Moreover, women from agricultural villages and itinerant laborers could earn competitive wages at tea refining plants. For these groups, the creation of a tea industry offered a path of transition from being subjects of feudal leaders in the Edo-period order to citizens of the new Japanese nation. To be clear, these men and women did not enjoy rights of suffrage and thus could not actively participate in Japan's political institutions. Nonetheless, they could identify in tangible ways with the slogans of the regime and the larger goal of creating a more cohesive national order.

In sum, the making of Japan Tea into a successful brand on the U.S. market provides one explanation for how a diffuse political polity, further divided by a decade of internal conflicts, emerged to become a more unified Japanese nation. With its victory in the Satsuma Rebellion, the Meiji leadership could also proverbially turn the page on what we can term Japan's post–civil war period.

By coincidence, 1877 marked the end of Reconstruction in the United States. The inauguration of President Rutherford B. Hayes in March emerged from a compromise that resolved disputes about the previous year's election returns. Hayes recalled to barracks federal troops still stationed around the capitals of some Southern states, thus signaling that remaining federal troops would no longer play a role in political affairs. As the historian Eric Foner explains, "1877 marked a decisive retreat from the idea, born during the Civil War, of a powerful national state protecting the fundamental rights of American citizens."[89] He notes how the federal government remained aggressively involved in suppressing a growing labor movement and in guarding the rights of corporations. Yet leaders in Washington cast the fate of Black Americans, so recently granted citizenship, into the hands of Southern state and local authorities. Although not reviving slavery as an institution, Southern states imposed regulations on voting as well as political participation and economic opportunity that crippled the socioeconomic and political status of Black Americans for nearly a century. In contrast to Japan, vanquished Southern white elites found some success in restoring aspects of the previous social order. They achieved this not only because of the hands-off approach of federal leaders that allowed discriminatory legislation and legal codes to be passed but also through the Ku Klux Klan's campaigns of violent intimidation.[90]

As the United States moved away from the goal of a more inclusive Union championed during Reconstruction, it is not surprising that anti-Chinese sentiment, which had shaped the U.S. tea market during the 1870s, would remain strong. Although Japan's nascent tea export industry had benefitted from such views, American acceptance of racial prejudice and stereotypes would, in the coming decades, open the door for demeaning images of Japanese, introduced by British tea traders, to influence the U.S. tea market in new ways.

4

THE MIDWEST

Green Tea Country

*In the last fifty years a vast change has taken place in the
lives of our people. A revolution has in fact taken place.
The coming of industrialism, attended by all the roar and
rattle of affairs, the shrill cries of millions of new voices that
have come among us from overseas, the going and coming
of trains, the growth of cities, the building of the interurban
car lines that weave in and out of towns and past farmhouses, and now in these later days the coming of the auto-
mobiles has worked a tremendous change in the lives and
habits of thought of our people of Mid-America.*

—SHERWOOD ANDERSON, *WINESBURG, OHIO* (1919)

The convergence of trends that the novelist Sherwood Anderson
termed a revolution would shape the U.S. tea market in the 1880s
and 1890s. Tea intersected with urbanization in the emergence
of Chicago as a grand emporium where the "roar and rattle of affairs"
was loudest. Similar to the more prominent commodities of meat, lumber, and wheat, tea came to be increasingly shipped through the indus-
trializing city. Because of Chicago's important role, more wholesale and

retail shops opened to sell to some of the "millions from overseas" living there, as they did in other cities and towns that had sprouted on the Midwest prairie. With the "going and coming of trains," merchants in the Chicago rail hub could more easily and efficiently ship tea to rural towns like Galva, Illinois. Thanks to the confluence of these trends, the Midwest emerged as America's definitive "green tea country" (to coin a phrase), a place where green tea became "democratized," within the reach of all social classes.

Across the Pacific, Japan witnessed, on a more modest scale, economic expansion that led to the construction of a rail network connecting much of the archipelago. Although not experiencing an influx of foreign immigrants, Japanese cities also saw steady upticks in population, with more moving from the countryside to take jobs in factories. This chapter will detail how amid these developments, the teahouse remained a key social institution throughout Japan while at the same time cafés began to appear in these growing urban centers. Focusing on coffee, the new cafés offered alternative spaces of social interaction. Meanwhile, the nascent Japanese tea export industry faced two major challenges: American concerns about the quality of Japanese teas and emerging competition from British colonies in South Asia, trends that shaped how Japanese merchants presented their teas at the Columbian Exposition held in Chicago in 1893.

REGIONAL VARIATIONS ON
THE U.S. TEA MARKET

In the early 1880s, clipper ships still brought a modicum of tea to New York City. Yet contemporary observers noted how the steamship had recast maritime transport of the leaf. Whereas a clipper could sail from East Asia to New York in about one hundred days, a steamer coming via the Suez Canal could make the journey in about half that time and carry a larger cargo.[1] Akin to the stories of clipper ships delivering teas in record times during the 1850s, newspapers took note of steamships that competed to be the first to bring to New York, by early August, prized new teas picked in May in the fields of Japan.[2]

New York also received a larger volume and wider range of teas from China, notably oolongs from China's Fujian Province and increasingly from the island of Taiwan. As was the case in Nagasaki, in Taiwan British interests played a key role in advancing production tailored almost exclusively for the U.S. market. In 1869, John Dowd, a British merchant, established the first refining plant on the island, and other Western firms followed suit. Within a decade, Taiwan would export 10 million pounds of tea annually, almost all of it oolongs sent to the United States.[3] New York and New England emerged as the main oolong consuming areas.[4] Stories of life in small New England farming communities told of people meeting over cups of "steaming oolong," and some stores listed oolong as their only variety of tea for sale.[5]

In the South, green tea remained popular. In North Carolina, stores sold mainly Japan Tea and Chinese green tea varieties but also some oolongs and black English breakfast tea.[6] Retailers in Californian cities offered essentially the same choices.[7] Americans moving into territories west of the Rockies, such as cowhands tending herds of cattle, drank primarily coffee on the trail. Native Americans in many parts of the Mountain West apparently also chose coffee, marketed by Arbuckle, a growing national coffee retailer.[8]

Midwesterners became the biggest consumers of Chinese and Japanese green teas. Thanks to that demand, Chicago emerged as a center of the national tea trade, receiving teas by rail from New York and, later, San Francisco, after the opening of the transcontinental railway in 1869. In 1875, the *Chicago Daily Tribune* marked the new year with an overview of the city's grocery and wholesale trades, stressing that thanks to the transcontinental railway, Chicago was receiving an increasing proportion of the tea shipped across the Pacific from Yokohama. The newspaper reported that cargoes brought by rail from San Francisco, about half of which were teas from Japan, proved fresher than those carried entirely by maritime routes. In 1887, the *Tribune* boasted that Chicago had become the "largest tea mart in the United States." Whereas previously Eastern firms such as the A&P had dominated through their

branch stores, the city now included twenty-five Chicago-based importers and wholesalers, up from zero just fifteen years before. These wholesalers sold teas primarily west of the Appalachian Mountains, which
proved a more lucrative territory than points east.[9]

It is doubtful that Chicago's trade had supplanted New York, but the
city had certainly become an emporium that supplied Japanese tea
throughout the Midwest.[10] Realizing its importance, Frederick Hellyer
moved there permanently in 1888, settling in the suburb of Riverside, a
planned community designed in part by the prominent landscape architect Frederick Law Olmsted. Hellyer worked first as a broker, initially with
his brother, Thomas. Within a few years, he had established his firm as an
importer and wholesaler of teas. One of a cluster of tea and coffee companies occupying a section of Wabash Avenue, Hellyer and Company competed with roughly forty other importers and wholesalers. During the
1890s, a growing number of tea and coffee retail stores also set up shop
throughout Chicago, rising from seventy-six in 1892 to 204 by 1896.[11]

Hellyer and Company operated a factory and office in Kobe, where
tea became the most prominent export. Thomas apparently lived permanently in Kobe and ran operations there. Before moving to Chicago, Frederick had married Georgianna Tirrell, whose father owned warehouses
in Boston and, and, thus possibly, had connections to shipping firms
that assisted Hellyer and Company in expanding its export channels to
the U.S. market. In advance of the harvest each spring, Frederick (who
became a U.S. citizen) and his family traveled by rail to San Francisco
to board a steamship to Kobe, remaining there until the late fall to
oversee the refining and shipments of tea.[12]

The season's first teas would be shipped from Kobe in April, an event
noted in the local press.[13] Around the same time, representatives of
Hellyer and Company fanned out across the Midwest. These salesmen
would confirm orders with wholesalers in major cities, many of which
also dealt in grains and other commodities. A Hellyer salesman
would also visit large grocers, such as Roundy, Peckham, and Company
in Milwaukee, which in 1895 purchased the largest amount of Japanese
tea in the city. Other Milwaukee grocers had display rooms where customers could browse varieties of Japan Tea.[14]

FIGURE 4.1 Chests of tea are apparently stacked on the left side of the quay waiting for lighters to transport them to ships in the harbor. Stereoscope, Griffith & Griffith, Philadelphia, Pennsylvania, circa 1900.

Milwaukee-based jobbers also made the rounds to smaller tea retail stores. Everett A. Smith Company dispatched "a staff of popular salesmen" on routes to visit retail stores throughout Wisconsin, Minnesota, Michigan, and Iowa.[15] A salesman would schedule his visits via mail. As figure 4.2 shows, the categories of importer, wholesaler, and jobber were not rigid, with some firms fulfilling multiple market roles.

We can speculate that an Everett A. Smith salesman or one of his competitors visited a Milwaukee shop run by a man of apparent German ancestry, Peter Klingelhoefer, described in a directory as simply selling "teas." He may also have called on Austin Eli, who is recorded as dealing in "teas" in his shop in the village of Sheboygan Falls, about fifty-five miles north of Milwaukee. Sheboygan Falls was described as having experienced substantial growth since its founding in 1854. The village of just over one thousand people was said to contain "the largest woolen mill in the State, a large tannery, 2 machine shops, a plow factory, a chair factory, planing mill, lime kiln, 2 banks, 1 newspaper, 5 churches, a public library of about 400 volumes, [and] an excellent opera house, seating capacity 600." As if to confirm it as a quintessential Wisconsin village,

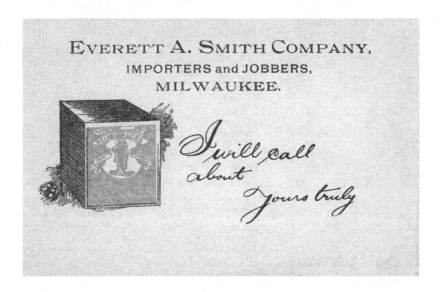

FIGURE 4.2 Appointment postcard, Everett A. Smith Company, Importers and Jobbers, Milwaukee, Wisconsin, circa 1890. Printed on the flip side of a prepaid postcard, the company's salesmen evidently mailed this card to schedule appointments to sell Japan Tea to retailers throughout the Upper Midwest.

Sheboygan Falls supported the "usual number of stores" but held "probably more tributary cheese factories than any village in the State."[16] These accounts from Wisconsin suggest that while not supplanting coffee, tea, the sale of which men like Eli and Klingelhoefer held as a defined profession, occupied a confirmed place in the everyday lives of many Midwesterners.

Meanwhile, in coordination with their central government, in the 1880s Japanese tea producers and merchants had created the Japan Central Tea Association to advance Japan's tea trade. In 1895, the association dispatched two representatives to the Midwest to learn more about the region's tea market and Japan Tea's place in it. In their report, the pair charted how Japan Tea had gained significant shares of markets throughout the region. Farmers surrounding Milwaukee, many recent immigrants from northern Europe, often consumed more coffee. Yet over the past few decades, the area's tea drinkers had begun to turn away from Chinese teas, buying instead uncolored, pan-fired Japan Tea, which sold for between 16 and 25 cents a pound. In the Twin Cities, which the Japanese tea men marveled had surged to include fifty thousand souls in recent years, residents had also been increasingly drinking uncolored, pan-fired Japan Tea. Over the past thirteen years, Japan Tea, previously rare, had come to occupy 90 percent of all the tea consumed in not only the Twin Cities but also much of the rest of Minnesota.[17] The Swedish Mercantile Company in Worthington, a small town near the Iowa border, reflected this in its advertisements, which included both coffee and teas but highlighted the varieties of Japan Tea selling for between 30 to 50 cents a pound.[18]

During roughly the same span of time, uncolored, pan-fired teas had also displaced Chinese teas in Omaha, Nebraska. The team concluded that the residents of Kansas City, Missouri, by contrast, preferred basket-fired teas, finding them especially suited to the city's hard water. Overall, their report emphasized the conclusions presented in the previous chapter: that the poor reputation of Chinese teas, and no doubt prejudice against Chinese in the United States, had spurred Japan Tea's recent gains across the Midwest.[19]

Further south in Galva, Illinois, Japan Tea had become a mainstay at stores by the late 1870s. One grocer advertised "Good Japan Tea" for 40 cents a pound, while a competitor in a neighboring town sold it for the same price, along with young hyson, oolong, and imperial (the latter two at slightly higher prices). By 1895, grocers offered those same varieties but had reduced the price for Japan Tea, a pound of which could now be procured from 25 to 40 cents.[20] In Chicago, the lowest grades of Japan Tea were sold for a mere 17 cents per pound.[21] This sampling demonstrates how tea prices overall had dropped since the 1860s, when Japan Tea and other green teas sold for between 50 cents to $1.50 a pound.

In central Illinois as well, some of the "new voices from overseas" were likely among the consumers of Japan Tea. During the 1850s and 1860s, Galva and nearby towns had swelled with Swedish immigrants, their significant numbers indicated by the emergence of Swedish-language newspapers.[22] In the rail hub of Galesburg, Swedes worked as laborers on the railroad, on farms, and in newly constructed factories. The city's

FIGURE 4.3 A tea package, estimated from the 1880s, used by a retailer in the town of Tecumseh (population around 2,000) in southeastern Nebraska. The package exemplifies not only the diffusion of Japanese green tea throughout the Midwest but also the wide variety of brands coined by importers and retailers, in this case "Excelsior Japan Tea," which the reverse side of the package states that customers can recognize by its distinctive label: a sailor with the American flag.

railway and factory workers organized labor unions, which the heads of the railway, in conjunction with city leaders, aggressively opposed. Galesburg's divisions, which at times included armed clashes surrounding issues of labor organization, mirrored those then emerging throughout the Midwest and other parts of the United States.[23]

JAPANESE GREEN TEA IN MIDWESTERN LIVES

How would Midwesterners purchase Japan Tea and other varieties at their local tea shops or grocers? Like other staples, most retailers appear to have sold their teas in bulk, with customers asking for specific amounts from a clerk behind the counter.[24] Advertisements before 1900 generally still listed teas by variety but emphasized the "fresh" new teas of the season.[25]

Hamlin Garland, a Wisconsin native who profiled the lives of Midwestern farm families in novels and short stories, crafted characters who found comfort in a cup of green tea, especially one made from "fresh" tea. In a short story set somewhere in the rural Midwest, we meet the Haskinses, who had lost their farm in Kansas after grasshoppers devastated their crops. One evening they appear, desolate, at the doorstep of the Council family, who invite them to stay the night. Mrs. Council welcomes them with food and drink: "Mis' Haskins, set right up to the table an' take a good swig o' tea whilst I make y' s'm toast. It's green tea, an' it's good. I tell Council as I git older I don't seem to enjoy Young Hyson n'r Gundpowder. I want the reel green tea, jest as it comes off'n the vines. Seems t' have more heart in it, some way. Don't s'pose it has. Council says it's all in m' eye."[26] In this case, Mrs. Council may have been referring to either a basket-fired green tea or, more likely, a green tea colored by additives, given that she wanted a tea "just off the vines" but one that, as her husband noted, was apparently only green in appearance.

In another story profiling the homecoming of a wounded soldier, Garland vividly describes an abundant one o'clock dinner convened on a Wisconsin farm at which a "long table was piled with boiled potatoes, cords of boiled corn on the cob, squash and pumpkin pies, hot biscuit, sweet pickles, bread and butter, and honey." The women who set the table tell the "young uns" to enjoy as much of the corn on the cob as they like. They are cautioned that "the tea is for the women-folks, and 'specially f'r Mis' Smith an' Bill's wife. We're a-goin' to tell fortunes by it." By two o'clock, the "women alone remained around the débris-covered table, sipping their tea and telling fortunes" in the tea leaves.[27]

Guidebooks for housewives also noted the practice of reading tea leaves. Christine Terhune Herrick, a prolific writer on cooking, home-making, and social etiquette, stressed that in the past, "young girls" would delight "in telling fortunes from the mass of sediment in the bottom of the cup." Yet after the wider use of strainers, which pre-vented pieces of leaves and stems from being poured into cups, such practices had become less popular. Herrick also described tea as a markedly feminine beverage, a woman's "comfort" that is "frowned upon by the stronger sex as 'weak, sloppy stuff.'" She opined that "men as a rule prefer coffee—possibly because the proper mode of preparing it is more generally understood, and, consequently, the chances are in favor of its palatableness."

Criticizing the practices of boiling tea common earlier in the century, Herrick instructed readers that to brew tea correctly, the requisite amount of the leaf must be covered with boiling water, steeped for just three min-utes, and then covered with more boiling water and left to stand for one minute before being served. These more effective brewing techniques, she stressed, would serve as the foundation of a successful tea party. Describing practices reminiscent of those employed during colonial times, she urged a hostess to make and dispense the tea with her own hands, while "a young girl visitor, or the son of the house, or any privi-leged guess passes the biscuit-jar."[28]

Tea as a light meal taken between a noontime dinner and evening sup-per was offered by Chicago restaurants such as the Gardner House, which gave patrons the option of tea from six p.m. to nine p.m., followed by supper from nine p.m. to midnight.[29] Americans also convened "Five O-Clock Tea" gatherings in their homes and gardens, which some painted as a practice "indulged in only by the idle or wealthy classes in

America."[30] Herrick offered tips for how housewives of means could host teas, noting which tasks would be left to a servant. She also outlined how Midwestern women could hold tea gatherings at reduced cost, especially when on outings made by train or bicycle. For such forays to enjoy nature, she confided that an English tea basket, made to hold the proper equipage, would work best. Yet given the high price of such an accessory, a resourceful homemaker could draw on Yankee ingenuity and instead employ a common basket with a cloth cover to carry the food and drinks—iced tea or coffee—to be enjoyed on the grass or under a tree. Housewives should also consider packing a "pocket stove." Sold by druggists, it was a device replete with a kettle, teapot, cups, and saucers. She explained how a small alcohol lamp could be used to boil water and a tea ball, packed with the requisite amount of tea leaves, subsequently inserted to brew a pot of tea.[31]

Beginning in the late nineteenth century, household-advice columns increasingly mentioned iced tea as a beverage option. One such column in a Montana newspaper offered a recipe for iced tea along with suggestions for making rhubarb pie as well as curds and whey. The author advised making a strong brew in the morning and keeping it chilled in the refrigerator, serving it over a small amount of ice. He or she implored readers to avoid pouring hot tea over ice, which would lead the iced tea to be "weak, insipid, and a libel on its name." The sociologist John Shelton Reed concludes that iced tea had become an "all American drink" consumed throughout New England, the Midwest, and the South and provided (along with lemonade) to members of Congress during the hot summer days.[32]

MORE "THINGS JAPANESE"

During the 1880s and 1890s, more Americans, and increasingly those of lesser economic means, began to purchase Japanese tea sets and other "things Japanese." Yet as was the case in the 1870s, only a small portion seems to have followed the practice of drinking only Japanese teas in their Japanese-made tea ware. Advice columns, such as those penned by Herrick, provide indications of how Japanese tea sets and other Japanese-made accessories were broadly used in many situations and apparently to consume many types of teas. In her advice to readers, Herrick noted various Japanese wares that would complement both indoor and outdoor teas. For an indoor event, she suggested that "for fifty cents one can get a bit of pretty Japanese ware that would grace any board" and that accompanying cosies could be purchased at "Japanese stores."[33] For a tea picnic, she advised packing imported Japanese paper napkins, then used as an inexpensive substitute for cloth and linen table napkins.[34]

Below Herrick's article, the editors of the column "What Women Talk and Think About" described in detail possible uses for the napkins, which sported "dainty flower designs," along with other "Jap Tea Table Novelties" such as pots and cups appropriate for luncheons and teas. A fern dish or lily bowl as the centerpiece, complemented with Japanese lanterns hung from the chandelier, would add further "Japanese" flavor to the room.[35]

In the 1890s, middle- and lower-class Americans purchased more such "Japanese" accessories, using them to create idiosyncratic "Japanese" styles in their home. The influence of *The Mikado* and Japanese-themed villages had percolated throughout the country in the form of Japanese novelty stores that sold fans, silks, china, cloisonné ware, and a dizzying array of knickknacks. Shopkeepers, only a handful of them Japanese or Japanese Americans, peddled some goods imported from Japan, but more often, the items were made in the United States, China, or Europe. Japanese novelty stores popped up across the United States, including in Texas and Western states and territories—one town in New Mexico with a population of just under three thousand people supported two such establishments.[36] In Wisconsin, bookstores and drug stores, which did not sell tea, peddled Japanese wares.[37]

Tea retailers throughout the country also got into the act, offering Japanese tea pots and other wares as gifts accompanying the purchase of large amounts of tea, although not exclusively Japan Tea.[38] In so doing, they continued to expand the practice of premiums begun earlier by the A&P's George Gilman and the owners of other large firms. Tea packages ordered by mail, which in the 1860s and 1870s held collectable lithographic prints as premiums, could now include stamps, which customers could exchange for china, glassware, and other household goods. Tea stores would also provide such wares for customers visiting their shops. In addition, the A&P and other large firms initiated wagon services that sold tea and coffee door to door, especially in rural areas.[39]

In sum, we can make several broad observations about tea in the American "heartland" during the closing decades of the nineteenth century. Midwesterners overwhelmingly preferred green over black teas and were beginning to show a preference for uncolored varieties. Japan Tea had gained further market share at the expense of competing Chinese varieties and was sold at markedly lower prices compared to its debut in the early 1860s. Earlier in the century, tea parties, but not the beverage of tea per se, had often been seen as affairs reserved for women. Now tea generally had come to hold a more distinctly gendered quality, portrayed by many as a feminine beverage drank at meals, on picnics, and at more formal gatherings. Restaurants also confirmed the place of tea in the U.S. gastronomic landscape by making tea, enjoyed between four p.m. and seven p.m., a defined meal option. Although most tea was consumed hot, iced tea was becoming more popular during summertime.

What made Midwesterners avid drinkers of Japanese green tea at a time when their countrymen on the Eastern Seaboard were embracing oolongs and later, as will be described below, varieties of black tea? Over roughly a generation, the Midwest moved from a sparsely populated prairie to a region dotted with booming cities and towns connected by modern railroads. Living in an area of new wealth and prominence, Midwesterners sought to place themselves on a social and cultural level commensurate with that of their counterparts in the East. In Chicago, the new elites constructed grand mansions and established institutions, like the Art Institute, to showcase their appreciation of the art and sophistication of Western Europe and the classical age. The elders of Sheboygan Falls built an opera house and library to announce that their small, cheese-producing village appreciated culture and learning. It seems safe to conclude that the consumption of green tea was part of this larger and deliberate embrace of "traditional" practices. In their

selection of green tea, Midwesterners appropriated an aspect of the established American tea culture that had emerged during the early days of
the republic.

Thanks to the wide range of teas imported from China and Japan,
men and women lower on the socioeconomic ladder could also consume
green teas and thereby join the established American culture of tea consumption. A family operating a small farm in Minnesota, or one living
in Chicago with a father employed in a factory, could purchase a pound
of lower-grade or colored green tea—"poor-man's tea"—for around 20
cents a pound. Twenty years earlier, the same type of tea would have sold
for 50 cents a pound. Thus, in the 1880s green tea had become democratized, a product within the reach of Americans across the social
spectrum.[40]

TEA CONSUMPTION IN MEIJI JAPAN

During the 1880s and 1890s, silk and tea, shipped to the United States,
continued to be the mainstays of Japan's export trade. Nonetheless, Japan
began to expand its commerce with East and Southeast Asian nations.
Nagasaki and other Kyushu ports loaded coal, much of it transported
to Shanghai to feed steamships calling at that thriving treaty port. New
export sectors also emerged, such as the production of matches, sent to
China and India.[41] Textile and other manufacturing factories opened
throughout the country, and financial cliques (zaibatsu) that operated
mines, factories, and banks to finance their operations came to dominate
much of the economy. Iwasaki Yatarō, who had traded with Alt in Nagasaki, developed Tosa's trading company into one zaibatsu, Mitsubishi.
Mitsui, a trading house that had prospered since the middle of the Edo
period, emerged as another.

As the head of its trading arm, the Mitsui Trading Company, Masuda
Takashi helped the firm profit from sales of army supplies to the government during the Satsuma Rebellion and in the export of Kyushu coal
to Shanghai. With his new wealth, Masuda became a patron of the tea
ceremony (chanoyu), which in the wake of the Meiji Restoration had

reached a nadir. Japanese elites, embracing Western cultural practices, showed less interest in the "old" elegance of the tea ceremony, exemplified by the fact that prized utensils used in the tea ceremony were selling for low prices at auctions. Masuda began studying the tea ceremony during the mid-1870s and soon became an avid collector of tea ware. His interest, and that of other men of wealth and power in business and government, helped restore the status of the tea ceremony as a cultural pursuit.[42]

Japanese leaders, meanwhile, began to build an empire in Asia. Seeking to assert greater control over Korea, they embarked on a war with China in 1894. Most Western observers believed China would prevail given its size and level of military advancement. Yet Japan shocked the world with triumphs on land and sea. In 1895, the Qing relented, signing the Treaty of Shimonoseki, which granted Japan control over Taiwan and its tea industry (a point that will be explored later in more detail). Japan received another territorial prize: the Liaodong Peninsula. Fearing an emerging rival to their own imperial ambitions in China, the leaders of France, Germany, and Russia forced their Japanese counterparts to give up control of that stretch of Chinese territory. Japanese intellectuals and leaders would remember that humiliation and mark it as exemplifying Western hypocrisy: Western nations could enjoy a free imperial hand in China, but not upstart Japan. Nonetheless, the Treaty of Shimonoseki granted a tremendous boost to the Japanese economy in the form of a huge indemnity, paid by the Qing in silver, which the Meiji government used to finance new industrial projects.

Thanks in part to that financial infusion, Japan's expanding economy engendered urban growth, though not on the scale of that witnessed in the U.S. Midwest. In 1900, close to 85 percent of Japanese lived in rural areas, compared with 60 percent of Americans.[43] In villages throughout Japan, farm families faced hardscrabble lives. Men often took jobs in distant locations to earn extra income, thereby increasing the burden on wives and other women in the household to farm while also raising children. In the 1880s, many families, confronting severe debts, lost their land and became tenant farmers, increasing the rate of tenancy throughout the country to around 40 percent.[44] Needless to say, most rural families raised much of their own food, including their daily tea. Thus, rural consumption still centered on *bancha* grown and produced at home using methods described in chapter 1. In Tokyo, the number of tea shops grew modestly during the late Meiji period. In 1891, the city supported 463 shops; by 1900, that number had risen to 495. By contrast, the number of establishments selling Japanese alcoholic beverages, such as rice wine (sake), increased from 884 to 2,128 over the same period.[45]

Sencha, the tea comprising a good portion of the exports to the United States, continued to make up the majority of tea produced commercially in the late Meiji period, more than double the amount of *bancha*. As before, most commercially produced tea was exported—for example, roughly 85 percent in 1892.[46] Given that the majority of *sencha* was shipped overseas, *bancha* no doubt dominated menus at the teahouses that continued to operate, using categories generally unchanged since the Edo period. Nonetheless, at rural roadside establishments some *sencha* also seems to have been served, as an American visitor noted drinking "pale yellow tea" at a rustic teahouse.[47] The British globetrotter Isabella Bird described visiting a roadside teahouse when she made her way through northern Japan. The coolies, as she called them, assisting her travels would choose a teahouse at which they "bathed their feet, rinsed their mouths, and ate rice, pickles, and 'broth of abominable things'" before taking out small pipes for an after-meal smoke. Rice was often served cold, and patrons poured hot tea on it to make a Japanese dish still common today: *ochazuke*. At one such establishment, Bird received tea in a small pot, holding about "an English tea-cupful." She noted that the tea was allowed to steep for only a minute and produced "a clear, straw-colored liquid with a delicious aroma and flavour, grateful and refreshing at all times."[48] Given the color, it is safe to conclude that she too received *sencha*.

Yet other accounts suggest that *bancha* was brought to guests' tables. An Australian observer was more specific, describing how Japanese drink tea with a "delicious aroma" that "is very delicate in flavour; its colour is that of very pale manzanilla sherry," which holds a brown color more like *bancha*. The author also noted the prevalence of tea in daily life. "Tea is offered to drink on all occasions in Japan; when paying or receiving a visit, when making purchases of any length in the inner room of a shop or store, at every meal, when resting on a journey at seven-mile stages. It is supplied free in the first-class railway carriages, and is brought round at the railway stations."[49]

The Australian author could experience a rail trip in Japan because as part of its larger plans for economic expansion, the Meiji government continued to invest heavily in infrastructure, including the construction of railways. Beginning in the 1870s, national and, later, private railways gradually expanded Japan's overall network, initially carrying mainly freight. In the 1890s, railways focused more on transporting passengers, and the number of people using the rails surged from 23 million to 114 million annually between 1890 and 1900.[50]

Vendors at station kiosks and on platforms began to sell food, including boxed lunches. According to one account, in 1885 an innkeeper running a Japanese-style inn near Utsunomiya Station, just north of Tokyo, created the first station boxed lunch (*ekiben*) tailored for rail passengers. Other accounts suggest that workers made redundant by the completion of the Tokaidō rail line in 1889 found employment selling passengers boxed lunches and snacks, usually made from well-known local foods.[51]

The first sale of tea at a kiosk is said to have occurred at a Shizuoka rail station in 1885.[52] Vendors often sold tea in small earthenware pots, which held roughly a half-liter of liquid. The pots sported rudimentary wire handles and came complete with a small cup. Shizuoka tea vendors initially used pots from two regions in central Japan famous for their pottery, Shigaraki and Mashiko. Within a few years, other regions produced pots expressly for use on railroads, many times adorned with the name of the station at which they were sold. Some travelers saved pots as souvenirs of their rail journeys.[53]

COFFEEHOUSES IN URBAN JAPAN

In major cities, teahouses fulfilled many societal roles. In the red-light district of Tokyo, some teahouses served as intermediaries between brothels and clients, as they had done during the Edo period.[54] Conventional

teahouses offered urbanites quick cups of tea and snacks. A 1900 newspaper account noted that teahouses were "everywhere in Japan" and
were places "where a customer can rest and eat cakes or, in the summer,
ice with lemonade poured over it."[55]

As is the practice at many Japanese restaurants today, customers were
often served a cup of tea immediately upon taking their seat. Western
visitors noted that the tea and any other snacks were provided without
charge but that patrons customarily left a modest tip in addition any
amount incurred for additional food and beverages ordered. At inns,
customers were expected to leave an envelope of "tea money" (chadai)
as a token of thanks for service during their stay.[56]

Japanese cities also came to include coffeehouses. Tei Ei-kei, the
adopted son of a Taiwanese man who worked for the Japanese foreign
ministry, opened the first coffeehouse, the Kahiichakan, in Tokyo in
1888. Tei had a penchant for languages, speaking Chinese, French, and
English, and had attended Yale University before illness forced him to
return home without earning a degree. After working as a teacher and
for a time for the Meiji government, he decided to create a café modeled
on what he had experienced in London, where people of all ages and
classes could share conversation and ideas over a cup of coffee. Tei's coffeehouse included books, foreign newspapers, and billiard tables, which
the mostly male patrons could enjoy free of charge after purchasing a
cup of coffee. With his coffeehouse, he created a new space for social
exchange but not a viable business—the Kahiichakan closed after only
five years in operation. More successful imitators followed, and by 1901,
there were 145 Western-style coffeehouses, cafes, and eating establishments in Tokyo.[57]

The coffeehouse offered a novel social environment for Japan—one
often based on anonymity. As the anthropologist Merry White has
shown, for the price of a cup of coffee, patrons could enjoy a time of
respite—to read or simply relax. For those from the countryside, especially men working as laborers, urban coffeehouses offered relief from
what for many must have been the overwhelming "roar and rattle of
affairs" brought by new technologies, such as street cars, which were
introduced in Tokyo and Osaka early in the twentieth century. Many

also found in such establishments a suitable space to commiserate about and better understand life in the big city.[58]

Although some appropriated the Western term "café," a good portion of the new establishments came to be referred to as *kissaten*, a term developed from the Chinese characters for "drinking tea" (*kissa*) matched with the character for shop (*ten*). As will be explored in subsequent chapters, a *kissaten* usually had tea on its menu. Yet for those seeking to embrace the trappings of a Western lifestyle, coffee became the drink of choice. The consumption of tea as a focus of social interaction (outside of the tea ceremony), as well as its identification as a health beverage, both diminished in significance as the Meiji period progressed.

QUALITY CONCERNS IN JAPAN AND THE UNITED STATES

As the export trade ramped up, officials in Shizuoka realized the importance of maintaining quality standards for exported teas. In 1873, they issued a directive urging farmers to avoid underhanded practices, such as adding coloring agents to mask poor-quality or bogus leaves. Brokers unwittingly purchasing such spurious tea suffered financial losses, hurting the overall integrity of the trade. Appealing to a sense of cooperation, the edict cautioned that such dishonest practices would set back the hard work—the clearing of land and planting of tea—contributed in recent years by so many in the newly formed prefecture.[59]

Yet by 1880, Western merchants began to express concerns that such directives were having little effect. One lamented that year by year, the quality of exported teas had deteriorated as producers "looked to nothing but the immediate profit to be obtained, and cared nothing about the future. The only market for Japan teas is America; let Japan lose that—and lose it she will, if the existing state of affairs continued [*sic*]— and the export of Japan teas would then stop."[60] A U.S. consul in Yokohama concluded that widespread adulteration had led to a steady decline in prices on the Yokohama market and thus a nearly 40 percent drop in the value of teas exported between 1874 and 1881, although an oversupply of tea at points during that period also may have contributed.[61]

Meanwhile, U.S. newspapers continued to print claims that Chinese merchants liberally adulterated their teas before shipment, for example by adding cheaper willow leaves. Reports also circulated that Americans had joined the act. In New York City, devious merchants allegedly collected used tea leaves from restaurants, drying them and selling them as the veritable product to unsuspecting consumers.[62]

For decades, Americans had expressed doubts about the quality not only of tea but also milk and other beverages, foods, and drugs.[63] Yet during the early 1880s, such concerns became part of the zeitgeist. Prominent U.S. newspapers and magazines chronicled assaults by the "fiend of food-adulteration," which included mixing "chicory, peas, rye, beans, and a dozen other base counterfeits" into coffee and selling "a decoction of tannin" in place of tea. Reports also detailed the widespread addition of alum as a cheap substitute for cream of tartar in the manufacture of baking powder, an indispensable good in most U.S. kitchens.[64]

What made the early 1880s a tipping point? One factor was the role of prominent health advocates, such as John Harvey Kellogg, whose intriguing health remedies stimulated more discussion of the American diet. A physician, Kellogg opened a popular sanitarium, which operated well into the twentieth century. Its patients, who included captains of industry and a former U.S. president, received enemas and adopted strict vegetarian diets to conquer various ailments. Kellogg published health guides and along with his brother created an iconic breakfast cereal, Corn Flakes. As part of a path to healthy living, he called on Americans to stop drinking tea and coffee, which he believed "excited animal passions."[65]

In Washington as well, officials began to see food and beverage quality as an area of governmental concern. In 1883, Harvey W. Wiley became chief chemist of the Bureau of Chemistry in the U.S. Department of Agriculture. Over the next two decades, he emerged as a forceful advocate for state and federal regulation to keep adulterated foods and beverages off the U.S. market, eventually playing a key role in the adoption of comprehensive federal legislation, instituted with the Pure Food and Drug Act of 1906.

Given the increased public discourse and influence of men like Kel-logg, it would be reasonable to conclude that popular outcries prompted U.S. government officials like Wiley to advocate for regulation to assure the quality of foods and beverages on the U.S. market. In fact, several years would pass before Wiley and other bureaucrats would assume such roles. Moreover, there is little evidence of consumer or health advocate groups, which would later emerge as important forces in pushing for fed-eral food and drug regulation, advocating for government oversight of tea in the early 1880s.

Instead, U.S. congressmen, prompted by tea merchants, took the initia-tive. In February 1883, the Committee on Ways and Means of the U.S. House of Representatives began debating regulations of imported tea. The committee eventually recommended legislation to protect consumers from teas "deprived of their proper quality, strength, or virtue by steep-ing, infusion, decoction, or other means." It affirmed that tea merchants supported the measure, stating that an executive committee of New York tea traders, the Philadelphia Board of Trade, and others engaged in the tea business had given their "unanimous endorsement." These parties backed the bill because it had been framed "to prevent any seri-ous inconvenience by sudden changes in manner of trading to those engaged in the sale of tea in the United States."[66] Making few revisions to the committee's report, in March Congress issued "An Act to Prevent the Importation of Adulterated and Spurious Teas." It stipulated that custom-house officials reject any shipments not meeting quality stan-dards and directed that disputes be adjudicated by a three-man arbitra-tion board—with one member selected by the merchant, another by the custom-house official, and a third by consensus of the two parties.[67]

The pro-business flavor of the act is evident in its failure to ban col-oring agents, instead directing that tea with "so great an admixture of chemicals or other deleterious substances as to make it unfit for use" be stopped at ports. It was thus weaker than a New York State statute passed in 1881 that made it a misdemeanor to sell teas that had been "colored, or coated, or powdered" to conceal damage or to make them appear of higher value.[68] In addition, Congress apparently also responded to con-cern that the U.S. market had become a dumping ground for poor-quality teas following Britain's decision to ban the import of adulterated teas in 1876.[69] Rising anti-Chinese sentiment, which had helped Japan Tea gain market share, does not seem to have had any direct influence in bringing about the new guidelines, despite the fact that the previous year Congress had passed the Chinese Exclusion Act, prohibiting further Chinese immigration to the United States.

In the months after the tea act's passage, the *New York Times* reported on the rejection of Chinese and Japanese teas at New York ports, as well as the abrupt halting of a tea auction because of concerns over quality.[70] Perhaps to offer journalistic balance, the *Times* subsequently ran an article in which several tea merchants offered their perspectives on the quality of imported teas and the use of coloring agents. Like the boy travelers on their visit to a Yokohama refining factory described in the previous chapter, the *Times* reporter showed distaste for uncolored tea, portraying it as having a "dirty yellowish black or deep brown" color. He or she expressed understanding for the decision of merchants, in East Asian ports and in New York, to add color to make their teas green and more pleasing in the eyes of consumers. One tea man interviewed stressed that coloring remained prevalent, even with teas labeled as "pure" or "uncolored," but that tea drinkers should not worry, as only small amounts of Prussian blue and other minerals were added at Japanese and Chinese packing facilities. New York wholesalers also added colors, he revealed, but only in the form of "safe" dyes such as indigo. Another New York tea man stressed that the new act's efficacy was clear given that it was now impossible for anything but the "pure leaf" to be brought into the country. He assured that federal regulation benefited both the consumer and the tea merchant.[71]

INCREASING MEIJI GOVERNMENT INVOLVEMENT

In a speech to an agricultural association, Tada Motokichi identified increased U.S. regulation as part of a global trend, stressing that the British government as well as the colonial authority in Victoria, Australia, had recently passed similar measures. Although noting that Western merchant houses had initially employed Chinese refining and coloring methods to meet the tastes of American consumers, he concluded that those firms now used coloring in ways that blurred the distinction between premium and low grades of Japan Tea. Yet given the dominance of the Western merchant houses over the trade, Japanese producers had limited influence concerning such issues. Tada exhorted Japanese producers and merchants to focus on the factors under their control, detailing ways to improve cultivation, harvesting, drying, and storage practices. He asserted that if followed, such steps would enhance the luster and flavor of Japanese teas and help the industry overcome the challenges posed by the negative critiques that had prompted the U.S. legislation.[72]

A few years before the speech, the Meiji government, in the spirit of the slogan "rich country, strong army," had already begun to sponsor domestic exhibitions in an effort to enhance the quality of goods produced for domestic and foreign markets. Such events, often centered on works of art, had occurred in many regions during the late Edo period.[73] Displaying the increasingly prevalent hand of the central government in the national economy, in Tokyo in 1877 Meiji leaders convened the first national event focused on the promotion of Japan's trade, agriculture, and industry. Ōkubo Toshimichi, a prominent member of the ruling Satsuma-Chōshū clique, proclaimed that by expanding knowledge in those areas, the exhibition would boost the economy of a Japanese nation under the benevolent rule of Emperor Meiji.[74] Matsukata Masayoshi, who subsequently served as a finance minister, pushed the government to open competitive, commercial exhibitions centered on key goods, along the lines of events he had observed in Europe. He shepherded the creation of the first such events, focused on Japan's top exports: silk and tea. Opening in the autumn of 1879, a month-long, competitive tea exhibition drew over eight hundred producers, merchants, and brokers. The judging committee, headed by Tada Motokichi, included another Tea Office official, Kanbayashi Kumajirō, from the famous Uji family, and nine tea merchants and producers, among them three familiar names: Ōtani Kahei, Maruo Bunroku, and Nakayama Motonari. The lineup judged the submitted tea samples based upon their luster, shape, and flavor, as well the on tea's current wholesale and market prices. Six participants received first prize for their teas, including Maruo and Nakayama—a puzzling development, given their status as judges. In remarks offered at the awards ceremony, Matsukata expressed satisfaction, marveling at the number of producing areas represented and the variety of teas on display. He effused that the fragrant and green assemblage glittered as a source of wealth for the nation.[75]

Kyoto leaders also convened exhibitions with the aim of boosting their city's economy by showcasing its manufactured goods and artistic wares. During the city's inaugural exhibition, held in 1872, the organizers offered entertainments, first in the form of the Miyako Odori, dances performed by women from the city's Gion entertainment district, a performance that became a permanent part of Kyoto's cultural calendar. Heads of prominent tea ceremony houses also created displays to introduce the tea ceremony, especially to the handful of Western visitors in attendance. In displays replete with tables and chairs to accommodate Westerners, onlookers could view the tea ceremony and taste samples of *matcha* prepared in the "traditional" way. At subsequent Miyako Odori, female entertainers performed the tea ceremony as a sideshow, later conducting it at city exhibitions as well. The tea ceremony, previously an elite domain practiced largely in private, thus became a more public ritual facilitated by young women, a part of Japanese culture to be presented to the outside world.[76]

Meanwhile, tea producing areas pursued measures to enhance quality. In 1880, Nakayama hatched plans to set up a training facility in Sashima that would teach advanced cultivation methods and another that would impart knowledge about improved refining techniques. Around the same time, an area farmer developed a hand-processing technique that he proclaimed produced a tea of superior flavor. A training office to teach new harvesting and hand-processing techniques soon opened, and teas made using the new methods won first prize in a prefectural competition.[77]

A second national tea competition opened in Kobe in September 1883. Maruo again garnered the competition's first prize and would join a committee of tea producers and merchants that later traveled to Tokyo to offer ideas to improve standards. Early the following year, the Agriculture and Commerce Ministry, the Home Ministry, and Shizuoka Prefecture called for the creation of prefectural and national merchant associations. "Tens of thousands" of tea producers and merchants reportedly thereafter mobilized to assure that harvested teas would meet newly revised U.S. quality standards. In December 1887, the central government issued further directives, which codified links between prefectural tea associations and the newly christened national merchant organization, the Japan Central Tea Association. Government bureaucrats stressed that the newly formed merchant organizations would focus on the production of quality teas to meet the desires of American consumers and thereby once again allow Japanese teas to regain their strong reputation.[78] The Japan Central Tea Association, born in large part from the passage of regulatory legislation in the United States, would thereafter play a vital role in the nation's tea trade. Maruo, Ōtani, and Nakayama served as officers as the association began operations.[79]

In many respects, the Japan Central Tea Association represented an effort by the Meiji government to amalgamate the regional initiatives, in places like Shizuoka and Sashima, which had driven the development of the export industry during the decade following the Meiji Restoration. As later events showed, tea merchants and government officials hoped that the new association could assist regional producers who had previously encountered challenges when trying to break the dominance of Western export firms and sell their region's teas directly on the U.S. market.

Such was the case with the Sayama Company, which, using funds from local investors and loans from the Meiji government, moved to begin direct exports of teas from the region in 1875. The company worked with Satō Momotarō, a Japanese man educated in San Francisco who had sold teas at a San Francisco shop following his graduation from an area business school. He later studied in Boston before opening a trading office in New York, apparently with assistance from the prominent entrepreneur and educator Fukuzawa Yukichi. Along with Japanese silk, Satō aimed to sell Sayama teas to U.S. wholesalers.[80] In 1877, he received a U.S. trademark for his "basket" teas and created a label that proclaimed his teas "guaranteed absolutely pure and genuine." The label notably presented the tea as essentially his private brand and did not include a reference to Sayama or the familiar Japan Tea moniker. The Sayama Company (including Satō's private brand) and similar firms established in the 1870s and 1880s in the Kyoto area, as well as in the treaty ports of Nagasaki and Kobe, all ended in failure. Although the individual circumstances varied, in general the firms confronted limited capital, poor internal organization, and declining export and market prices. During 1873 and 1874, export firms bought teas at an average price of $33 for 100 *kin* (approximately 132 pounds), but that had dropped to $20 per 100 *kin* in the period from 1878 to 1881.[81]

THE RISING INFLUENCE OF SOUTH ASIAN TEAS ON THE WORLD MARKET

In late February 1876, Tea Bureau officials decided to remove Tada from the group that would represent Japan at the Philadelphia Centennial Exhibition. Coming less than a month after his selection, Tada may have been disappointed to miss a chance to visit the United States. Nonetheless, his superiors showed faith in his abilities by sending him, just a few weeks after returning from China, on a six-month junket to survey the rapidly expanding tea industry in British India.

Beginning in the 1830s, colonial authorities in Bengal and officials in the English East India Company initiated efforts to develop tea plantations in Assam. In the late 1840s, the company dispatched to China a Scottish botanist, Robert Fortune. Traveling in disguise as a Qing official, he visited several Chinese tea regions to study tea production and clandestinely acquire tea plants for shipment to India.[82] Colonial officials (the company was dissolved in 1858) subsequently fostered the development of plantations in Assam that eventually grew a hybrid of Chinese and native Indian tea plants. In 1850, India's sole tea plantation occupied just under two thousand acres, producing approximately 200,000 pounds of tea. By 1873, 75,000 acres were under cultivation, producing 14.6 million pounds of tea, most of it shipped to Britain and other British colonies.[83]

Tea Office officials in Tokyo charged Tada with gathering information about how British plantations were cultivating the native Assam plant and using machine technology to refine black teas. Upon his return to Japan, Tada shared what he learned about Indian tea production. He became an instructor of "Indian Style Tea Refining" at a training office set up in Shizuoka in 1877, purveying information about the new refining machines employed by British planters.[84] The following year, he was a joint author of the Japanese translation of an award-winning British study of tea production in India.[85]

Despite the rising interest in Indian techniques, the Industrial Promotion Bureau continued to disseminate information about Chinese cultivating and refining practices. It commissioned the translation and publication of a guidebook penned by Hu Binghsu from the Lingnan region in southern China. In this treatise, Hu offered information about cultivation in different terrains as well as about refining and packaging green and black teas. He also included illustrations of the pan-firing process. In the introduction to the translation, Oda Kanshi, a ministry official, stressed that the text would allow tea growers and, by implication, Japan overall to exploit its tea resources as China had done for centuries.[86]

As production using Chinese and Indian techniques began to rise, the Tea Office identified Australia as a potential new market. At the time, the British colony consumed 6.6 pounds of tea per capita, above that of even Britain (4.6 pounds per capita). To gain a proverbial beachhead on the Australian market, Japanese merchants displayed their teas at the 1880 Melbourne International Exposition. The Tea Office aimed to develop black tea exports, reflected in the fact that seven of the nine merchant groups in the Japanese contingent offered only black teas.[87] Nevertheless, Japanese black teas proved unable to gain a market share, first because of their reputed poor quality vis-à-vis other national varieties. Writing in an Australian newspaper in May 1883, one J. O. Moody concluded that "Japan teas have not given satisfaction, as most of the samples to hand have been too highly fired." He stressed that by con-trast "Indian teas now take the lead in quality over all other growths." Second, Moody presented statistics revealing a prodigious rise in imports of Indian teas into Australia over just three years: from a mere three thousand pounds in 1880 to 2.3 million pounds by the end of 1883.[88]

In 1889, the Japan Central Tea Association helped mount a new effort to export black teas, including those in brick form, to Russia, at the time one of the world's leading tea consuming nations. Aware of the recent failures of prefectural and regional firms to achieve direct sales on the U.S. market, the new enterprise brought together six existing firms work-ing to export teas produced in Shizuoka and the Kyoto area. With Ōtani as president, the Japan Tea Company set up a main office in Tokyo with a branch in Kobe and secured loans from the Meiji government. Ōtani and the directors began to implement steps to commence sales in Russia and to explore expanding exports to the United States. Based on those plans, the company moved to make an initial public offering of its stock, but problems arose concerning the schedule by which the company would repay its government loans. In addition, investors remained timid, partly because of the continued decline in retail tea prices in the United States. Amid these concerns, the company, briefly headed by Maruo after Ōtani resigned, closed in 1891, adding to the list of failures in diversifying export markets and expanding sales of black teas. As a result, the United States, where green teas still dominated, would remain Japan's chief foreign market, with the refining and shipping of Japanese teas kept largely in U.S. and European hands.[89]

DUELING TEA ROOMS AT THE GRAND COLUMBIAN EXPOSITION

Back in Chicago, the thriving economy prompted civic and govern-ment leaders to organize the second world's fair in the United States, the Columbian Exposition of 1893. Packaged as a celebration of the four-hundred-year anniversary of Columbus's arrival in the Americas, the grand, six-month event showcased Chicago's economic prowess and, its promoters hoped, the city's cultural charms. Millions visited the neoclassical buildings and exhibit halls laid out by Frederick Law Olmsted and a team of designers.

The Japanese committee's exhibits stood out among the forty-six participating countries because of the sheer amount of goods on display—topping even Britain. American visitors reveled in the splendor of antique Japanese items on view but lamented that many Japanese at the fair wore Western instead of "exotic," "oriental" attire.[90] Attendees could also see samples of green tea prepared by over 170 Japanese individual farmers as well as local and prefectural tea associations. Maruo displayed his prize-winning teas, and Ōtani offered samples of basket- and pan-fired varieties.[91]

In addition, the Japan Central Tea Association included public displays of tea preparation and tasting similar to those developed at the Kyoto city exhibitions. It operated an "authentic Japanese tea house" to show "the people of the United States and visitors to the Exposition how tea is prepared and drunk in the Land of the Rising Sun." The house included three tea saloons, the first a "common" one, with a 10-cent admission, where young Japanese men served visitors cups of "genuine Japanese tea" (*sencha*), accompanied by a Japanese cake, and giving them a parting gift of "some Japanese article." Paying 25 cents allowed one to enter the "special tea saloon" and enjoy high-grade *gyokuro*, served in "pure Japanese style with a Japanese cake; accompanied with a present of a sample of genuine tea." For those willing to part with 50 cents, there was the "ceremonial tea saloon," offering *matcha*, "the best quality of powdered tea, served with the 'chanoyu' ceremony," along with a cake and a present of packaged Japan Tea. The association aimed to make the teahouse a venue to not only serve *sencha* but to also introduce *gyokuro* and *matcha*, two high grades of Japanese green tea that had "never been known in foreign markets." M. Murayama, a bureaucrat in Japan's Department of Agriculture and Commerce, also alluded to that strategy in a pamphlet, published around the opening of the fair, that gives descriptions of how various types of Japanese tea were made. After detailing the refining process for both varieties, Maruyama stressed that *gyokuro*, like *matcha*, were "served without milk and sugar to bring out their real flavor."[92]

Accounts of the fair, narrated by fictional characters intended to be representative visitors, describe the teahouse and garden and the types of Japanese teas offered. A "history" presented "Maria and her mother" making the rounds of exhibits. Reaching the gate of the Japanese tea garden, they hesitate, "scandalized" at the prospect of paying fifty cents for a single cup of tea. Caught up in the spirit of the fair, the mother decides to enter and join other "curious people who have drunk tea all their lives, just as they have eaten steak and pie, and have regarded it perhaps as a necessary filling for their depleted interiors, but certainly as nothing more." In glowing albeit condescending terms, the mother relates tasting *matcha* "so startling green that the visitor is almost afraid of it" in an ornate ceremonial teahouse followed by a chaser of *sencha*. Sitting on a cushion perched on a porch overlooking the garden, the mother and daughter watch "the little tea-makers hopping about like a bevy of amiable and highly intelligent hoptoads." Those interested in tasting one of the other available teas—the "common herd who just drink tea"—did so in the "big, cool, shady retreat" of one of the other tea rooms. In another account, fictional youths making the rounds of the fair with their tutor take a requisite stop at the tea garden, receiving a cup of the highest-price "ceremonial tea" as well as a "half-pound of the tea, a wafer, some sweetmeats, a souvenir, and elaborate courtesy."[93]

These fictional accounts illustrate the popularity of the Japan teahouse, a fact that Japan Central Tea Association representatives relayed to their superiors in Tokyo. As the number of visitors grew in June 1893, teahouse staff anticipated a shortage of *sencha* and requested more be dispatched from Japan. As they waited for the shipment to arrive, the teahouse staff contacted Hellyer and Company, whose Chicago office supplied enough *sencha* to allow the teahouse to continue to offer both brewed tea and samples packed in paper bags.[94]

With less detail, the aforementioned fictional history also recreates the experience of visiting the nearby tea room operated by the India Tea Association of Calcutta. Tasked with introducing their black teas to Americans, the room's attendants, "great swarthy fellows clad in crimson and gold" with uniforms "adapted from that of a viceroyal bodyguard," encouraged guests to bring their lunches and consume as much tea as they liked, free of charge. In separate rooms for men and women, visitors enjoyed apparently only one grade of Indian black tea, described as having a "rich amber color" and the aroma of "a hay field in July."[95]

Using funds from the colonial government and raised from tea planters, the Ceylon commission constructed its own teahouse to offer samples of the island's new export good. As tea had only recently come to be cultivated on the island, the Ceylon commission members had no specific tradition of tea consumption upon which to draw. It is therefore unclear why they chose an architectural style that employed grasses and reeds to construct a rustic hut near the Lake Michigan shore. An exposition album described the hut as displaying the "ingenuity with which the Cingalese utilize such primitive materials in their building operations." The album called the teahouse a refuge from the hot summer weather and a place where Americans could compare Ceylon teas with those from China and Japan. Tea was also available at the Ceylon Pavilion, where for example, the Spanish royal infanta Eulalia sampled it during her celebrated day at the fair. An estimated six million people visited the Ceylon Pavilion, consuming 4.5 million cups and taking home over one million packets of Ceylon teas.[96] Over the course of the exposition, many Midwesterners probably tried their first cups of India- or Ceylon-produced black tea at the India and Ceylon tea rooms.

Given that national displays formed a key part of the Chicago and other world exhibitions of the late nineteenth century, it is understandable that teas were offered to Americans within distinct national categories. Yet such a strategy also fit the strong American preference for established varieties of teas, which included the "national" brand of Japan Tea. This manifested in an apparent American dislike for blended teas, a consumption pattern that contrasted with their British cousins. Joseph Walsh, the Philadelphia tea merchant, noted that U.S. dealers and the general public viewed blending as "dishonorable and about on a par with other methods of adulteration." Hoping to counteract such views, he offered numerous recipes for blending various green, oolong, and black teas.[97]

Based upon their offerings of tea, it is safe to conclude that the leaders of Japan Central Tea Association viewed the Columbian Exposition as an opportunity to expand sales of Japan Tea beyond the now well-established pan- and basket-fired varieties. If Midwesterners, typified by the fictional Maria, could come to appreciate *gyokuro* and *matcha*, they might begin to purchase such high-end varieties of Japanese green tea, which could be sold at higher prices. The failure to export black teas to markets like Australia and Russia probably also played a role in prompting such a strategy tailored for the U.S. market. Following the fair, the association established offices in New York and Chicago to maintain Japan Tea's foothold and track the emerging competition from India and Ceylon.

The years surrounding the Chicago fair also witnessed a changing of the guard in the leadership of Japan's tea industry. In 1892, Maruo, who held posts in the Shizuoka government, became involved in the national political scene, winning a seat in the Lower House of the Diet, a bicameral national legislature. In 1889, Emperor Meiji had promulgated a constitution, a "gift" to the nation that paved the way for the creation of the Diet. The Meiji government made the move to quell strong opposition that had coalesced in a Freedom and Popular Rights Movement, which called for the adoption of more representative forms of government.

In 1892, Nakayama passed away at the age of seventy-five. Two years later, Tada Motokichi retired from his government post, choosing to return not to Chiba, his birthplace, but to his tea farm in Shizuoka. Although retired, he remained an active participant in the Shizuoka tea industry, giving talks and offering advice, before passing away in 1896, the same year as Maruo.[98]

Of the three men, Tada lived a life that perhaps best exemplifies the rupture and new possibilities of the Meiji period. If not for the tumult and social change of the 1860s, he would have known an existence encapsulated within his native Chiba and nearby Edo. Yet because of the tea export trade, Tada, a man who had fought against the nascent Meiji regime in Boshin War, could create a new life in Shizuoka. He would later journey to China and India, destinations he could have only dreamed of visiting as a young man. The fact that Tada, as a government official supporting the nation's tea trade, would travel to other parts of Asia underscores again the international nature of Japan's tea export trade.

As the nineteenth century drew to close, Japan's takeover of Taiwan began to make the Japanese tea industry a more integrated, imperial enterprise, although as will be explored in the following chapter, Japanese and Taiwanese teas continued to be sold in the United States as distinct categories. Overall, Japan's tea export trade remained defined by exports to the United States, despite attempts to cultivate interest in other parts of the world. Because of the continued prominence of the American market, Ōtani, who lived well into the twentieth century and became president of the Japan Central Tea Association when the post was created in 1909, would repeatedly travel to Chicago and other parts of the Midwest, aiming especially to keep the Midwest green tea country.

5

THE BLACK TEA WAVE
HITS AMERICA

In March 1895, Richard Blechynden, representing the Calcutta Chamber of Commerce, trumpeted the remarkable success of India and Ceylon teas in displacing Chinese varieties in Britain, mirroring what had unfolded in Australia. In 1866, Britain imported 96 percent of its teas from China, but by 1894, 88 percent of teas consumed in Britain came from India and Ceylon. Blechynden asserted that the United States would soon witness a similar change because the "American people are quick to appreciate a good thing when they see it" and are "fast learning the superiority of teas raised in India and Ceylon to those of China and Japan."[1]

During the 1890s, more Americans would in fact begin to consume black teas from Ceylon and India. Yet as this chapter will explore, this was not simply because the newcomer black teas were superior in price or quality. Rather, as was the case with the rise of Japan Tea two decades earlier, racial prejudices and images played a central role.

CREATING NEGATIVE IMAGES OF CHINESE
AND JAPANESE TEAS

As British troops engaged Chinese naval and army units around Canton at the start of the Opium War, a missionary journal, introducing

THE BLACK TEA WAVE HITS AMERICA 125

aspects of China to Anglo-American audiences, published an account of tea cultivation and production. Drawing upon Chinese publications and apparently firsthand experience, the unnamed author gave a generally positive appraisal of Chinese refining methods, describing how a worker "with his bare arm" stirred the tea before "dexterously" removing it from a firing pan to be cooled before packing. He or she outlined the remaining stages necessary in preparing chests for shipment, noting that a Chinese merchant might sometimes use inferior grades to make imitations of superior varieties. Yet the author intimated that a Chinese merchant would employ such practices not to deceive but to meet the extraordinary European demand for a particular type of tea. He or she also mentioned that brokers at the London market had recently received some of the first shipments of Indian Assam teas. Unfortunately, the "unskillfulness of the [Indian] workmen had spoiled the quality of the tea, as it had a smoky and strong flavor." Yet the author believed that the quality of the teas would soon improve, thanks of the presence of better qualified Chinese workers, who would advance standards in Assam's tea fields and factories.[2]

The historian Erika Rappaport has illustrated how in subsequent decades, British merchants, scientists, journalists, and novelists increasingly offered far less generous portrayals of Chinese production practices and Chinese tea overall. They warned British consumers that Chinese manufacturing techniques were dirty and fraudulent, leveling particularly harsh attacks against colored Chinese green teas. Such negative pronouncements helped India and Ceylon black teas gain dominant shares of the British and Australian markets by the 1880s. During the same decade, representatives of Indian planters began to circulate throughout the United States, developing marketing strategies that they hoped would lead Americans to turn to their black teas.[3]

In this changed British view of the Middle Kingdom, Chinese factories came to be populated not with skilled workers but with dirty coolies, half-clad, sweaty, and neglectful of quality. A British traveler in the 1880s described a tea factory as full of the "hum of the busiest activity— when indeed are Chinese labourers otherwise than desperately busy?— but there is an entire absence of English order, cleanliness and method." He noted the "crowds of half-naked coolies," which were "shambling about with heavy burdens, getting in each other's way, and claiming 'by leave' in constant discordant cries."[4]

Similar portrayals soon appeared in U.S. newspapers. A Portland, Oregon, newspaper published an interview with an apparent tea expert who had visited a Chinese tea factory. "Just outside one of the largest establishments, I saw a half-naked coolie who had pulled off his gown and was picking out of the seams certain unquestionable animals, which he cracked between his fingers and ate." The man went on to describe how because of the warm weather, "perspiration was rolling down their [the workers] yellow skins, and was, I judge, readily absorbed by the tea in the boxes." He claimed that at a major port "I was told that a vast amount of the tea was spoiled about a year or so ago. It was so ruined by dampness or something that the Chinese would not use it. The factors then spread it out on the dirty wharves, where it was mixed with all kinds of foul stuff, and dried for shipment to America and England."[5]

In a similar vein, a San Francisco newspaper presented an interview with F. A. Hines, a tea merchant, who cautioned readers that Japanese also refined tea using underhanded and unsavory methods. Although offering some positive assessments, Hines suggested that such practices emerged from a general lack of morality and ethics in Japan. He roundly criticized the widespread practice of poor rural families selling their daughters into prostitution and concluded, with little explanation, that an average Japanese man could expect to live about twenty years less than his American peer because of Japan's low moral standards. Although not using the term, Hines took the dirty coolie of the Chinese tea factory and placed him in a Japanese one, describing watching "a perspiring Jap, who is stripped to the waist, stir[ring] the tea with his hands. The peculiar flavor [of Japanese tea] which is admired by many people is largely derived from the streams of moisture which pour from the superheated native who operates the firing-pan."[6]

Such portrayals undercut the image of the industrious, artistic, and thus unthreatening Japanese presented in previous advertisements and viewed by many Americans at Japanese villages and world exhibitions. The Japanese and Chinese refining tea became laborers at the lowest end of the wage scale, toiling to complete base, physical tasks.[7] In addition, such descriptions eliminated distinctions between Japan Tea and Chinese varieties that had helped the former gain market share in previous decades. Instead, both were presented as an amorphous and suspect group of sweat-laced green teas, sowing seeds of doubt in the minds of U.S. consumers.

Advertisements appearing throughout the United States began to employ the specter of the dirty coolie in an effort to convince Americans to purchase India and Ceylon black teas. In Chicago, an advertisement for the Monsoon brand asserted that its Ceylon and India black teas were the result of "civilized labor and intelligence," which brought "greater perfection." It boasted that "there can be no question as to the result when civilized man's intelligence, backed by capital, is placed in competition with the pauper and Coolie labor of China and Japan."[8] Other advertisements stressed the superior methods of British-run plantations in Ceylon and India, producing teas, such as those sold under the Blue Cross brand, which were "carefully prepared under white supervision—China and Japan teas are not."[9]

The colonial government of Ceylon took the lead in instituting levies on its teas to fund further print advertising. The Indian colonial government later followed suit. The Indian and Ceylon promotion boards would thereafter work together, often forming a unified lobby to promote their teas.[10]

British tea men hoped to entice Americans to switch to Ceylon and India teas also by taking on the road versions of the exhibits presented at the Columbian Exposition. In August 1893, a St. Paul grocer, no doubt in coordination with a British supplier, offered customers a complimentary tasting of Indian tea, proclaiming that "never before has such a glorious drink been sipped in St. Paul." The grocer hung "handsome Indian draperies" in a temporary tea room equipped with "cozy tea tables" and "comfortable seats." "Polite natives of India" would wait upon customers as they sampled the tea, with sugar and cream supplied for those interested in adding them to their cups.[11] Blechynden also brought "native experts" with him when he traveled around the Midwest offering samples of Indian black teas. For good measure, he asserted that India and Ceylon teas held a higher caffeine content than Chinese varieties. Japanese teas contained only traces of "that essential princi-ple."[12] Other British observers, quoted in U.S. newspapers, stressed that India and Ceylon teas could produce more cups per pound than Chinese teas.[13]

British subjects involved in the promotion of Ceylon tea at the Colum-bian Exposition took the promotion a step further by founding their own companies, optimistic that Americans would soon take to the island's black teas. John J. Grinlinton, Ceylon's commissioner at the fair, opened the Chicago Tea Store, but the venture soon ended in failure.[14]

Vincent Tissera, another member of the fifty-person Ceylon contin-gent, also decided to remain in the United States and try his fortunes in the tea trade. A native of Colombo, Tissera presents a story akin to that of Satō Momotarō: an Asian man attempting to sell his homeland's teas on a U.S. market dominated by white-owned and -operated Anglo-American firms. With a partner, Tissera set up the American Ceylon Tea and Produce Importing Company in Davenport, Iowa. Tissera aimed to circumvent the usual trade route that saw goods going first to Britain and instead directly import teas, spices, and other Ceylon products into the United States.[15]

To drum up sales, Tissera traveled throughout the Midwest, includ-ing a stop in Milwaukee in January 1895. In an interview with a local newspaper, he cautioned U.S. tea drinkers that green teas were treated with gypsum or Prussian blue and Japan Tea with a coating of graphite to give it polish. Tissera extolled that Ceylon black teas were pure, com-posed only of tender leaves from the first picking of the year.[16] The tour took him to St. Louis, where on the evening of February 5 he boarded an eastbound sleeper on the Louisville & Nashville Railroad. Upon checking the tickets, the conductor, taking "him for a negro," demanded that Tissera move to the segregated "smoker" car. Tissera refused, pro-ducing a ticket and even offering to pay his fare a second time. When forced off the train at Belleville, Illinois, Tissera scuffled with the train staff, in the process losing $100 in cash and a ticket for his baggage, which was apparently stuffed with tea samples.[17]

Details of the incident soon appeared in newspapers and magazines throughout the United States. The *Congregationalist* noted how the inci-dent revealed "probable complications" that would result from recent laws in Southern states stipulating racial segregation on railcars, no doubt referring to a Louisiana law that would be upheld by the U.S. Supreme Court in the famous *Plessy v. Ferguson* case the following year. The magazine lamented that "the world is full of dark-skinned races and America is attractive to them. Must every man with a swarthy skin carry a certificate of eligibility for the comforts of a Kentucky railroad car?" The *Congregationalist* urged Tissera to sue for damages, a path he did not take because the Louisville & Nashville Railroad quickly offered a $1,500 settlement. Tissera seemed to revel in the attention and gave the conductor the benefit of the doubt, asserting that he had erroneously believed Tissera had held a counterfeit ticket.[18]

Tissera later split with his partner and moved his share of the company to Chicago. His brand of Ceylon tea soon became available at Chicago retail stores, although in at least one instance, it sold at a higher price (43 cents a pound) than basket-fired Japan Tea, which retailed for 35 cents a pound, and Japan Tea in bulk, sold for as low as 19 cents per pound.[19] Tissera embraced life in Chicago, becoming an active member of the Masons and later a U.S. citizen, relating in one interview his ardor for his adopted land, which had sprung forth after witnessing Independence Day celebrations for the first time. To advance his business, Tissera tirelessly pursued expanding direct trade between the United States and Ceylon via transpacific routes. Over the span of several years, he made numerous appeals outlining the economic benefits that such trade could bring to Chicago, as well as to Seattle.[20]

Tissera's experiences in Chicago and across the United States reveal a strange duality: an individual hungry for publicity in almost any form but facing repeated challenges as a man of color. In December 1896, he personally campaigned for the life of Gypsy, a circus elephant that had killed its keeper. No doubt looking to create an event for which tickets could be sold, the elephant's owner requested permission to electrocute Gypsy in public on January 1, 1897. The Chicago police chief refused to allow the spectacle, but Gypsy's fate remained in the balance. Professing a reverence for all living things gained from the Buddhism practiced in his native land, the Episcopalian Tissera visited the offices of the *Chicago Daily Tribune*. There he asked for a campaign to be mounted to send Gypsy to India, an effort he felt should be championed by the

Republican Party because of the party's use of an elephant as a mascot. (It is unclear what happened to the animal.)[21]

A few weeks after the sinking of the USS *Maine* in Havana Harbor, the event that triggered the Spanish-American War, a man approached Tissera on a Chicago street, asking if he spoke Spanish. When Tissera replied yes, the man attacked him. Making no mention of the possible role of jingoistic, anti-Spanish sentiment, the *Tribune* hinted that Tissera's ethnicity was to blame, writing that his "swarthy skin nearly precipitated an international imbroglio."[22] His "coppery complexion and dark optics" were also suggested as contributing to the decision of custom's officials to search Tissera "down to his socks" for allegedly smuggling jewels when he arrived in New York in 1900. Tissera lodged complaints over the incident, noting his rights as a naturalized U.S. citizen.[23]

Despite facing racial prejudice on numerous occasions, Tissera continued to operate, apparently with success, his tea company in Chicago. He forged ahead with selling Ceylon tea, a product then being aggressively marketed through a campaign built on contempt for other Asians: Chinese and Japanese and their tea refining practices.

U.S. TEA MERCHANTS AND THE CAMPAIGN FOR INCREASED FEDERAL REGULATION

As the India and Ceylon campaign to create a negative image of Japanese and Chinese teas continued, tea merchants in New York and Chicago began to call for expanded federal regulation. Thomas A. Phelan, a prominent New York importer, became the front man in an initiative to push members of Congress to enact stricter laws related to imported teas.[24] In February 1897, E. A. Schoyer, the head of a Japan-based firm, organized a meeting of Chicago tea merchants, who agreed to support Phelan's call for greater federal oversight. The group resolved to telegraph the Illinois congressional delegation a statement of support signed by twenty-one Chicago tea merchants. They also formed a committee, which appealed to the Chicago Board of Health to take steps to stop the flow of damaged and harmful teas into the city's market.[25]

As had been the case with the passage of the 1883 act, the initiative of tea merchants proved decisive. In March 1897, Congress passed legislation "to prevent the importation of impure and unwholesome tea."[26] Taking effect two months later, the act made it unlawful "to import or bring into the United States any merchandise as tea which is inferior in purity, quality and fitness for consumption." Essentially scrapping the existing regulations imposed in 1883, the new law directed that the secretary of the Treasury appoint a board of seven tea examiners. Meeting annually, the board would "set uniform standards of purity, quality and fitness," which involved not merely written instructions (as was the case in 1883) but also the selection of samples of acceptable varieties of tea that inspectors could reference when examining teas entering specified U.S. ports. The inaugural tea board included Phelan, Schoyer, and A. P. Irwin, the head of a large New York house that imported teas from China, Japan, Ceylon, and India. Frederick Hellyer would later serve a number of years on the board.[27]

As we can see, a cross-section of U.S. tea merchants, not simply those importing Chinese and Japanese teas, had supported the push to enact new legislation. Yet the India-Ceylon lobby showed particular dissatisfaction, exemplified by the decision to run a new wave of negative advertisements in prominent newspapers. The advertisements proclaimed that the new legislation would have little impact because of the deplorable refining processes employed by Japanese and Chinese producers. As shown in figure 5.1, such advertisements simultaneously stressed the better quality of India and Ceylon teas that resulted not from legislation but from the mechanized process employed to refine them. The advertisement punctuates the "filthy process" reputed to be used in refining Japanese and Chinese green teas with an image of two coolies, with almost animalistic faces, hand rolling teas on a table, oblivious to the pigs feeding beneath them. In addition, making use of a quotation from Shakespeare, it suggests how sweat from the toiling coolies added more "impurities" to Japanese and Chinese green teas.[28]

Accounts from proclaimed experts also continued to appear in major newspapers, affirming that consumers should be wary of green teas. In July, the New York Times featured an interview with Fred C. Williams, an advertising agent.[29] Williams argued that the act would improve the

CEYLON AND INDIA TEA

Needs no Legislation to keep it pure, being prepared by

Legislation cannot eliminate the impurities in China and Japan tea imparted by the filthy process shown below.

"Let them (tea drinkers) lick not the sweat which is in their poison."—Coriolanus, Act III , Scene I.

F. B. F. Grocery Co.

SOLE AGENTS.

For Sale by All First-Class Grocers.

One teaspoonful of Pure Machine Rolled Tea goes as far as two of the impure hand rolled. Use boiling water; infuse five minutes.

BEST BRANDS.

India and Ceylon Teas

PURITAN,
KNICKERBOCKER,
COLUMBIA,
B. & B., (Green Packet.)

FIGURE 5.1 This and similar advertisements for Ceylon and India tea appeared in newspapers and magazines throughout the United States in the spring and summer of 1897. This version ran in the *Bellows Falls Times* (Bellows Falls, Vermont) on August 14.

Source: Chronicling America, Library of Congress, Washington, DC.

overall quality of tea on the U.S. market by eliminating disparities between Japanese and Chinese teas and those produced in India and Ceylon. He asserted that Japanese tea merchants had reluctantly confirmed the veracity of doubts about the quality of their teas.

> It is a case of an absolutely pure article manufactured in a scientific way against an impure and adulterated article manufactured in an unclean and unscientific manner. The people of this country are beginning to demand only pure food products, and judging from the enormous increase in the sales of Ceylon and India teas, they propose to have the best.

Some New York merchants also appealed to their congressional delegation to address their concerns that the new regulations often unjustly excluded Ceylon and India teas of good quality.[30]

Speaking as the head of the new Board of Tea Experts, Phelan held his ground and refused to revise the new regulatory process. He argued that the law had put all importers on notice, and thus low-grade teas from any country could no longer enter the United States. He stressed that in recent years such low grades, "little more than weed," had been occupying a large market share, imported for around 15 cents a pound and selling for 25 cents retail. Phelan hinted that tea merchants overall would benefit from the new law and the opportunity to import higher-grade and therefore more expensive teas. In so doing, they could combat what had been a steady decline of wholesale and retail tea prices over the past two decades. The secretary of the Treasury later weighed in, asserting that the new inspection regime was improving the overall quality of imported teas.[31]

FIGHTING RENEWED TARIFFS

Although the new tea act mollified many involved in Japan's export industry, a proposal to slap a 10-cent tariff on tea floated by members of

Congress in May 1897 caused consternation among Meiji government and Japan Central Tea Association officials. Maeda Masana, a bureaucrat who played a role in the development of the prefectural and national tea associations a few years earlier, hastily traveled to the United States as a special envoy, tasked with lobbying to keep tea tariff free. Maeda met the secretaries of the Treasury Department and the Department of Agriculture, members of Congress, and President William McKinley, making appeals that apparently prompted the shelving of the proposal in July 1897. Yet the situation changed suddenly in April 1898 when the Spanish-American War broke out. Looking to boost revenue to fund the war, Congress passed a tax on tea, which took effect in July that same year. To the frustration of tea merchants, Congress left coffee tariff free. Although the United States proved victorious in the war several months later, the tariff remained in place.[32]

In hopes of prompting a repeal, in the autumn of 1898 Ōtani Kahei traveled to United States as president of the Japan Central Tea Association to attend a meeting of Japanese and American businessmen in Philadelphia. En route, he made a brief stop in Minneapolis and St. Paul, where he conferenced with a number of business and city leaders. Ōtani described at length his conversation with James J. Hill, the railroad executive who had spearheaded the completion of the Great Northern Railway between Seattle and the Twin Cities five years earlier. Then working with the Japanese steamship company Nippon Yussen, Hill stressed the savings in transport costs of the Great Northern and thus its virtues as a route for U.S.-Japan commerce. Hill probably supported the Twin Cities' tea wholesalers and jobbers in their push to have a federal inspector based in Minnesota to check tea transported in bond from Seattle via the Great Northern. The Twin Cities contingent complained that the current system—with inspectors at Tacoma, San Francisco, New York, and Chicago—unfairly limited their profits from the lucrative tea trade. They voiced particular frustration at wholesalers and jobbers in Chicago, who had stymied efforts to bring an inspector to the Twin Cities. Firms in New York also opposed the new inspectorate, but the federal government decided to open one in St. Paul in April 1899.[33]

Ōtani spent a number of days in Chicago, where he again met with civic and business leaders and toured the Board of Trade. Japan Central

Tea Association officials working at the Chicago branch briefed him on current market conditions before he called at the offices of several import firms, including Hellyer and Company. He also made his way to a prominent advertising firm, marveling at the hum of a typewriters and phones in use by the employees on the eleventh floor of a large stone building. After attending the Philadelphia meeting, Ōtani visited the Japanese ambassador in Washington to seek his help in pushing for a repeal, asking him to stress to U.S. officials the strain that the tax had placed on Japan's tea farmers.[34]

On that trip, Ōtani failed to achieve a repeal of the tariff but nonetheless demonstrated that a more active stance of both the Japan Central Tea Association and the Meiji government more generally was emerging. As he sought to expand direct sales by Japanese firms, Ōtani displayed a commitment, which tea association representatives would continue to follow, to work closely with the U.S. trading houses like Hellyer and Company that maintained a hold over the distribution and sale of Japanese teas in the United States.

As had been the case with the push for greater federal regulation, U.S. tea importers and wholesalers came together to continue to fight the tariff on tea. In 1901, Phelan, then president of the Wholesale Grocers Association, helped form a National Tea Duty Repeal Association. In January of the following year, he presented the association's case to the Ways and Means Committee of the U.S. House of Representatives. Phelan and other tea men complained that Congress had maintained the tax on tea but not on coffee, a move that according to Department of Treasury statistics had led to a significant drop in per capita tea consumption: from 1.5 pounds per year in 1897 to a pound in 1901. One tea retailer stressed that the poor bore the brunt of the tariff, detailing how low-grade teas, which had sold for around 19 cents per pound before 1898, were now priced at 25 cents per pound. The tea men urged Republicans on the committee to not show undue favor to coffee and remember the slogan of the "free breakfast table," successfully employed to repeal tariffs on both tea and coffee in 1872. The tea men apparently made a persuasive case: two months later, Congress approved a repeal.[35]

As the secretary of the Treasury's report revealed, Americans were drinking less tea, perhaps because of the higher prices resulting from the tariff. Many may have instead chosen coffee because of its dramatically lower price, which according to some accounts had fallen from 15 cents to a mere 5 cents a pound in previous years. In fact, the years around 1900 witnessed a surge in U.S. coffee consumption as Brazil, a coffee producer since the mid-nineteenth century, ramped up exports. By 1902, per capita coffee consumption reached 13.2 pounds a year, up from ten pounds annually just a few years earlier.[36]

Yet we should be cautious about seeing consumers as choosing between tea and coffee simply because of price. The 1890s also witnessed the appearance of Postum, which captured much of coffee's market share, thanks to aggressive marketing efforts. C. W. Post, the enigmatic creator of Postum, challenged coffee by claiming it to be detrimental to one's health, not merely by undercutting it on price. Post revealed how effective advertising could be in shaping beverage consumption, a point not lost on anyone involved in the U.S. retail tea trade.[37]

PROMOTING "AUTHENTIC" JAPANESE TEA

Maeda, Ōtani, and others involved in Japan's export industry lamented the damage done to their exports by the short-lived tariff. To make matters worse, some U.S. importers still complained about the poor quality of Japan Tea, contending that the blame lay on the other side of the Pacific. Thomas Hellyer numbered among such critics, asserting that the Japan Central Tea Association must devote its full attention to improving the quality of the teas sent to the United States or fear losing the trade to their competitors from India and Ceylon. Hellyer's cautionary words, reminiscent of those offered by U.S. merchants decades earlier, indicated that creating sustained quality remained an abiding challenge for Japan's tea industry.[38]

Nonetheless, around the turn of the century Japan's tea merchants found themselves at a convergence of trends that presented fresh opportunities for their export trade. The India-Ceylon campaign had sowed further doubts about colored teas, which still composed a subsector of the Japan Tea brand. It is difficult to track the total share of colored teas, but it is safe to say that while the federal government and merchants did not explicitly ban coloring agents, their use was increasingly frowned upon on both sides of the Pacific. For example, U.S. Department of Agriculture chemists voiced their opposition in a report issued in 1892. Illustrating the increasingly active role of the federal government in food and beverage markets, the group tested a range of teas, concluding that common coloring agents, with the exception of salts of iron or copper, had little effect on a tea drinker's health. If present in tea, most would be removed during infusion. A consumer would therefore have to drink a large amount of colored tea daily to experience any ill effects. Although affirming the limited medical risk, the chemists categorized coloring agents as one of the deceptions they sought to eliminate to protect the American consumer from adulterated products.[39]

Maeda also expressed his dissatisfaction with colored teas and with the continued use of Chinese refining practices. "Westerners do not personally know Japanese tea. Until now, they have only experienced the Japanese tea refined by Western firms in the treaty ports. Put another way, the tea exported has been produced with the hard toil of Japanese workers, and changed into a strange hybrid [*bakemono*] before it is even shipped overseas."[40]

In the late 1890s, Japan's tea industry could begin to export in large volume what Maeda and others could categorize as a more "authentic" Japanese tea, refined with less firing and free of coloring, in other words, a tea with more flavor and a natural green color. The efforts of regional producers contributed to this shift. In Sashima, the prefectural government established more training offices, bringing experts from Shizuoka to teach hand-refining methods. After a period of instruction, farmers were tasked with refining roughly seventeen pounds of tea within a two-hour period. The instructor would thereafter judge the luster, flavor, and other attributes of the tea. If he deemed the resulting tea suitable, the farmer would receive a graduation certificate. The training offices indicate how prefectural authorities and tea association officials sought to enhance their production model, by which small producers first refined some teas before shipment to ports for further processing and export.[41]

Greater mechanization would prove even more influential in advancing production of this revised version of Japan Tea. In the 1880s, Takabayashi Kenzō, who had grown up in Kawagoe, developed one of the first refining machines. A few years later, Hellyer and Hunt both invested in the new devices, keeping them a trade secret. Another Japanese inventor, Harasaki Gensaku, subsequently created a machine that rolled tea to refine it, a machine later installed in many factories. In 1903, an observer of the trade noted that "the success achieved by British tea-manufacturers in the matter of tea-preparing machinery has warranted many progressive go-down owners at Kobe, Yokohama and elsewhere in Japan to attempt similar methods of manufacture, and at this time there are several plants that are manufacturing teas by machine."[42]

Because of the decline of coloring and the increased mechanization, which allowed for the production of less-fired teas, a greater proportion of Japanese teas exported to the United States were becoming more like the *sencha* widely consumed in Japan today. Instead of focusing on the physical appearance and color of a batch of Japanese green tea, U.S. consumers could now begin to appreciate more its taste and aroma when brewed. It helped that, as noted in the previous chapter, Americans had also moved away from boiling teas for extended periods. In addition, consumers were becoming aware of aspects of tea that tea drinkers today take for granted. An 1898 report advised that "the most prominent characteristics of tea are very probably due to a substance called caffeine in it."[43]

Amid these trends, the leaders of the Japan Central Tea Association also realized the growing value of print advertising, a fact illustrated by Ōtani's decision to visit an advertising firm in Chicago. In 1897, Ōtani successfully lobbied the central government to provide, for seven years, an annual financial stipend used to mount the first coordinated advertising campaign for Japan Tea in the United States. One of the campaign's initial advertisements ran in a prominent national magazine in February 1898. It boasted that Japan Tea was not only pure but had a "superior flavor and aroma resulting from the natural advantages of Japanese soil and climate, but equally so, perhaps, because of the clean and careful methods by which it is uniformly prepared for market." Along with the image of a Japanese woman in a kimono making tea, it listed the "official recipe," urging consumers to use one teaspoon of tea leaves for every cup desired and never to allow a pot to boil.[44]

Similar advertisements were linked with another Midwest fair: the Trans-Mississippi and International Exhibition held in Omaha, Nebraska, from June to November 1898. Compared to the Chicago extravaganza five years earlier, the Omaha Exhibition sported a far smaller foreign presence, and Japan, Ceylon, and India did not send official contingents. The Qing government operated a Chinese pavilion but apparently did not directly promote its teas, leaving a U.S. company to manage a separate "Chinese Tea Garden."[45] The Japan Central Tea Association undertook a more comprehensive effort, linking an advertising campaign to its tea garden at the Omaha exhibition. One such advertisement proclaimed Japanese tea to be "absolutely the purest, cleanest, most wholesome" and pledged that it was "officially inspected before exportation." It included a line urging readers to visit the Japanese tea garden at the Omaha fair.[46]

Association representatives implemented several steps to assure that visitors could appreciate the "true taste" (*shinmi*) of Japan Tea. Deeming Omaha's water to be unsanitary, they employed filters to assure better quality water for brewing. The representatives also offered a variety of Japanese and Western sweets to meet the widest demand. In addition, the contingent served iced tea, especially during hot days, hoping to overcome the perception that their green teas were ill suited to be served as a chilled beverage. Visitors gave the iced tea only mixed reviews. Finally, representatives sought to convince U.S. consumers to refrain from the common practice of adding cream or milk and thereby appreciate what the representatives believed was the fine, pure flavor of Japanese green teas. They therefore did not provide cream and milk and only when pressed gave guests a small amount of sugar to add to their cups. Stipulating so strongly to visitors the "proper" way to consume Japan Tea was a bold move that potentially alienated some committed tea drinkers. Japan Central Tea Association representatives apparently believed it a necessary step to demonstrate the inherent, fine flavor of "straight" Japanese green tea in light of the sustained negative campaign. We can only speculate how many tea drinkers changed their minds about Japan Tea because of this approach. Exhibition officials, however, judged that the tea garden staff had promoted Japanese teas in an impartial and fair way. They therefore presented the Japan Central Tea Association with a gold medal, one of the scant hundred awarded among the roughly 12,000 exhibits at the fair.[47]

Lipton Tea Company also ran a small tea stand at the Omaha fair.[48] At the time, the firm was beginning to sell its teas on the U.S. market. Determining that "the drinking of tea had become very much more general in Britain" in the 1880s, Thomas J. Lipton, who hailed from Glasgow, moved to expand his commercial empire beyond his chain of British retail grocery stores and meatpacking plants in the U.S. Midwest.[49] He purchased coffee plantations in Ceylon devastated by a plant fungus and converted them to tea. Selling his plantations' teas at his stores, he eliminated middlemen and their share of the profits, quickly achieving success on the British market.

In an autobiography published just after his death in 1931, Lipton stressed that the poor quality of green teas had allowed his company to gain a foothold in the U.S. market. He declared that around the turn of the century for "all intents and purposes there was *no* tea-trade in America," a claim supported by his failed attempt to order tea at an American hotel. The businessman described encountering a waiter who had never heard of the beverage and instead hurriedly brought coffee, hoping to pacify his customer. Perhaps aware of the dubious nature of his account, Lipton acknowledged that tea was indeed available in New York and Chicago stores, but "without exception they [the teas] were terrible—at least, to my taste. For the most part the teas sold to the general public were 'Oolongs' and 'Japans' common sorts of green teas, and most inferior 'China Congou.'"

Lipton also bemoaned that many "store-keepers regarded tea as on the same level with barley, rice, and maize, and kept their supplies exposed in all kinds of open receptacles. At a leading grocery establishment on State Street, Chicago, I saw tea being made to suffer the horrible indignity of complete exposure to all kinds of weather at the open shop door." He lamented that shops denied tea the appropriate "reverent handling" by giving it to customers in cheap paper bags.[50]

Lipton, while hyperbolic in his assessments of green teas, seems to have been correct in his contention that grocers continued to sell tea largely in bulk. Although Lipton and other large national companies were gradually gaining prominence, most U.S. consumers, upon visiting a local shop, would see various types of teas displayed in chests or kept in canisters behind a counter. After making their selection, the retailer would place the amount desired by the customer in a bag sporting the store's label.

Retailers also sold teas in prescribed amounts in tins or cans with proprietary labels. Writing in 1905, a guidebook for retailers outlined the process by which an importer, like Hellyer and Company, would act as a wholesaler, acquiring and refining teas in Japan and delivering teas to grocers:

> It is generally understood that, when accepting a tea-importation order from the retail merchant, the Wholesaler undertakes to purchase in the Oriental markets, on behalf of, and for the account of the retailer, a given quantity of one, or of several kinds or grades of tea, at a stated, or at a limited price for each grade, delivered at some designated distributing point in the United States. Each chest of tea so imported is to bear upon its label, or facing, the name and address of the retailer, together with his chosen brand or brands. When small packages, boxes or tins are to be imported, each package, box or tin is to bear a chosen brand together with the retailer's name as the importer of the tea covered by the label of the package, box or tin.[51]

In Milwaukee, grocers marketed their own brands, such as Milwaukee's Roundy, Peckham, and Company's "Red Clover Japan Tea," which was likely imported by Hellyer and Company or another Chicago-based firm.[52] In 1903 in Galva, Japan Tea was still sold (for 50 cents a pound), but now along with Lipton's "Best Tea," presumably a black tea, offered in a can for 40 cents a pound.[53]

The San Francisco–based Hills Brothers also imported teas and created labels indicating the brand names of local retailers throughout Western states. The labels include familiar categories of pan or basket fired and, in tune with the efforts of the Japan Central Tea Association, often referenced Japan Tea's purity. Like those etched in Japan in previous decades, some labels had images of flowers or objects but lacked representations of Japanese places and people. Most prominently printed the name or initials of the retailer, such as shown in figure 5.2, the Morris Roberts Company of Hagerman and Bliss, Idaho, and Quilici Brothers, an Italian American–owned store in Wells, Nevada, a town that became known for its gambling houses and saloons soon after the Central Pacific Railway founded it as a watering station in 1869. Revealing the diversity of retailers offering Japan Tea, Hills Brothers also prepared labels for the Union Lumber Company of Fort Bragg, on the coast of northern California. In addition, the company developed its own Japan Tea brands—O-Yama and Hilvilla.[54]

During the early twentieth century, versions of the now familiar tea bag also appeared. In restaurants, staff would employ cotton tea bags to brew individual cups and larger cotton "urns" for pots. A New York tea man also developed the "Certipure Tea Ball," made from "pure" aluminum foil. He boasted that aluminum was reputed to be the "only metal impervious to the actions of the acids of tea and coffee" and thus would not oxidize. The inventor suggested that his new creation would provide a "practical substitute for the unsanitary cloth bag container."[55]

As Hellyer and Company gained its footing in Midwestern markets during the 1890s, Frederick and Georgianna spent each year split between Chicago and Kobe, where Hellyer and Company continued to operate its tea refining factories in the foreign concession. In 1897, their eldest child, Marion, married John Liddell, a British merchant, and moved to Shanghai, where the couple lived for many decades. Marion's and John Liddell's children retained their British citizenship, but Marion's younger brothers, Walter, Arthur, and Harold (my great-grandfather), all became U.S. citizens and worked in the family tea business. The three took American wives and also made homes in Riverside and in Kobe. Their uncle, Thomas, apparently lived much the same life, as we learn from his appearance on a passenger list of a steamship arriving from San Francisco. On his way to Japan in April 1906, Harold was caught in San Francisco during the great earthquake that ravaged the city.[56]

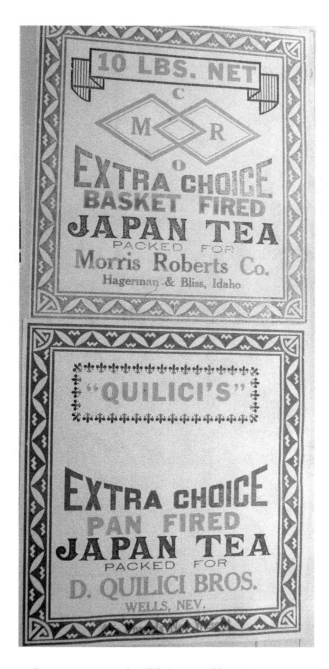

FIGURE 5.2 These circa 1910 retail tea labels, printed by Hills Bros. Company, exemplify those commonly affixed to tea chests of various sizes. The labels also illustrate how Japan Tea was widely available in small towns in Western states and marketed in both pan- and basket-fired varieties.

Source: Hills Bros. Coffee Company, Incorporated Records, Archives Center, National Museum of American History, Smithsonian Institution, Washington, DC.

FIGURE 5.3 Frederick Hellyer (seated) and his sons, from left to right, Walter, Arthur, and Harold, circa 1905.

RECREATING KYOTO IN ST. LOUIS

In 1904, yet another U.S. Midwest city hosted a world's fair: St. Louis. When the fair opened in April, Japan had been at war with Russia for two months. Japanese leaders had gambled in starting the conflict, believing that Russia aimed to gain control of Korea and perhaps later threaten Japan. Despite the war and its financial burden, officials in Tokyo did not consider withdrawing from the fair, given that government funds had already been allocated. The Japanese government assembled a large contingent that would occupy twice the space of the nation's exhibits at the Chicago world exposition. Ōtani, serving as head of all of Japan's exhibits, chose to showcase Japan Tea in a version of the iconic Golden Pavilion (Kinkakuji). The tea room, adorned with far less gold leaf than the original temple in Kyoto, formed the kernel of a larger garden that also included a reception hall constructed in the style of a medieval lord's estate and a bazaar selling Japanese wares. As Japan had expanded its empire in 1895 to include the tea producing island of Taiwan, the garden had a Formosa Tea House, which served varieties of oolong and other Taiwanese teas.[57]

In a newspaper interview just before the fair's opening, Baron Matsudaira, the vice commissioner of the Japanese contingent, drew attention not only to the tea garden but to all the exhibits, "which will excel [sic] anything of the kind we [Japanese] have attempted before."[58] In July, Matsudaira hosted exhibition administrators at a dinner held at the pavilion. The dignitaries enjoyed several courses of Japanese cuisine along with tea, a dessert of green tea sherbet, and "sake, sake, sake always." As entertainment, "geisha girls danced an allegorical charade. The performance was a dramatic epic of the tea fields of Japan, composed by Mr. Yamaguchi, concessionaire of the Kinkaku pavilion, and was a very pretty performance."[59]

For the Japanese contingent, such glib portrayals of women employed in the tea pavilion as "geisha" became a point of contention. At the St. Louis fair, Japanese representatives replicated a practice developed at earlier domestic exhibitions in Kyoto in which young Japanese women

FIGURE 5.4 Stereoscope of Japanese Tea House and Garden, Louisiana Purchase Exposition, St. Louis, Missouri, 1904.

provided entertainment to showcase tea. The pavilion's tearoom staff also included a number of young women to serve tea, which the Japanese organizers stressed were not "geisha girls" but rather "respectable and refined" young women, "daughters of educated and respectable parents."[60]

Accounts of the St. Louis fair offered some positive portrayals of Japan Tea. A widely read, fictional tale of Samantha, a woman from a rural town visiting the fair, described eating good but "queer" fare accompanied by "the best tea I ever drinked."[61] Many articles in the Missouri press lauded the ambience of the tea garden as well as the stalls and amusements around it that formed a cluster known as "Fair Japan."[62] In a piece published just before the fair's conclusion, the *St. Louis Republic* apparently sought to laud the Japanese contingent in stating that "while drinking tea with Japan [sic], the world learned to appreciate the sturdy little brown men."[63]

Nonetheless a few months earlier, the same newspaper ran an article proclaiming the beneficial attributes of the teas available at the Ceylon tea room. The article noted how the colonial government of Ceylon had funded the construction of the "attractive and picturesque Ceylon building" to display Ceylon products, including tea. The article's author quoted an unnamed dealer who echoed points about Ceylon tea highlighted in previous marketing campaigns. The dealer stressed how Ceylon tea's "virgin purity, greater strength (hence greater economy), its scientific manufacture, together with its delicious and delicate flavor," make it appealing to "all lovers of tea." The merchant concluded that British-grown tea would therefore soon displace Japanese and Chinese varieties on the U.S. market, just as had transpired in Britain. "Free from adulterants and deleterious substances," he affirmed, Ceylon tea is handled only by "approved and scientific machinery . . . another reason for its great popularity is because it is midway between the weak teas of Japan and the stronger teas of India."[64]

The following month, a newspaper in the town of Lexington, near Kansas City, reported that a London tea merchant had identified imperial patriotism as propelling the growth of Ceylon tea consumption in Britain. He affirmed that the success of the island's tea demonstrated that "the British people are willing to support each other, although they may be of different hue and thousands of miles apart."[65] A few weeks after the close of the St. Louis fair, the *St. Louis Republic* also ran an advertisement for a tea brand claiming that Ceylon tea surpasses Chinese and Japanese teas in purity and economy.[66]

Had a decade of often racist advertising trumpeting the superiority of South Asian black teas and questioning the quality of Chinese and Japanese green teas changed tastes in the United States overall? Based on available trade figures, in 1905 the answer is no. In that year, Japanese teas made up just over 40 percent of all tea imports into the United States. Chinese green and black teas composed another 45 percent, with India and Ceylon black teas only occupying around 15 percent. Japanese teas were thus still holding their own in terms of national trade figures. In fact, beginning the following year they would overtake Chinese varieties in the percentage of teas imported into the United States, a position maintained in subsequent decades. Analysts at the time noted that this change may have resulted in part from the codification of Japan's imperial networks with Taiwan. Namely since 1895, oolongs from the island had increasingly flowed through Japanese ports and thus began to be categorized as "Japanese" in U.S. trade statistics. Nonetheless, throughout the 1910s green Japanese teas outpaced other varieties imported into the United States, with most shipped to Chicago for distribution throughout the Midwest. Tea drinkers there continued to choose it as a "fresh" product, and many living in communities with hard water believed it brewed a better cup of tea.[67]

The India and Ceylon lobby had made inroads primarily on the Eastern Seaboard. Newspapers noted that this success resulted from the very points emphasized by the lobby over the previous decade: the superiority of South Asian machine-produced teas in quality, flavor, and economy. "Scientific machinery" used to refine India and Ceylon black teas made them pure, as opposed to the hand-processed varieties from China and Japan.[68] In general, newspaper articles and advertisements gave fewer descriptions tinged with racist imagery. It is unclear why the India and Ceylon lobby decided to stop using such portrayals. Perhaps the lobby realized that additional campaigns emphasizing such points were unnecessary given that negative views of Chinese and Japanese teas had been successfully planted in the minds of many U.S. consumers, including newspaper reporters. Japanese diplomats in the United States noted as much, recording how Midwestern newspapers continued to repeat the trope of Japan Tea as unclean, tainted by the sweat of the laborers refining it.[69]

Many American companies dealing in India and Ceylon black teas focused on increasing sales by advertising name-brand teas sold in packages. P. C. Larkin, the head of the Canada-based Salada Teas, described plowing profits into expanded newspaper advertising, a decision he believed helped convince Americans that Ceylon black tea, sold in "leaden packages," was the "tea of the future."[70]

Those companies, and the India Ceylon lobby, found the Midwest more challenging and charted renewed plans to expand consumption of their black teas there, efforts tracked by Japanese diplomats. In August 1910, an official at the Japanese consulate in Calcutta sent a report to Tokyo that included a clipping (along with a translation) from a Calcutta newspaper describing how the Indian tea lobby intended to expand sales in the United States. It told of the lobby's aim to build upon a magazine and newspaper advertising campaign recently initiated in Minneapolis and St. Paul in order to make inroads in what it called "Japan Tea Country."[71]

TEA ROOMS IN THE UNITED STATES, COFFEE SHOPS IN JAPAN

In 1905, Japan achieved another military victory that shocked the world—vanquishing not merely an Asian but a European empire: Russia. In the peace settlement, negotiated by U.S. president Theodore Roosevelt, Russia ceded the southern half of the island of Sakhalin and renounced its imperial interests in Korea. Thanks to its victory, Japan gained a freer hand in Korea, forcing the two nations to "merge" in 1910. The Japanese government also promoted national interests in Manchuria and would soon finance the Southern Manchuria Railway, which transported goods and people between points in the Chinese province and its terminus at the former Russian-held city of Port Arthur, at the tip of the Liaodong Peninsula. Americans took note of Japan's growing military prowess and voiced concerns that it had become a menacing, militaristic state.[72]

In 1906, Okakura Kakuzō, a Japanese art historian and staff member at Boston's Museum of Fine Arts, published *The Book of Tea*, which he hoped would assuage such concerns. Okakura sought to use the Japanese "religion of aestheticism," which he termed "Teaism," as a vehicle to introduce a more sophisticated and softer Japanese elite culture to American audiences. He aimed to increase the Western understanding of Japan to help prevent future conflicts, asserting that "the beginning of the twentieth century would have been spared the spectacle of sanguinary warfare if Russia had condescended to know Japan better. What dire consequences to humanity lie in the contemptuous ignoring of Eastern problems!"

Although geared for a U.S. audience, *The Book of Tea* makes no reference to U.S. consumption of Japan Tea. In fact, it mentions green tea only once in a discussion of sixteenth-century events and otherwise describes tea as a "brown" or "amber" beverage. By taking that approach, Okakura adroitly kept his story of tea and Japanese aesthetics free from the taint of an everyday U.S. beverage, one often consumed with milk and sugar. He gained intellectual longevity with his accessible introduction to elite tea culture and explanation of its important role in Japanese aesthetics; his book remains popular to this day.[73]

In the years surrounding 1900, commercial Japanese villages continued to appear, notably in California. Convened in San Francisco in 1894,
the California Midwinter Exposition included one such village, where
Japanese women were employed to serve tea and sweets. The art historian Kendall Brown notes how, consistent with the changing views of
Japanese outlined in the previous chapter, local newspapers gave favor-
able accounts of the Japanese women working at the fair but disparaged
the men for their short stature, brown skin, and "queer" ways. After the
fair's short run, the teahouse and garden were donated to the San Francisco municipal government and continued to operate in a corner of
Golden Gate Park.

Entrepreneurs looking to take advantage of the interest in "things Japanese" opened other gardens and tea rooms throughout California. In
1911, Henry Huntington, a railroad baron, acquired the buildings of a
former commercial tea garden, rebuilding them on his Pasadena estate
to form the centerpiece of a Japanese garden.[74] In 1919, the city government of San Antonio, Texas, converted an abandoned rock quarry into
a Japanese garden, and Jingu Eizō, a Japanese man living in the city, later
opened a tea room on the grounds.

In major cities, tea rooms also became fixtures in department stores
and hotels. During the first two decades of the twentieth century, they
served primarily the elite. Women especially patronized tea rooms as
U.S. society became less restrictive about women dining outside the
home without their husbands or other family members.[75] Some establishments were decorated in a Japanese style, such as one in the Hotel
Tulsa in Tulsa, Oklahoma, where the wives of Shriners gathered for a
social affair in March 1913.[76] A hotel in Eugene, Oregon, used its Japanese tea room to host groups of visiting dignitaries, and an Atlantic
City, New Jersey, hotel advertised its tea room as its main attraction.[77]
Wealthy families also created their own tea rooms, such as the New
York couple who donned Japanese garb for their wedding, held in a Japanese tea room constructed for the occasion. In Jefferson, Texas, near
the Louisiana border, a local social club celebrated the New Year with a
Japanese-themed party, in which the hostesses wore kimonos. In the
town's Carnegie Library, the organizers created a "tea room of matting,
poles, and bamboo." The room was also adorned with large Japanese

FIGURE 5.5 Postcard, Japanese Tea Garden and Sunken Garden, Breckenridge Park, San Antonio, Texas, circa 1925.

umbrellas and fans illuminated by Japanese lanterns. To set a mood, "an orchestra of six pieces rendered soft, sweet, Japanese airs." The local newspaper reported that one attendee gushed that "this is the most magnificent affair I have ever attended, and this place is indeed a fairy-land and too much praise cannot be given these excellent ladies."[78] Unfortunately the article does not explain what constituted "Japanese airs" in the musical selection or if Japanese green tea made it onto the menu.

This latest version of American fascination with "things Japanese," with its more specific focus on the tea room, may have helped Japan Tea hold its market share. Unlike the previous wave of interest in Japanese wares to decorate the home, Americans holding a tea in a Japanese-themed room or wearing Japanese clothing may have been more inclined to choose Japan Tea as a means of adding a finishing touch to their gathering, although such a choice was seldom reported on.

In fact, in most cases tea rooms, especially those that became permanent businesses, were places to enjoy "home-style" fare in a quaint and relaxed atmosphere. The tea rooms offered sandwiches, freshly baked breads, and desserts, often made according to family recipes. The upper-class women opening the rooms in New York succeeded by making their establishments places where patrons could enjoy the meal of tea, served around four to five p.m. In response to the wishes of customers, many expanded their hours to offer breakfast and lunch. Tea rooms also became "exchanges for women's work, antique furniture, pottery, embroideries and laces, which aid in decoration of the room." Although women were the chief clientele, men also took meals at such establishments, attracted by the simple yet hearty cooking and quiet atmosphere.[79] Thus in many respects, the tea room label was a misnomer: neither the drinking of tea nor the taking of the meal of tea was central in this new dining trend.

Tea parties also continued to hold a place in American society. In January 1912, wealthy men and women in Annapolis, Maryland, made the rounds during "Monday's teas," apparently regular events held on "the most popular society day of the week." Not to be left out, that spring fraternities at Dartmouth College convened teas as the warm-up for tennis matches against faculty, followed by an evening prom show featuring an operetta. The fraternities held more teas the following day, which members enjoyed while watching a baseball game.[80]

During the same period, the urban café, centered on coffee, also came of age in Japan. In many ways, the new wave of cafés represented the "modern" trends of the Taishō period (1912–1926), often exemplified by the trendsetting young men and women, sporting European clothes and haircuts, said to frequent them. The year before the new emperor began his reign, Café Paulista, a European-style coffeehouse, opened in Tokyo. It would soon welcome around seventy thousand patrons each month and later added branches in Osaka and Kobe. Its founder, Mizuno Ryō, had previously been involved in bringing Japanese contract laborers to work on Brazilian coffee plantations. Officials in the state of São Paulo provided Mizuno with free shipments of coffee for several years to express gratitude for assisting in their labor needs—and also in pursuit of developing a coffee-consuming culture in Japan.[81]

JAPAN'S TEA EXPORTS DURING WORLD WAR I

In 1911, the U.S. federal government banned the import of colored teas. A trade paper opined that the move was "no revolution" given that U.S. retailers and exporters of Japanese tea had already signaled their support. The publication also stressed that the difference between colored and uncolored green teas had become "quite slight," apparently because producers used less color and thanks to the machine-refining advances noted earlier. Describing the viewing of samples of the two varieties, the paper stated, "Both were green but the uncolored one was more of a grayish green than the other. No one not a judge could have told the difference unless the two samples were side by side."[82] Gone were days when Japanese tea, much of it fired in baskets or pans, needed coloring to mask a light hue.

When World War I broke out three years later, Japan joined the Allies, ostensibly to assist Britain, with which it had signed an alliance in 1901. The government in Tokyo ordered the Japanese Imperial Navy to secure shipping channels and move against German colonies in the Pacific, taking over the Marshall and Caroline Islands. Japanese forces also "liberated" German-held areas in China. Meanwhile, the Japanese economy grew increasingly entwined with China as Japanese firms opened factories in Japanese concessions in Chinese treaty ports. The war proved a boon for the nation's economy, partly because Japanese businesses could exploit opportunities in China with Western nations focused on the conflict in Europe.

The tea industry also thrived, with 1917 marking a banner year as Japan's exports of tea reached a record level in volume. Much of the tea was dispatched to U.S. ports and then transshipped to Britain. At the same time, the Dutch empire exported more of its black teas, produced primarily on the island of Java. Javanese teas gained a small share of the U.S. market but initially proved most popular in the Netherlands and, later, in Australia.[83]

During the war, the Japan Central Tea Association promoted Japan Tea at the Panama Pacific International Exposition in San Francisco in

1915, as well as at the Panama-California Exposition, which ran simultaneously in San Diego. As in St. Louis, the San Diego pavilion included a Japanese-style teahouse staffed with young Japanese women serving tea accompanied with rice crackers. The central government also provided funds to operate a San Francisco teahouse where visitors could sample Taiwanese oolongs, part of an effort to expand sales of the colony's teas.[84]

The fairs were held amid rising anti-Japanese sentiment in California and the West Coast as the number of Japanese immigrants increased. In 1907, President Theodore Roosevelt aimed to mitigate the influence of these jingoistic voices by developing a Gentlemen's Agreement with Japan's prime minister Saionji. With the deal, the Japanese government committed to drastically limit the number of its citizens emigrating to the United States.

Nonetheless, the measure did not dampen the calls of groups like the Asian Exclusion League of California. Its literature opined that the vast majority of the ninety thousand "Mongoloids" in the state "were gainfully employed while from forty to fifty-thousand white men have been tramping the roads of the State or lounging on the streets of our largest cities waiting for work that does not come."[85] Yet the league's publications made no mention of refraining from drinking Japanese or Chinese teas. For the league, the rising Asian "threat" to white jobs was the prime issue. Tea, a product neither grown nor refined using U.S. labor, merited little concern.

World War I also brought to fruition several trends in Japan's production and export practices. Factories continued to mechanize and therefore eliminated the seasonal jobs, taken mostly by women, of refining tea by hand. There is little evidence that the shift engendered social discord over the loss of what had no doubt been for many Yokohama and Kobe families a welcome addition to household income. We can speculate that the women who had worked in tea factories could now find employment in other industries, then expanding with Japan's economy overall.

Simultaneously, Shizuoka Prefecture emerged as not only the main producing but also the dominant refining region in Japan. In 1899, Shimizu, near Shizuoka, opened as a port for foreign trade, and a railway soon connected the two cities. Thereafter, Shimizu grew into a tea export hub, overshadowing Yokohama and Kobe. Following in the footsteps of Western nations that aimed to bring advances in science to agriculture, the central government established the Tea Experimentation Station in Makinohara. In 1917, Hellyer and Company relocated to Shizuoka City, setting up a refining plant there. To be near the new factory, Harold Hellyer, his wife, Dorothy, and sons George (my grandfather) and David moved from Kobe to Shizuoka. In their move, they were joined by the Tanimoto family, who had been employed in the Hellyer household.[86]

In 1915, Frederick Hellyer, chosen to serve once again on the Board of Tea Examiners the previous year, died at his home in Riverside. A trade journal noted his passing and lauded him for establishing a firm "known throughout the world as one of the most dependable tea houses in the business." The same publication ran an obituary for Vincent Tissera when he passed away the following year, describing him as "introducing Ceylon tea into the United States after coming to the World's Fair in 1893." It noted how he thereafter became an importer of teas and gained prominence as a lecturer. Representatives of Ceylon's colonial government provided a casket with a color scheme that was said to emphasize his efforts to build connections between Ceylon and the United States. Tissera was buried in Davenport, Iowa, where he had begun his tea firm nearly two decades before.[87]

Frederick Hellyer and Vincent Tissera were British subjects who chose to become naturalized U.S. citizens because of their involvement in the tea trade. Both achieved success thanks to the American thirst for tea, but Tissera unquestionably confronted more challenges because of the color of his skin. Hellyer probably never faced an indignity such as that which Tissera endured upon returning to the United States from overseas: being forced to undergo a search of his person and belongings. We can conclude that the Board of Tea Examiners also did not ask Tissera to serve as an examiner. Not surprisingly, that body, as with many aspects of the tea trade, continued to be defined by the racial barriers of the day.

6

DAILY CUPS DEFINED

Black Tea in the United States, *Sencha* in Japan

After World War I ended, Americans began to drink more tea, and in January 1920, the Eighteenth Amendment to the Constitution went into effect, prohibiting the consumption of alcohol.[1] Many in the tea industry anticipated that as Americans embraced dry lifestyles, tea would become even more popular. Yet a year later, industry insiders bemoaned that the impact of Prohibition had been less than expected. Instead, they noted the start of what would prove a watershed in American teaways: a significant rise in imports of Ceylon and India black teas and the decline of Chinese and Japanese green teas, a trend that accelerated as the decade progressed.[2]

Identifying a single factor behind the national move from green to black is challenging. The economic historian Teramoto Yasuhide sees multiple factors contributing to the decline in the consumption of Japanese green tea. He concludes that in the early 1920s the Japan Tea brand was, first, crippled by perceptions of poor quality, especially that it included more stems and lower-grade leaves than other national varieties. Second, the larger South Asian tea industry brought its economies of scale to bear by undercutting Japan Tea on price. In addition, the India-Ceylon lobby, drawing on funds gained through a tax on its producers, initiated a fresh advertising campaign that promoted brands of India and Ceylon black teas. The advertisements touted the superior taste and flavor of South Asian black teas and urged Americans to embrace British practices of teatime. Thus overall, more U.S. consumers, aware of the declining reputation of Japanese green teas, chose India and Ceylon black teas after reading glowing accounts about them in newspapers and magazines and after finding them priced lower at their grocers.[3]

Left out of this comprehensive analysis is the legacy of the India-Ceylon lobby's negative campaigns. Advertisements that questioned the quality of Chinese and Japanese teas, coupled with reports from reputed tea experts repeatedly published in U.S. newspapers and magazines over the preceding decades, set the stage for the triumph of black teas and the creation of a consumption pattern that continues to this day. In other words, the factors weakening Japan Tea's market share were present before World War I but had a lasting impact only because of the convergence of the aforementioned trends in the early 1920s.

The move to black tea, although national in terms of aggregate trade numbers, did not initially include the Midwest, where Japan Tea continued to hold its own. Leaders of Japan's tea industry worked to revive their waning export trade with advertising campaigns as well as renewed initiatives at world fairs. The chapter will follow the efforts of Jingu Eizō, who on behalf of the Japan Central Tea Association developed approaches to promote anew Japanese green tea as a complement to everyday American meals. Those endeavors, while failing to restore the level of exports to the United States, nonetheless shaped what became a surge in consumption of *sencha* in Japan, setting the stage for that green tea's wider adoption in Japanese teaways.

A RELAXING AND ENERGIZING BEVERAGE: RENEWED CAMPAIGNS IN THE UNITED STATES

In 1925, the Japan Central Tea Association, working with the Shizuoka Prefectural Tea Association, formed the Japan Tea Promotion Committee. Ōtani Kahei, now retired but with a wealth of information gained from his six decades of experience in the tea industry, served as the committee's honorary chairman. Along with prominent Shizuoka tea men, Walter Hellyer, who with his brother Arthur operated Hellyer and Company, joined the group. (Harold, their younger brother, had left the company several years earlier.) The committee received input from other merchants throughout Japan. William H. Ukers, editor of the New York-based *Tea and Coffee Trade Journal*, and representatives of U.S. retail firms also shared their views.[4]

In addition, Japan Central Tea Association officials commissioned fresh surveys of the Midwest tea market. Working with the prominent advertising firm J. Walter Thompson, association representatives visited homes and circulated questionnaires to tea wholesalers, jobbers, retail tea shops, and restaurants in Illinois, Iowa, and Ohio. To gauge urban tea consumption, the representatives focused on Chicago. The research team also canvassed two smaller cities, Peoria, Illinois, and nearby

FIGURE 6.1 A 1925 photograph of the Japan Tea Promotion Committee, which was tasked with developing advertising strategies aimed to restore Japan Tea's fortunes on the U.S. market. The committee's honorary chairman, Ōtani Kahei, is in the front row, fourth from the left. Walter Hellyer is in the second row, fifth from the left.

Burlington, Iowa, both of which supplied tea to surrounding farming communities. In those two cities and their rural environs, 80 to 90 percent of people consumed tea, both in the afternoon and evening. (This was in contrast to Chicagoans, who preferred to take tea at noon.) Green tea was most popular in rural Illinois and Iowa, while black tea had taken hold in eastern Ohio. Nearly three-quarters of consumers chose their teas based upon a specific variety—such as Japan Tea, oolong, or English breakfast—as opposed to a name brand. Green and black tea drinkers alike added lemon, milk, and sugar to their teas. In fact, only one in eight people liked tea straight.[5]

The survey also indicated that devotees of green tea preferred to purchase their teas in bulk, underscoring how in the Midwest at least, that retail practice remained widespread. As before, at a local shop, a customer could browse available varieties of tea from China, Japan, India, and Ceylon. Retailers would provide packaging, often a paper bag with their store's label, in which to place a customer's chosen amount of tea. Since the 1890s, large tea companies, such as Salada, Lipton, and Tetley's, had begun to challenge that retail model, building factories to package teas. Although usually including the country of origin of the tea, the packages emphasized, often with bold letters, the company's brand.

The *Tea and Coffee Trade Journal*, which had emerged as the tea industry's main trade publication, often ran articles discussing the virtues of the two retail methods. One such article stressed that a retailer benefited from selling name-brand, packaged teas because the consumer increasingly knew and trusted the quality of such brands. A shop focused on packaged teas could also reduce costs by keeping a smaller variety of teas on hand.

By contrast, jobbers and wholesalers sought to continue to sell teas in bulk, since fees were nominal for each shipment. They contended that prepackaged teas robbed a grocer or tea retailer of the chance to draw on his experience and salesmanship to convince customers that he or she could "furnish them with just the tea to suit their particular fastidious taste." Most of all, by selling in packages a retailer neglected the "intelligent buyer" who could "purchase bulk tea at 10 cents to 20 cents a pound below the price he must pay for package tea, and can buy what *he* wants and not what the packer wants to sell."[6] In sum, the sale of bulk teas allowed the seller to connect with connoisseurs who might prefer established and well-known categories like Japan Tea.

Those involved in the tea retail trade gave differing estimates of the percentages of tea sold in bulk versus that sold in name-brand packages. One estimate can be found in the personal album of R. W. Hills, a cofounder of Hills Brothers. Hills kept the album to organize information, gleaned from newspapers and trade publications, concerning his company's sales. He evidently also wanted to stay apprised of market trends in the tea and coffee retail trades. Resembling a scrapbook, the album is stuffed with various advertisements and articles from magazines and newspapers from the 1910s, including an advertisement for an advertising firm. Hills clipped it from a trade journal apparently because of its observations about the tea retail trade. The advertisement asserts that in 1919, 75 percent of all teas were sold in bulk. It calculated that of the remaining 25 percent, only a portion reached consumers in the packages of name brands.[7] A few years earlier, a St. Louis tea retailer offered another estimate, based upon the expanding role of wagon men who sold tea, coffee, and groceries door to door. He concluded that wagon men, who often peddled packages of their company's house brand of tea, controlled about 50 percent of the tea and coffee business of the country.[8]

Following World War I, the Chicago-based Jewel Tea Company emerged as a prominent wagon-delivery company. Jewel wagon men kept routes throughout the Midwest, selling, among other items, Jewel house brands of oolong, gunpowder, and English breakfast. Wagon men also offered three-quarter-pound packages of basket-fired Japan Tea for 75 cents and one-pound packages of pan-fired Japan Tea for 90 cents.[9] Jewel notably spent funds not on advertising but on premiums, calculating that consumers would buy more tea and other goods to receive decorative plates, cups, or other household items. The company's "cake-safes," which allowed one to carry a home-baked cake or pie to a neighborhood event, proved a popular premium. Jewel executives instructed their salesmen, who increasingly switched to trucks during the 1920s, to focus on assuring that housewives acquired from them their staple foods and beverages—most of all their house brands of coffee and tea. Company

FIGURE 6.2 Postcard, Jewel Tea Company delivery wagon, circa 1920.

executives feared that customers who did not purchase Jewel coffees or teas might venture to their local market and, while there, buy other sundries, instead of obtaining them from their Jewel deliveryman.[10]

Against this market backdrop, the Japan Tea Promotion Committee hired J. Walter Thompson to create a U.S.-wide campaign. The committee benefited from an obligatory tax levied on all chests of tea exported from Japan. Previous campaigns had been hampered by inconsistent financial support from the Japanese government and spotty efforts soliciting voluntary contributions from producers and merchants.[11]

J. Walter Thompson coined the slogan "the drink for relaxation" to advertise Japan Tea. Running in magazines such as the *Farmer's Wife*, a string of advertisements, such as shown in figure 6.3, presented Japan Tea as the perfect drink for housewives, office workers, and busy executives.[12] The advertisements emphasized that the ten to fifteen minutes spent enjoying a cup or two would not only be relaxing but allow one to feel energized throughout the afternoon, an oblique reference to the caffeine content. One advertisement appealed to housewives to enjoy Japan Tea after lunch as it would bring enough reinvigoration to allow a homemaker to be ready to dress for dinner a few hours later.

Another proclaimed that a stenographer gained the requisite energy to make it through the hour when she might lag—between four p.m. and the end of work at five. For the male executive, Japan Tea would promote efficiency.

> Ten minutes to restore the nervous energy you've been paying out all afternoon! Ten minutes to wind you up like a clock for the afternoon's work! Just ten minutes spent in genuine relaxation over a leisurely cup or two of Japan Green Tea after luncheon. Drink it slowly, *lingeringly*. Enjoy each separate mouthful. Can you afford the time? Try it once, this way, and see what it does for you! You'll make it a daily habit![13]

The India-Ceylon lobby also revised its advertising efforts. British campaigners alternated between promoting South Asian teas (and tea in general) as a "masculine" beverage, to stressing its Englishness in hopes of attracting U.S. consumers out a sense of shared Anglo-Saxon heritage. In the late 1920s, the India Tea Bureau, flush with funds following an increase in its collections from growers, began to market its teas anew in major newspapers and magazines, often using a new emblem that splashed the words "India Tea" across a silhouette of a map of India.[14]

TEA ROOMS IN CITIES AND ON "INTERURBAN CAR LINES"

During the second decade of the twentieth century, tea rooms became more prevalent in major cities; in New York City, the number increased from a dozen in 1913 to sixty by 1921.[15] Numerous tea rooms, most run by women, opened in Greenwich Village, attracting male and female clienteles from throughout the five boroughs. At the time, many in the tea industry concluded that the proliferation of such establishments resulted not from Prohibition but rather because they offered family-style surroundings and the quality teas and coffees sought by New Yorkers.[16]

FIGURE 6.3 Japan Tea advertisements developed by the J. Walter Thompson advertising agency. The advertisement on the left typifies the "Drink for Relaxation" campaign and appeared in the July 1927 issue of the *Country Gentleman*, a farm periodical. The advertisement on the right, which presents Japan Tea as a health beverage high in vitamin C, ran in a competing farm periodical, the *Farm Journal*, in February 1930.

In downtown Chicago, Le Petit Gourmet, "a transplanted bit of France," attracted patrons with continental flairs and lunches featuring main dishes like "Lobster Farcé," creamed fresh lobster meat packed in lobster half shells and covered with breadcrumbs and cheese before being baked golden brown. Its owner noted that the meal of tea "brings the women-folks, shoppers and gossipers and entertainers, with their guests. Luncheon and supper, however, bring men in almost the same proportion as women, and that says a lot for the food and the comfortable atmosphere of the place, for you won't find men where either is poor." Baltimore's Chimney Corner, which welcomed customers for tea from three p.m. to half past five in the evening, sported a black interior enlivened with Japanese color prints hanging on its walls and "gayly painted trays and china."

Opened in 1916, Polly's Place in Colebrook, New Hampshire, ten miles from the Canadian border, proclaimed itself the first tea room in the "great North Country." Its guests could enjoy tea "*freshly made for each person*" accompanied by "freshly made hot toast, buttered with golden butter or redolent with strained honey and cinnamon." Polly's Place overwhelmingly attracted customers arriving by car and therefore bought advertising space in travel guides, automobile touring maps, and on roadside signs.[17] The tea room thus illustrated another trend noted by Sherwood Anderson in 1919 (in the passage cited as the epigraph to chapter 4). "The interurban car lines that weave in and out of towns and past farmhouses" had brought "a tremendous change in the lives and habits of thought of our people of Mid-America," including in reshaping American teaways.[18]

HEALTHY GREEN TEA FOR JAPANESE AND AMERICANS

As they moved forward with efforts to restore market share in the United States, Japan Central Tea Association officials confronted a glut of *sencha*. Production levels remained at the robust levels of the mid-1910s, but

POLLY'S PLACE, TEA HOUSE, COLEBROOK, N. H.

FIGURE 6.4 Postcard, Polly's Place Tea House, Colebrook, New Hampshire, circa 1925.

because more Americans were choosing India and Ceylon black teas, the percentage exported had dropped nearly in half.[19] Association officials therefore charted plans to expand sales at home. They chose to target urban areas, first because those living in the countryside generally continued to produce their own *bancha* and other teas. Moreover, the number of Japanese residing in urban areas was steadily increasing. Between 1920 and 1930, over five million more made their homes in cities, pushing the national percentage to 24 percent. The urban population would continue to rise during the 1930s.[20]

To better understand Japan's urban markets, the Japan Central Tea Association assembled a team of researchers who examined the transport, sale, and consumption of tea in Tokyo. In the report of their findings, the researchers offered a bleak assessment of tea consumption in the capital, stressing that because of the growing influence of Western practices, such as a preference for coffee, the denizens of Tokyo had forgotten the enjoyment of tea. Cherishing less the culture of tea drinking,

Tokyoites showed limited interest in high-grade teas, notably *gyokuro*. Consumers also drank smaller amounts of *sencha* and *matcha*. Instead, they bought low-quality teas, especially *bancha*, a trend that had accelerated after the Great Kanto Earthquake in 1923, which devastated the Tokyo metropolitan area, killing over one hundred thousand people. The authors speculated that financial hardships following the earthquake caused Tokyoites to choose such less expensive options. They noted that those varieties sold well especially in the summer months, probably because customers used them to brew iced or chilled teas. The authors also noted that *sencha* was not a popular gift, with many Tokyoites instead preferring to send department store gift certificates.[21]

Around the same time, the Shizuoka Tea Association polled tea shop owners and invited representatives of prefectural tea associations from throughout the country to Shizuoka to meet and assess market conditions. Echoing the conclusions of the Tokyo report, association officials discerned a decline in the consumption of high-grade teas. Several prefectural representatives identified another reason for the prominence of *bancha*—elite families viewed it as a healthier choice than *sencha*. To counteract this perception, many prefectural representatives saw potential in advancing slogans tied to a recent scientific study that identified high amounts of vitamin C in *sencha*.[22]

The merchants were referring to two Japanese scientists who in 1925 had published research indicating significant levels of vitamin C in refined Japanese green tea. In their laboratory, Tsujimura Michiyo and Miura Masataro fed guinea pigs an infusion of a common variety of green tea purchased at a retail store. Their subsequent observations led them to conclude that the green tea prevented the animals from contracting scurvy for at least two months. The scientists stressed that because of their higher level of oxidization, black teas failed to hold the same vitamin C content and thus efficacy against scurvy.[23]

With the cooperation of the Shizuoka Tea Association, tea merchants distributed advertising materials emphasizing the high amount of vitamin C in *sencha*, often referencing Miura and Tsujimura's research. A pamphlet issued by a Shizuoka tea company offered a chart showing the vitamin C content in common foods including meat, potatoes, bananas, and peaches. It also showed the amount in various beverages—orange juice, soda pop, and beer—along with tea's most immediate competitors: coffee and oolong and black teas. The chart emphasized how refined *sencha*, like that purchased at stores, contained by far the highest amount of vitamin C. In addition, it demonstrated that refined *sencha* had more vitamin C than not only high-grade *gyokuro* but also *bancha*, an appeal to counteract the perception of that tea as a healthier option.[24]

The Yamashiro Tea Company, located in the Kyoto area, produced a more detailed pamphlet, *The Wisdom of Tea*, which covered a range of topics, including the history of tea in Japan, the tea ceremony, and even the use of tea in cosmetics. The pamphlet sported a similar chart emphasizing *sencha*'s high vitamin C content in comparison to other foods and beverages. In addition, it offered examples of the wonders inherent in green tea in any form, describing it as effective in preventing the spread of contagious disease. One chapter focused upon events in the city of Nagoya the previous year. Referencing an article in the *Asahi* newspaper, it noted that a prefectural hygiene officer had described tea as a powerful disinfecting agent against cholera. Going even further, the pamphlet suggested that because of the popularity of the tea ceremony and therefore the greater consumption of powdered green tea (*matcha*) in the city, it is not surprising that since the mid-nineteenth century, Nagoya, a large city in central Honshu, had avoided a major cholera outbreak.[25]

At the direction of Japan Tea Association officials, J. Walter Thompson created advertisements to run in U.S. magazines and newspapers that highlighted the broad array of health benefits brought by Japan Tea's vitamin C content. As shown in figure 6.3, they often included bold headlines that referenced recent scientific research and emphasized how Japan Tea was one of the "very few foods" that contain vitamin C. These advertisements would usually proclaim (as is the case in figure 6.3) that a cup of Japanese green tea was the perfect elixir to "safeguard against needless fatigue and several common ailments."[26] Receiving them from the Japan Central Tea Association, Jewel Tea Company passed on the new findings about vitamin C in Japanese green tea to its wagon men and retailers to employ in peddling packages of Jewel's house brands of Japan Tea.[27]

Writing a few years later, Ukers commented that advertising men never warmed to emphasizing the health benefits of Japan Tea. They instead found the "non-controversial character" of the "relaxation campaign" more appealing. He noted that the health campaign was hampered by a series of experiments undertaken by U.S. scientists that failed to replicate Tsujimura and Miura's findings of high levels of vitamin C.[28]

In 1929, the U.S. Department of Agriculture conducted one such study. Department scientists gave guinea pigs infusions of two teaspoons of Japanese green tea each day, while others received a quarter-teaspoon of orange juice. The guinea pigs that consumed orange juice thrived, but those on a diet of green tea soon developed scurvy, indicating a lack of vitamin C in their diets. In their report, the scientists asserted that "there can be no doubt that green tea is a poor and unreliable source of vitamin C even when consumed in relatively large quantities." The report stressed that "the evidence tends to show that the claims made that this Japan tea 'is rich in vitamin C' are not substantiated."[29] In the end, although the Japan Central Tea Association continued to promote it, the health campaign gained little traction in the United States. Yet as we will see, vitamin C and health would soon figure prominently in campaigns to sell more *sencha* on the Japanese home and imperial markets.

TEA CONSUMPTION PRACTICES IN JAPAN DURING THE 1920s AND 1930s

In 1926, Emperor Shōwa (Hirohito, as he was widely known in the West) took the throne upon the death of his father, commencing the longest imperial era of modern times, the Shōwa period (1926–1989). Following the stock market crash in 1929, Japan would soon navigate the challenges of the Great Depression. Successive finance ministers searched for policy remedies, returning the country to the gold standard in 1930 and then abandoning it the following year. On the continent, the Kwangtung Army, established just after the Russo-Japanese War to protect Japanese interests in southern Manchuria, played an increasingly aggressive role.

In 1928, Kwangtung officers ordered the assassination of the Chinese warlord controlling Manchuria. Three years later, the army's leaders, without consulting the civilian government in Tokyo, created a pretext to mount a full-scale invasion. Within a few months, Kwantung Army troops had conquered all of Manchuria. Showing the increasing dominance of the military, Tokyo leaders blessed the move and later established the puppet state of Manchukuo, with the last Qing emperor, Henry Puyi, as its titular leader.

As their nation's empire expanded, Japanese further embraced the café as a space for social interactions. In the now numerous urban cafés, a patron might listen to jazz while sipping a cup of coffee.[30] Many cafés continued to be called *kissaten* (tea shops) even though coffee was clearly the dominant beverage on their menus. Nonetheless, some offered a variety of teas. As part of a periodic column offering advice about operating a *kissaten*, a board member of the Association of Confectioners of Western and Japanese Sweets outlined in his association's trade journal the optimal ways to prepare various types of tea. He advised that *bancha* should be carefully roasted to protect its flavor. (When consuming it at home, many Japanese would roast *bancha* before brewing.) After the initial serving, any remaining amount of tea in the pot should be warmed over low heat to prevent it from boiling. He declared that *bancha*, thanks to its low caffeine content, was well suited for expecting mothers and those battling illness. In addition, the author offered detailed explanations for how to brew green and black teas, the latter, which he noted had become increasingly popular during winter months, enjoyed with sugar, milk, and lemon slices.[31] Although not widely consumed, imported black teas held a niche, especially among the wealthy. Elite hotels and restaurants, as well as steamship lines, commonly served India and Ceylon black teas.[32]

At home, many families consumed *bancha* as their everyday beverage and would stop to drink a cup of a *bancha* or *sencha* at urban and roadside teahouses.[33] Japanese riding trains could still obtain a pot of green tea to accompany their boxed lunch. However, in 1921 the Railway Ministry moved to limit the use of earthenware teapots following complaints that they damaged easily in shipment and that a consumer could not readily determine the amount of liquid inside.[34] The ministry urged that green tea instead be sold in glass bottles. During a trip to Japan, Ukers marveled at the bottles, explaining that they contained "about a pint of hot tea and are provided with a glass-cup top from which the beverage can be drunk or sucked, which is the popular but noisy way of drinking tea in Japan."[35]

As before, the drinking of numerous cups of tea remained an integral part of Japanese teaways. Japanese were said to still believe in the superstition, dating back to the Edo period, that they might meet with an accident if they failed to drink a cup of tea every morning. Moreover for many, tea needed to be fresh brewed as any kept overnight also held negative connotations—in the past it had been served to prisoners awaiting execution.[36] The American humorist Will Rogers noted the daily prevalence of tea during a 1932 visit, proclaiming: "No matter what you do in Japan you must have tea, then after you do what you was going to do you have tea again."[37]

During the 1920s and 1930s, only a few voices emerged to question that established, daily consumption pattern. In 1920, a commentator appropriating the pen name "A Young Man of Resolute Constitution" proclaimed that Japanese drank too much tea. In a short article, "The Negative Effects of Tea Drinking," the author noted that Japanese were wont to drink tea soon after getting up in the morning, during and after meals, if tired at work, and when meeting with family and welcoming guests. He or she lamented that this constant stream of tea, replete with stimulating caffeine, led to impatience, the inability to concentrate, and short tempers. Given their proclivity to consume cup after cup of *bancha*, *sencha*, and other green teas, Japanese also risked digestive problems and should therefore consider moderating their daily intake.[38]

A health institute founded by Ishizuka Sagen, who pioneered the idea of "food education" and macrobiotic diets during the Meiji period, published the journal in which the article appeared. It was therefore not a mainstream publication read by average Japanese. Nonetheless, the article is instructive in its critique of Japanese daily consumption patterns and for its focus on the connection between tea and health.

Japanese tea merchants zeroed in on both as they mounted campaigns to increase domestic *sencha* consumption during the late 1920s and 1930s.

In trying to expand sales of *sencha* on the home market, the Japan Central Tea Association sought not only to dislodge *bancha*'s prevalent place in daily life and its association with a healthy lifestyle but also to revise long-held views of tea as merely an accompaniment to a meal or a beverage downed quickly over the course of a day. The association moved on several fronts. It began to promote *sencha* as a gift offered at the end of the year, when Japanese often send presents to express their gratitude for favors received. Employing slogans tried on the U.S. market a few years earlier, the association also published pamphlets targeting groups within Japanese society, such as young women, urging them to discover the enjoyment of pausing to drink a cup of *sencha* with family and friends. Association officials, all of them men, also sought to have women conceive of the act of drinking tea (*kissa*) as a leisurely and, by implication, refined practice.[39]

Newspapers and women's magazines from the period give little indication of the success of these campaigns. Instead, when discussing tea prominent publications offered articles focused more on brewing methods and economizing strategies.[40] One article revealed the "secrets" of brewing delicious *sencha* and *bancha*, while another outlined ways for a housewife to efficiently use a small amount of *bancha* to serve five people.[41]

Another magazine detailed how men and women from throughout Japan had found renewed health by drinking alternatives to standard teas, including one Abe Komao, who espoused the virtues of green tea mixed with roasted brown rice (*genmaicha*).[42] The origins are obscure for this type of tea, today popular throughout Japan. According to one oral account, the tea blend was developed in a hospital in Pyongyang (now the capital of North Korea but then under Japanese colonial rule) as a medicinal beverage for patients.[43] Although no written record exists, the account seems consistent with views that increasingly connected tea with health during 1920s and 1930s. It also suggests why the Japan Central Tea Association published scholarly articles affirming not only the

amount of vitamin C in *sencha* but also its other health benefits.[44] Not
to be left out, the Shizuoka Tea Association incorporated such points into
its advertising campaigns. An association pamphlet stressed that *sencha*
offered a valuable source of vitamin A (in addition to vitamin C) while
its caffeine content acted as a mild heart stimulant and its tannins as an
astringent; it also claimed that recent studies had found that green tea
was even effective in treating diabetes.[45]

Meanwhile, mirroring trends unfolding simultaneously in the United
States, Japanese consumers in major cities also began to purchase more
packaged teas, often sold as name brands. Writing several decades later,
a Yokohama tea shop owner asserted that until the 1920s his customers
had traditionally disliked prepackaged teas. They instead valued the ritual of selecting from teas offered in bulk in open containers, enjoying
even the sound of their chosen tea being emptied into a bag at his store.
Because of economic challenges brought by the Kanto earthquake in
1923, the shop's customers came to embrace the convenience of prepackaged teas, a trend that accelerated thereafter.

No doubt aware of such trends, large tea companies in Kyoto and Shizuoka created *hōjicha*, a type of green tea still popular today. Ōyama
Yasunari identifies 1924 as the birth of *hōjicha*, which includes more
stems than other green tea varieties and is roasted to produce a brown
brew with a stronger flavor. Companies including the Yamashiro Tea
Company found in *hōjicha* an avenue to sell in packages lower-grade
teas, especially those that included stems, grades rejected by American
consumers. With the birth of *hōjicha*, Japanese producers commercial-
ized a tea that, like *bancha*, had previously been largely grown, picked,
and roasted at home.[46]

Large domestic companies would also soon promote their brands of
sencha. The Hayashiya, an Uji retailer, sold via mail order three types of
sencha, as well as *gyokuro* and black tea with lemon peel added. In 1940
and 1941, a major Tokyo newspaper included advertisements for *sencha*
sold by Meiji Seika, a prominent confectionary firm.[47]

Overall, the 1920s and 1930s proved seminal decades in the recasting
of Japanese teaways. The decline of exports after 1920 prompted Japanese
tea firms to focus on the domestic market as never before. Gradually,

sencha was becoming a more established, everyday beverage, with merchants emphasizing its health benefits whenever possible. New types of green teas—*hōjicha and genmaicha*—also appeared, diversifying the types of green teas consumed constantly throughout the day.

TEA AND SANDWICHES: JAPAN TEA AT
U.S. WORLD FAIRS

To assist in its U.S. advertising campaigns, the Japan Central Tea Association analyzed the number of magazines and newspapers distributed to urban and rural areas. Association officials also estimated the consumption of various teas in each U.S. state. In the South, black teas had come to dominate, while oolongs remained popular in New England. In California, Japan Tea held its own in rural areas and San Francisco; the denizens of Los Angeles and San Diego drank more black tea. The Midwest remained Japan Tea country, with consumption high in Chicago, northern Illinois, Nebraska, Wisconsin, Minnesota, and Michigan.[48]

During the 1920s, large British firms selling India and Ceylon black teas revived a category of black tea used sporadically since the late nineteenth century: orange pekoe. Lipton, Tetley's, and other companies marketed orange pekoe as a better-quality and especially fragrant tea.[49] Although in the early 1920s India and Ceylon black teas had sold at slightly lower prices than Chinese and Japanese teas, that price differential does not seem to have continued in some of the Midwestern markets we have examined. In Wisconsin, stores sold Japan Tea for half the price of Lipton's orange pekoe tea. In Chicago, a consumer could purchase basket-fired Japan Tea, orange pekoe, and oolong for the same price per pound. In Galva, the Larkin Economy store sold Japan, gunpowder, and English breakfast teas for roughly the same price.[50]

In Shizuoka, Hellyer and Company and a handful of other foreign and Japanese firms operated factories that together employed thousands, despite the increased use of mechanization in the refining process. In 1932, my grandparents, George and Ethel Hellyer, moved to the city.

George learned from his uncles the craft of tasting and judging samples of tea brought by Shizuoka-area brokers and farmers. (A process illustrated in the photo at the top of figure 6.5.) Hellyer and Company would offer a price, which a broker or farmer could compare to that given by another export firm. After being processed in the Hellyer and Company factory, the tea would be dispatched to the nearby Shimizu port for shipment to the United States. Figure 6.5 illustrates how the processing of tea had become mechanized even as sorting and packaging remained labor intensive. As the image shows, young women, usually in their early to mid-twenties, were hired to remove stems and place refined tea into packages for export.[51]

As before, the Japan Central Tea Association continued to promote Japan Tea at world fairs. At the Philadelphia Exposition of 1926, which celebrated the sesquicentennial of American independence, the association expanded its approach. Jingu Eizō, a Japanese man operating the Japanese-themed tea room in San Antonio, Texas, introduced in the previous chapter, devised specific presentation strategies. Following Jingu's advice, the Japan Pavilion's tea room did not distribute free samples but instead sold cups for a nominal fee, anticipating it would prevent chaotic scenes during busy days. Jingu decided to serve Japanese green teas accompanied by "Japanese style sandwiches," a departure from previous fairs where tea was offered with Japanese sweets and rice crackers. Although packaged as Japanese, the fare would have been familiar to American patrons—ham and chicken sandwiches along with tomato and chicken salads. Special crab salads and sandwiches were also on the menu, made from the tinned Japanese crab displayed in an adjacent room. Among the teas, guests could choose from hot and iced *sencha*, lemon tea (presumably served hot), and teas with slices of pineapple, peach, and lemon. The tea room was constructed on the shore of a small lake, which Japan Central Tea Association officials concluded would bring a pleasant breeze on hot days. To add a "Japanese touch," Jingu hung paper lanterns around the outside of the room. The association dubbed the establishment a success, noting especially the popularity of ice cream flavored with *matcha*.[52]

In 1933, the Japan Central Tea Association tapped Jingu to run a tea hall within the Japan Pavilion at Chicago's Century of Progress World

HELLYER & COMPANY: TEA TASTER AT WORK — SCENE IN THE PACKING DEPARTMENT — TEA SIFTING DEPARTMENT —
PACKING TEA IN CHESTS — MECHANICAL TEA FIRING PLANT AT SHIZUOKA

FIGURE 6.5 Views of Hellyer and Company's factory, Shizuoka, circa 1918. The image in the lower right demonstrates how mechanized refining techniques had advanced in factories of Western export firms.

Source: W. H. Morton Cameron and W. Feldwick, *Present Day Impressions of Japan* (Chicago: Globe Encyclopedia Company, 1919), 336.

Exposition, which was also held the following year. Apparently leaving his family to continue to operate the San Antonio tea room, he supervised the creation of a tea hall that served fare similar to that of the Philadelphia fair, but with the addition of American and Swiss cheese sandwiches. Jingu intended for the sandwiches to be only snacks, partly because the exposition board did not grant him a license to serve complete meals. Yet he also wanted to make sure that Japan Tea would be the most prominent item. As in Philadelphia, the menu included hot green tea but with an expanded iced tea selection that centered on the use of *matcha*, dubbed "ceremonial tea" (as it was in Chicago in 1893). Jingu also served a type of "cold brewed" iced tea, made with *matcha* stirred into a pitcher of cold water, ice, and sugar.[53]

The association employed a "traditional culture" approach, first used at the Columbian Exposition in 1893, to promote its teas, exemplified by the addition of a teahouse of a sixteenth-century Japanese lord. American

FIGURE 6.6 Views of the Japan Tea Hall and Tea Sales Room, Japan Pavilion, Century of Progress International Exposition, Chicago, Illinois, 1933. Jingu Eizō is seated (on the right) in the photo to the left.

Source: Katō Tokusaburō and Nihon Ryokucha Hanro Kakuchō Rengō Tokubetsu Iinkai, eds., *Shikago shinpoisseiki bankokuhakurankai kinen shashinchō* [A commemorative picture book of the Century of Progress Chicago World Exposition, 1933] (Tokyo: Nihon Ryokucha Hanro Kakuchō Rengō Tokubetsu Iinkai, 1934).

and other foreign guests were periodically invited to partake in the *chanoyu* tea ceremony at what was dubbed the House of Friendly Neighbors. Masuda Takashi, the tycoon whose earlier patronage had helped revitalize interest in the tea ceremony in the wake of the Meiji Restoration, presented the house as a gift to the Japan organizing committee. The house was disassembled in Japan and shipped to Chicago, where Japanese laborers and artisans reconstructed it on the fairgrounds. A few months before the fair's opening, Chicago labor unions lodged a complaint about this "importation of Japanese labor" with the secretary of labor in Washington. In response, exhibition officials replied that a special act of Congress had permitted the Japanese to legally enter the United States and work at the fair.[54]

TEA PROMOTIONS AMID ANTI-JAPANESE SENTIMENT

Although seemingly a minor issue, the question of who would build the pavilion was one of many points of friction related to Japan and its presence at the fair that unfolded in Chicago before and during the Century of Progress exposition. Japanese military moves in China in the early months of 1932 evoked much negative sentiment. From late January until early March of that year, Japanese naval and army forces battled units of the Chinese Nationalist Army in and around Shanghai in what came to be known as the First Shanghai Incident, or the January 28 Incident. Angered by Japanese military actions, students at Chicago-area universities resolved to act. In mid-February, first-year female residents at a Northwestern University dormitory pledged to boycott Japanese tea at "restaurants, sorority parties, and sorority 'rushes.'" Although a small-scale effort, the move apparently marked the first defined boycott of Japanese tea in the decades-long history of imports into the United States.[55]

On March 12, students from the University of Chicago joined Communist Party members in a protest on Chicago's bustling Michigan Avenue outside the Japanese consulate. As explained in an article in the

Chicago Daily Tribune the following day, protesters unfurled banners demanding an end to the "Robber War in China." In small groups, they attempted to enter the consulate but were blocked by police. During an ensuing melee, three policemen were wounded by shots fired from a protester's pistol. Another protestor and her teenage son were injured when the officers returned fire. Police arrested one protester in the lobby of the building containing the consulate, stymieing his effort to appeal directly to Consul-General Mutō Yoshio, who later issued a statement thanking police for their help in keeping the protesters at bay.[56]

Chinese-American groups in Chicago also lodged complaints against the Japanese government's decision to include a pavilion at the fair, adjacent to that of Japan, operated by the South Manchuria Railway Company. Although officially an independent concern, the company received government aid to support its transport and commercial activities in Manchuria. The organizers presented the railway pavilion's exhibits as intersecting with the fair's general theme of progress, especially by highlighting the rail lines built in Manchuria in recent years. In hopes of appealing to American visitors, the exhibit also emphasized the region's trade with the United States. Overall, the exhibit was a thinly veiled presentation of the newly "independent" state of Manchukuo and, with it, a celebration of the "virtues" of Japanese imperialism.[57]

The Chinese Consolidated Benevolent Association of Chicago, a branch of an organization that boldly claimed to include, as members, every Chinese living in the United States, complained not only about the South Manchuria Railway Company's exhibit but also about a series of lectures, with a pro-Japanese slant, given by Garner Curran. Described as a "noted traveler and lecturer," Curran used slides to profile aspects of life in Japan as well as the new Manchurian colony, connecting his travel experiences to items on display in the Japan Pavilion. For one, he urged attendees to visit the Japan tea hall to enjoy a cup of "green tea lemonade rich in vitamin C."[58]

In light of the protests, the head of the South Manchuria Railway Company's pavilion decided to hire a U.S. representative to more forcefully present the Japanese case in the U.S. media. In the summer of 1933, Felix Streyckmans, whose father served as an exposition official, became the company's spokesman, promoting the Japanese position while noting "erroneous" points in the press coverage and in exhibition materials. He found one such objectionable line in the fair's official guidebook: the description of the women involved in a demonstration of the tea ceremony as "dainty geisha girls." Streyckmans asserted that the women were not simply "ordinary entertainers." Rather, "the young ladies participating in the tea ceremony are girls of good family from Japan," echoing points stressed by Japanese officials during the 1904 St. Louis exposition.[59]

Ruth De Young, a reporter who interviewed two young Japanese women involved in several teahouse events, also emphasized their elite backgrounds. De Young stated that the two young women, Kondō Chikage and Takahashi Hiroko, had expressed little interest in visiting Chicago because they had been "having too gay of a time in their home country." Masuda, the donor of the aforementioned House of Friendly Neighbors, had persuaded them to make the journey to participate in events held at the Japan Tea pavilion as part of his plans hopefully to improve U.S.-Japan relations.[60]

The House of Friendly Neighbors was the site of many receptions and events at which the Japan Central Tea Association aimed to increase interest in Japan and its teas. In late August 1933, a ceremony was held to welcome Tokugawa Iesato, who as a boy had served as the last lord of the Shizuoka domain as its tea production ramped up immediately after the Meiji Restoration. On "Japan Tea Day" (one of the many special days on the fair's calendar), the organizers brought to the house eleven "queens," young women representing their respective countries at the Chicago fair. Wearing the traditional clothing of their home countries, they participated in a *chanoyu* tea ceremony performed by Kondō. Other Japan-related events at the fair placed young Japanese women, wearing kimonos, in prominent positions. To open the exposition's Japan Day on the morning of July 8, Mitsuhashi Chizuko, taking the title of Miss Japan for the day, cut a ceremonial tape at the fair's central gate.[61]

The Japanese delegation obviously wanted to offer a distinguished and elegant presentation of their country, and as discussed in earlier chapters, young women had been employed to serve tea at domestic and international exhibits since the 1880s. Yet given the tensions surrounding Japan's aggressive empire building in East Asia, the "softer touch" of

Japan Tea
Hall at A
Century of
Progress

Under
Management
of The Japan
Central Tea
Association

Tea Girls
in Native
Costumes

FIGURE 6.7 This postcard was probably offered to visitors to the Japan Pavilion during the Century of Progress International Exposition, Chicago, Illinois, 1933.

Japanese women presented at the teahouse and tea hall could also hold a political value by challenging perceptions of Japan as a menacing, military state.

In 1935, the Japan Central Tea Association opened a tea room at the California Pacific International Exposition held in San Diego, in the same building constructed for the 1915 fair. Members of the Asakawa family, who had run a business and farmed near the city for a number of years, operated the tea concession.[62] The Japanese tea room offered *sencha* presented with rice crackers, and patrons could also enjoy "American food" along with a "wide variety of Japanese food that Americans like." For example, "Japanese girls in native costume" served American-style "oriental" foods such as chop suey and chow mein to accompany Japanese teas.[63]

In his assessment of that fair, Jingu noted that American visitors generally preferred straight black teas or a blend of black and green varieties. He was surprised to find that *matcha*, especially when served in ice cream, again proved popular. Jingu offered a note of optimism, conjecturing that given this emerging American preference, producers in

Kyoto, long famous for *matcha*, could anticipate expanding sales in the future.[64] Remaining an advisor to the Japan Central Tea Association, Jingu continued to run his tea room in San Antonio until his sudden death in 1938. His family thereafter operated the establishment and oversaw maintenance of the surrounding garden.[65]

Overall, under Jingu's initiative during the 1920s and 1930s the Japan Central Tea Association sought to present Japan Tea as a beverage that would complement everyday American foods, whether a ham sandwich or a chicken salad. As such, Jingu developed a strategy that aimed to recapture an American view of Japan Tea as an everyday beverage downed with a meal. In essence he worked to revive the perception of green tea encapsulated in the stories of Hamlin Garland of life in Wisconsin in the 1890s and by the fictional Maria, who noted in her visit to the Japanese tea room at the 1893 Columbian Exposition that "people who have drunk tea all their lives, just as they have eaten steak and pie, [regard] it perhaps as a necessary filling for their depleted interiors, but certainly as nothing more." In other words, the Japan Central Tea Association, which had attempted to expand American interest in high-grade teas at the 1893 Chicago fair, now simply needed to recapture the everyman's and -woman's previous associations with Japan Tea.

The advertising campaigns and promotions at the world expositions during the 1920s and 1930s may have helped Japan Tea hold its market share in the Midwest. In addition, it seems to have remained competitive in price. In Galva in 1937, the A&P sold basket-fired Japan Tea for less than Lipton's orange pekoe. In Chicago, Japan Tea could be purchased for ten cents less than black Ceylon teas, and it was less expensive than tins of other black teas as well.[66]

MORE BLACK TEA—HOT AND ICED

Nonetheless, as Jingu noted, the American preference for black teas was increasing. Gertrude Ford, a well-established New York tea seller, also recorded the change. Ford related that when she had entered the

FIGURE 6.8   A billboard advertising Japan Tea on a street in Grand Island, Nebraska, 1930.

Source: *Chagyōkai* [The tea journal, Shizuoka Prefecture
Tea Association], August 1930.

business three decades before, the U.S. tea market was defined by its geographic parameters: "Westerners" preferred greens, while those on the East Coast drank black teas. Yet in recent years, Americans had largely embraced black teas, especially orange pekoes, which they drank not only at home but also while dining out. Ford calculated that 42 percent of Americans consumed their tea straight, 19 percent enjoyed it with a slice of lemon, and 38 percent added milk or cream.[67]

The move to black teas was aided by additional marketing campaigns mounted by an organization founded by British and Dutch colonial growers. Its advertisements, which included color cartoons that ran in newspapers and magazines, presented black teas as ideal for iced tea. Also adorning billboards, the advertisements portrayed iced tea as a beverage that would not only cool on a hot summer day but also "pep you up." In a related effort, the Indian Tea Market Expansion Board cooperated with lemon growers and major sugar companies to encourage the addition of lemon and sugar to iced teas, thereby helping further popularize what was increasingly being described as a distinctly American type of tea.[68]

In 1939, a market analyst, drawing on surveys conducted in six northeastern cities and in Columbia, South Carolina, concluded that iced tea was second only to lemonade in popularity during the summer months (Coca-Cola came in third). Newspaper columns discussing household menus often suggested that iced tea be served at lunch. Society pages advocated preparing both hot and cold teas for gatherings after tennis matches.[69] Unlike hot tea, which had developed connotations of being a feminine beverage, iced tea was apparently suitably masculine. Soldiers training to be shipped to the Western Front in the summer of 1917 were served iced tea with every evening's supper. "Strong men" were reputed to "think nothing at all of consuming three or four glasses [of iced tea] for supper on a hot night."[70]

The tea party, where more black teas were now undoubtedly served, also remained a part of American society, with commentators often stressing that gatherings over tea should be guided by the simplicity that defined the "Yankee" tea parties convened in early nineteenth-century New England. Extolling readers to realize that there is "nothing quite so comfy and relaxing as a good cup of tea," the author of a household advice column for a West Virginia newspaper recommended that when planning a tea party, a host should focus on creating a genial gathering of friends and not worry about having the proper set of china and silverware.[71] Emily Post, the famous syndicated columnist who advised about matters of etiquette, counseled that an informal afternoon tea party, at which hot tea and a cold tea punch would be served, would offer an inexpensive means to "bring out" a young woman to society.[72]

As the 1930s drew to a close, most Americans also apparently now purchased tea in half- and quarter-pound packages instead of in bulk, marking a significant change in purchasing practices over the previous two decades.[73] In addition, American tea drinkers had shed an earlier aversion to blended teas. Tetley's published a pamphlet advising Americans that most tea sold in their country had been blended to assure quality and consistency in taste. The pamphlet explained the various grades and varieties of orange pekoe teas, underscoring the prominent market position that type of black tea had come to hold. The dual trends of blended teas and the shift toward orange pekoe also helped strengthen the standing of name brands like Tetley's and Lipton.[74]

All told, by 1939 Japanese and U.S. merchants dealing in Japanese green tea faced a bleak market outlook. With black tea ascendant and increasingly sold in the packages of named brands, they struggled to maintain the relevance of the Japan Tea brand, which was based upon green teas, usually unblended, produced solely in Japan. American concerns about Japan's military moves to expand its empire complicated those efforts.

AN IMPERIAL FRONTIER FOR *SENCHA*

As they worked to regain market share in the United States, the leaders of the Japan Central Tea Association actively explored alternative overseas markets. They hoped to increase shipments to the Soviet Union, with which Japan had restored trade following a warming of diplomatic relations. More ambitiously, association officials also explored exports to South America and sent a research team to North Africa to gauge potential markets there.[75]

Shizuoka and Japan Central Tea Association officials saw particular potential in selling their green teas in Manchukuo. In 1933, a Shizuoka delegation traveled there to assess market conditions, stopping in Manchukuo's capital to present a gift of Japanese green tea to Emperor Puyi. The group noted that because of Manchukuo's newly "independent" status, Japanese tea could more effectively compete with Chinese varieties. Previously, Chinese teas had entered Manchuria tariff free, but they would now be assessed at a rate equal to that of Japanese tea imports.[76]

Yet association officials realized the challenges in front of them: Manchurians and ethnic Mongols living in Manchukuo preferred Chinese varieties of black and brick teas. Ikegaya Keisaku and Koizumi Takeo, who visited northern Manchuria on a junket in February 1936, observed that many poor Manchurians had no access to vegetables during the long

winter months and therefore lacked vitamin C in their diet. They concluded that in order to expand sales, Japanese merchants should convince Manchurians to adopt nutrient-rich *sencha* as part of their daily
fare. They argued that when this had been accomplished, green tea sales
would naturally grow as Manchukuo stabilized economically in the
coming years.[77]

Another Shizuoka Tea Association official later optimistically concluded that because they had been recently drinking more Japanese rice
wine (sake), using soy sauce in their meals, and learning Japanese, Manchurians would, as a matter of course, soon include Japanese green tea
in their diets.[78] The Shizuoka Tea Association subsequently developed
posters asserting that Japanese green tea was bringing unity and strength
to the peoples of East Asia, united under the Japanese Empire. One such
poster shows three women, distinguished as Chinese, Japanese, and
Manchurian by their national clothing, smiling at the prospect of cups
of Japanese green tea. Flags of their respective states wave in the background, with the Japanese flag above the others.[79]

The campaigns achieved some success: the amount of green tea
shipped to Manchuria rose from 492,000 pounds in 1935 to nearly 4.5
million in 1939. Nonetheless, the U.S. market, of which the Midwest was
key, remained more important, receiving nearly 14.5 million pounds
in 1939. [80]

RETHINKING TEA DURING A TIME OF WAR

In the summer of 1937, Japanese forces began an invasion of China.
Although gaining control over significant parts of Chinese territory, the
Japanese advance failed to topple the regime of Chiang Kai-shek, who
transferred his capital further inland to Chongqing and continued the
fight. The war became one of attrition, with Japanese troops holding
much of northern China and major southern coastal cities but stymied
in their efforts to expand those gains in the face of sustained Chinese
resistance.

As the Sino-Japanese conflict raged, on September 1, 1939, war broke out in Europe when Germany invaded Poland. Japanese tea merchants speculated whether events on the other side of the world would influence their industry. In June 1940, the Japan Central Tea Association's monthly journal, *Cha* [Tea], included an editorial discussing the impact of Britain's recent decision to close its tea auctions, at which teas from around the world were sold. Britain thereafter allowed imports only from the British colonies of India and Ceylon. In addition, the British dominions of Australia and New Zealand no longer permitted imports of Japanese tea. While these had been small markets for Japanese teas, many speculated that their loss might add to the glut of *sencha* then facing Japan's tea industry. The editorial stressed that association members should, however, not lament these developments but instead see the opportunities brought by them. For example, Japanese tea merchants could now actively explore the potential of "friendly" national markets such as Italy, which entered into an alliance with Germany and Japan in September 1940.[81] Moreover, as shown in figure 6.9, the Japan Central Tea Association, aware of the impact of declining exports, used the national flag as a backdrop to strengthen appeals for Japanese citizens to patriotically drink more Japanese tea during the current national emergency caused by their nation's state of war. The association also continued to promote tea as a gift, especially high-quality sencha that could be packaged as an "exclusive tea" (*meicha*).

Noting the pessimism about U.S.-Japan relations voiced by Foreign Minister Matsuoka Yōsuke in a speech the previous month, an editorial in the February 1941 issue of *Cha* offered another strategy for counteracting a further expansion of the glut of tea that would result from a possible loss of the U.S. market: sending green tea to Japanese soldiers at the front. The editorial stressed that this would provide an outlet for green teas not shipped to the United States and, by the same stroke, help Japan's fighting men. "It is said that even *bancha* has three times the vitamin C of the Japanese radish [*daikon*]. Therefore we must not forget to send Japanese tea to the soldiers at the front." To support the increased provisioning of green tea, the editorial offered stories of armies throughout history crippled by scurvy because of a lack of

FIGURE 6.9 Likely distributed beginning sometime in the late 1930s and into the early 1940s by the Japan Central Tea Association, this advertisement proclaims that in this "time of emergency," namely, Japan's state of war, Japanese should not only drink more Japanese tea but also give it as a gift. The woman holds a package of "exclusive tea" (*meicha*) gift wrapped with ribboning.

Source: The Ad Museum Tokyo, Japan.

FIGURE 6.10 This late 1930s or early 1940s advertisement produced by the Shizuoka Prefecture Tea Association declares in bold letters that "tea brings health" and urges that tea therefore be included in "comfort bags," which were care packets of food and toiletries prepared by civilians for soldiers at the front.

Source: The Ad Museum, Tokyo, Japan.

vitamin C in their soldiers' diets. It told of French soldiers in the Franco-Prussian War, Russians fighting in the Russo-Japanese War, and British troops involved in the invasion of Gallipoli in 1916 all stricken with scurvy. For further proof, it provided several examples of how scurvy had weakened soldiers during wars in China dating back to the Tang empire (618–907). The point was clear: not just any beverage, but Japanese green tea was vital to soldiers' health and therefore the war effort.[82]

The healthy attributes of Japanese tea were also highlighted in a campaign initiated by the Tokyo Organization of Patriotic Housewives that later spread to other parts of Japan: collecting used tea leaves from residences and shops and transporting them to military bases for use as fodder for military horses. The article explained that the campaign was important not merely because horses liked tea leaves but also because of tea's medicinal qualities, which had been shown effective in animals as well. As support, it offered two anecdotes, the first being trainers of racehorses who had discovered that feeding thoroughbreds *gyokuro* before a competition increased their energy and stamina. It also told the story of a soldier who lamented the serious injury his favorite steed had suffered in battle. Grieving, he was slowly gathering his belongings to move out with his unit, leaving the crippled horse behind, presumably to die. Meanwhile, unbeknownst to him, the animal had found its way into a tea field. After munching upon tea leaves, it was miraculously restored to health and came galloping back to his delighted master, ready to again carry him into the fray.

The article detailed how the Japan Central Tea Association backed a national patriotic plan to gather as large of a volume as possible of the used leaves of the approximately 82 million pounds of tea consumed annually in Japan. To illustrate the scope of the effort, it provided photos and reports of campaigns throughout the country. For example, the Organization of Patriotic Housewives in Ishikawa Prefecture was said to have gathered the leaves of a good portion of the estimated two million pounds of tea consumed annually in the prefecture, leaves that it emphasized would invigorate army horses by providing, of course, ample vitamin C.[83]

FIGURE 6.11 Children collecting used tea leaves for horse fodder. The sign posted in the center of the chest indicates it is a receptacle for used tea leaves. The signs on both sides of the chest read: "Horses Are Cute, so Let's Feed Them Used Tea Leaves." March 1, 1942, Kyoto, Japan.

Source: The Mainichi Newspapers/AFLO.

Despite its outward sense of patriotic fervor, the campaign revealed the obstacles in assuring basic supplies for the military as Japan's war in China dragged on. On the Japanese home front, shortages of basic food-stuffs also became common, with rice rationed in Tokyo and other major cities beginning in April 1940.[84]

Arthur Hellyer described similar hardships facing the Japanese populace upon arriving in San Francisco from Shizuoka in August 1941 on a Japanese vessel carrying two hundred thousand pounds of tea. He detailed shortages in food: bread was impossible to obtain and eggs rationed. Hellyer and Company also found it difficult to secure enough labor to continue operations at its Shizuoka plant, which meant the firm could ship just half the amount of tea as the previous year. Hellyer stressed that the freezing of Japanese assets held in the United States, as ordered by President Franklin Roosevelt the previous month in response to Japanese military moves into French Indochina, had made doing business in Japan nearly impossible for U.S. firms. Sensing a U.S.-Japan military conflict on the horizon, Arthur and other members of the Hellyer family no longer remained in Shizuoka for the entire tea season but instead made short trips there to conduct necessary business.[85]

In October, Tōjō Hideki, who had risen to prominence as a general in the Kwantung Army, became Japan's prime minister. Acknowledging that relations with the United States had reached an impasse, Tōjō and his cabinet embraced plans for a bold offensive to the south. Assuming a best-case scenario, they anticipated that Japan could secure the necessary oil and raw materials to allow it to deliver a knockout blow in the war with China. Aiming to gain control of the resource-rich Dutch colonies in Southeast Asia, on December 8, 1941 (the date in Japan), Japanese forces launched coordinated attacks on U.S. bases in Hawai'i as well on U.S., British, and Dutch colonies in Southeast Asia.

The outbreak of the Pacific War (as it is often known in Japan) of course brought an abrupt cessation in Japan's tea exports to the United States, a trade that had experienced booms and declines since the first shipments arrived in New York in the early 1860s. It also marked the end of the durable Japan Tea brand, developed by New York tea retailers and used and promoted by Japan Central Tea Association officials, Japanese government officials, and American tea companies for nearly eighty years.

Following the Pearl Harbor attack, Japanese Americans faced the wrath of racism in the form of Executive Order 9066, which led to the internment of Japanese and Americans of Japanese descent, primarily on the West Coast. The Jingu family was not compelled to enter an internment camp, but in 1942 the city government told them to vacate the tea garden they had called home for nearly two decades. San Antonio officials invited a Chinese American family to run the tea house, and the facility was renamed the Chinese Garden.[86]

As businessmen, the leaders of the Japan Central Tea Association no doubt felt keen disappointment at the loss of a U.S. market that had sustained their industry for generations and on which they had fought to retain a foothold in recent years. Yet with Japanese forces achieving a string of military victories in the Pacific and Southeast Asia, they focused on articulating how their organization would contribute to the war effort and the twin goals of total victory in China and the preservation of the Japanese empire.

In April 1942, the association's new president, Mitsuhashi Shirōji, emphasized the need, first, to sustain production levels despite shortages of labor and supplies. Second, he affirmed that the association would maintain tea collection and distribution systems throughout the homeland and, third, implement reforms in line with government efforts to streamline the national agricultural system to assist the war effort. Mitsuhashi's fourth point was one that occupied many pages of subsequent issues of *Cha*. In line with the government's goal to create a Greater East Asian Co-Prosperity Sphere, the association should focus on developing a coordinated tea production zone that included Japan, Taiwan, occupied China, and the recently "liberated" areas of Southeast Asia. Of particular interest was production on Java, now ruled by Japan and that, before 1940, had contributed significant amounts of black tea to the world market.[87]

Into 1943, *Cha* continued to publish a string of stories about efforts to reform internal distribution networks and to create a larger tea production sphere connecting East and Southeast Asia. In its January issue, Viscount Oda Nobugaki, who had taken over as president of the Japan Central Tea Association, highlighted the ambitious plans for that tea production sphere to one day assert control over the world tea market.[88] With few trade statistics to report, especially the export figures that had been a mainstay of earlier issues, the editors seemed hard pressed to find content, running articles that largely reiterated earlier patriotic initiatives and themes. In September 1943, *Cha* returned to discussing the health benefits of Japanese green tea, offering articles emphasizing its high amounts not only of vitamin C but also "healthy" tannins.[89]

In late 1943, a Tokyo newspaper advised readers that university researchers had identified a simple home remedy for burns to the skin: one should mix ash from burned paper, *sencha*, and water and apply the concoction to affected skin. The newspaper reported that the Army Ministry was disseminating such information so Tokyoites would be ready in the event of aerial bombing or other emergencies.[90] The following year, as U.S. bombers became more numerous in the skies over the city, newspapers described the ways that *sencha* could offer sustenance for people to stay healthy as they combated air raids. Along with consuming dried tofu as an enriching substitute for meat, Tokyo denizens were told to embrace *sencha* as a "marvelous" (*rippa na*) substitute for scarce vegetables and their vital vitamin content. Interestingly, the newspaper drew on the experience of then enemy Britain, where during World War I citizens were said to overcome wartime shortages of vegetables by consuming more Indian black tea.[91]

Yet as the war situation grew increasingly worse, *sencha* would have become harder to obtain. In 1943, the central government ordered a reduction of tea production in favor of foodstuffs to support the war effort. Shizuoka tea farmers dutifully dug up parts of their tea fields to make way for the planting of food crops deemed more vital in the goal of achieving total victory. As the Pacific War entered its final brutal year, marked by U.S. bombing campaigns that destroyed large parts of Tokyo, Shizuoka, and other major cities, the level of tea production declined still further.[92]

TEA PRODUCTION IN JAPAN DURING THE U.S. OCCUPATION

On August 15, 1945, Japan surrendered, ending a fifteen-year string of wars in Asia and the Pacific that began with the invasion of Manchuria in 1931. The victorious Allies dissolved the Japanese empire and restored Japan's national borders to those of the late nineteenth century. The U.S. military, under the command of General Douglas MacArthur, established an occupation government, which set about disarming Japan and implementing economic, political, and social reforms intended to create a nation with a durable democracy.

Occupation officials devised plans to restart tea production and exports in order to help revitalize the war-damaged economy. The task was formidable: in 1947, the acreage of tea fields had declined 30 percent from that of 1941. Japan was now producing only 54 million pounds of tea, compared to as much as 130 million before the war began. In 1948, the occupation government introduced a plan to expand areas under cultivation by 3,700 acres per year. To assist, it provided fertilizer, which was then being rationed, specifically for farmers to use in new tea fields. It also instituted measures to spur exports, and some optimistically believed that the United States could again prove a valuable market for "vitamin rich" Japanese green tea.[93] Overall, these measures helped revive tea production, which began to increase in 1948. Japan shipped some tea to the United States, but annual imports reached only half of those recorded during the late 1930s. States in northern Africa started to purchase more Japanese green tea, commencing a trade that remained steady until the 1970s.[94]

In 1951, Japanese green tea was included in meal rations for South Korean troops fighting in the Korean War, a conflict that jumpstarted the Japanese economy.[95] The U.S. military used Japan as a staging area for its operations during the war, purchasing goods and services from Japanese companies. U.S. military demand helped initiate a period of high-speed economic growth that continued after the U.S. occupation ended in 1952. During the 1950s, the tea industry would further stabilize. Yet the amount of tea exported from Japan, especially in comparison to the halcyon prewar days, remained small: in 1958, only 13 percent of the tea produced in Japan was shipped abroad.[96]

Overall, in the decades after 1945, Japan's tea industry maintained a trajectory that had emerged in the 1930s: producing *sencha* primarily for sale on the Japanese home market. By the 1960s, Japanese living in large cities, the target of the campaigns of the 1920s and 1930s, overwhelmingly preferred *sencha*, although *bancha* continued to hold its own in parts of western Japan.[97] *Sencha* would thereafter steadily gain market share, today composing close to 90 percent of all tea consumed in Japan.[98]

Another aspect of the tea consumption pattern described by the Young Man of Resolute Constitution in 1920 also remained intact. Japanese drank tea throughout the day and were less inclined to stop and enjoy a cup, as they might do with coffee. Moreover, a point about which the Young Man also voiced concern held little resonance: that one's health could be damaged by drinking too much tea. In fact, thanks largely to the campaigns of the Japan Central Tea Association during the 1920s and 1930s, *sencha* had come to hold a firm reputation as a health beverage.

The historian Susan Hanley, who has researched Japanese daily life and material culture, concluded that the despite the dramatic changes witnessed throughout Japan during the Meiji period (1868–1912), significant changes in the diets of ordinary Japanese occurred in the subsequent Taishō period (1912–1926).[99] As this chapter has shown, the adoption of *sencha* as a definitive daily beverage emerged in the closing years of the Taishō period and increased steadily thereafter, creating a consumption pattern that continues to this day.

JAPANESE GREEN TEA: A NOVELTY IN THE UNITED STATES

In September 1946, the *Wall Street Journal* ran a short article heralding the first shipment of Japanese green tea into the United States since 1941. It described "thirsty tea drinkers and old ladies who consider it essential to their health" anxiously awaiting the opportunity to again purchase green tea. Many in the American tea industry were said to be watching whether American consumers would again demand Japanese green tea after having access only to India and Ceylon black teas during the war.[100]

American tea sellers hoping for a revival of tea imports from Japan were disappointed. Americans did not regain their thirst for Japanese green teas, and in subsequent years, imports failed to rise. By 1954, the United States imported just over 105 million pounds of tea; of that, 88 million was black tea from Ceylon, India, and Indonesia (in that order of volume). Japanese green tea was a proverbial drop in the bucket: 1.8 million pounds.[101]

In response to the changed market, Hellyer and Company, which slowly restarted its operations soon after the war ended, began to sell more Japanese black teas through its Chicago office.[102] Jewel continued to operate its home-delivery service, which now composed just under one-quarter of its overall business. Retail stores, which numbered 184 in the Chicago metropolitan area in 1957, had come to make up the bulk of the company's operations.[103]

Jewel's Chicago stores sold name-brand orange pekoe in tea bags. In Galva, the town's A&P advertised three types of orange pekoes, sold for between 31 to 39 cents for a half-pound, but no green teas, which had been available a decade earlier. Like many Americans, the residents of Galva enjoyed iced black tea during the summer months. The local paper offered numerous advertisements for name-brand black teas, such as Salada, packaged in teabags tailored for brewing iced tea—but listed no green teas for sale.[104]

In the summer of 1959, Galva welcomed home Ann Blout, a native daughter who had spent a year living and working in Tokyo with her children while her husband was stationed at a U.S. military base in South Korea. During a chat with a reporter from the Galva newspaper, Blout showed souvenirs from Japan—woodblock prints, a kimono, a fan, and assorted Japanese foods—while serving some of her cache of "strong and slightly bitter" Japanese green tea, pointing out that Japanese often served it with rice crackers. Blout probably also offered Japanese green tea at the open house organized by her parents a few days later (and publicized in a column adjacent to the interview), which "all friends" were invited to attend.[105]

In Galva and throughout the United States, Japanese green tea had ceased to be an everyday beverage. It was instead reserved for special occasions, such as the Blouts' open house, to experience "exotic" Japan. Long a mainstay, green tea had become a novelty in American teaways.

CONCLUSION

In the autumn of 1987, the American pop star Michael Jackson visited Japan to commence his worldwide Bad tour (promoting the album by the same name). Although busy with preparations and interviews, Jackson took time to be a tourist, dressing up in Edo-period samurai armor and riding on the bullet train from Tokyo to Osaka. The mayor of Osaka gave the singer a key to the city, noting in a short address to dignitaries and journalists that it was the first time that a chimpanzee, Jackson's companion Bubbles, had been received as a guest of the Osaka City government. During the informal ceremony, the gathered dignitaries sat around a large oval table, each with a cup of what was no doubt *sencha* in front of them. Despite his guest status, Bubbles was not provided his own cup of tea. When Jackson paused to take a sip from his cup, Bubbles pestered him for a taste.[1]

By beginning his world tour there, Michael Jackson affirmed the global economic status Japan had achieved in the 1980s. For our purposes, the story of Jackson and tea illustrates a point argued throughout this book: the prevalence of tea in so many contexts within modern Japanese society. Placing a cup of tea in front of everyone gathered to greet Jackson was common, accepted practice and, in this case, a means to show the level of Japanese hospitality to the world.

Yet that Jackson's cup—and the many other cups Japanese consume throughout the day—to be filled with *sencha* cannot be put down simply to Japanese tradition. As this book has illustrated, *sencha* had been consumed in Japan since the eighteenth century. Nonetheless, that type of tea only gained the prominent place it occupies today because of the need for Japanese leaders, in the wake of the Meiji Restoration, to create a tea export industry that could boost the national economy while also providing employment for a samurai class and others dispossessed by the early Meiji-era reforms. Japan's tea industry could thereafter grow to feed U.S. demand, by the 1910s producing record volumes of *sencha* for shipment across the Pacific. The changing of U.S. tastes in tea beginning in the subsequent decade meant that Japanese merchants would instead promote *sencha* to their home market, helping it achieve its dominant place in Japan today. Thus, the rise of *sencha* was intimately connected to major developments both within Japan and in the American market.

The contemporary emphasis on the high vitamin C content in *sencha* harks back to another legacy of the 1920s. In Japan today, tea is largely consumed in ready-to-drink cans and plastic bottles, disposable containers pioneered in the 1970s. In vending machines found seemingly on every corner, consumers can choose from various green teas (along with black and oolong teas), available hot or cold. Many bottled green teas indicate the vitamin C content on their labels.

Parts of the tea industry also continue to emphasize that attribute of *sencha*. On its homepage, the Tea Research Division of the Kyoto Prefectural Government includes a chart, reminiscent of those published in the 1920s, demonstrating that *sencha* has a higher amount of vitamin C than strawberries, cabbage, and lemons.[2] Moreover, Japanese tea merchants of the 1920s succeeded in making more common the practice of offering *sencha* as a gift. Today, large department stores such as Mitsukoshi and Takashimaya market a wide variety of *sencha* from throughout Japan, packed in decorative containers.[3]

In the 1980s, it was not just pop stars like Michael Jackson who took an interest in Japan. Many Americans read what would become a bestseller, Ezra Vogel's *Japan as Number One*. Vogel, a Harvard sociologist, provocatively included a subtitle, *Lessons for America*, suggesting how

Americans could find in Japan's rise ideas upon which the United States could restore its sputtering economy.[4] During the 1980s, American firms were urged to adopt Japanese business and management techniques.[5] Popular culture also weighed in on how the United States was learning from its former enemy. In 1986, Ron Howard directed *Gung Ho*, a comedy that portrayed workers in a western Pennsylvania auto factory trying to learn Japanese production methods while navigating cross-cultural frictions with their new Japanese bosses.

Intrigued by the newly ascendant Japan and its growing place in U.S. discourse, some Americans took a renewed interest in things Japanese, including green tea. A turning point in green tea's rediscovery came in 1994, when major newspapers published a study, conducted in Shanghai, which showed that drinking it reduced rates of esophageal cancer. Accounts quickly followed detailing that Japanese scientists had found that those consuming green tea daily could prevent cancers of the lung and stomach, as well as lower their cholesterol levels. The *New York Times* reported that green tea was high in vitamin C: two small cups held the same amount as a glass of orange juice.[6]

In the following decade, green tea consumption expanded, but its overall share of the U.S. market remained small. In 2005, green tea composed 12.5 percent of all the teas drank in the United States, with black tea occupying 87 percent. Oolong and herbal teas combined mustered just 0.5 percent of the total. Japanese teas remained essentially a novelty, composing less than 1 percent of all U.S. tea imports. Nonetheless, thanks to the health wave and the growing interest in Japan and East Asia, the number of tea rooms offering green and other specialty teas grew from two hundred to two thousand.[7]

New firms, such as AriZona Beverages, founded in 1992, succeeded in selling a wide range of flavored green teas in cans and bottles, including green tea mixed with lemonade. The company's teas, available at convenience stores and gas station food marts, include labels, such as a woman in a kimono, reminiscent of those found throughout the United States in the late nineteenth century.[8]

Anticipating a surge in U.S. consumption, in 2006 a Japanese entrepreneur ambitiously established green tea–focused cafés, based on the

Japanese *kissaten* model, which offered assorted hot and cold drinks made from *sencha* and *matcha*. After some early success, in 2008 the company closed the doors of its shops in Seattle and Tokyo.[9]

Since the 1990s, scientists have conducted numerous studies that suggest the ways that green tea consumption can improve health and possibly inhibit the growth of cancers in the body. Although many results are promising, the National Cancer Institute does not recommend for or against consuming green tea to reduce the risk of any type of cancer.[10]

Nonetheless, an increasing number of Americans are adding green tea to their diets and have more recently embraced *matcha*. U.S. ice cream shops and Asian restaurants have long served *matcha*-flavored ice cream, but in a new twist, the powdered tea has now begun to be used as a condiment. On the eve of her 2018 marriage to Britain's Prince Harry, a British newspaper reported that the American actor Meghan Markle was a devotee of *matcha*, sprinkling it on salads and cereals and mixing it with hot water to make a "refreshing, cleansing drink." The newspaper stressed that many had embraced *matcha* because it is "packed with antioxidants and is said to help with everything from weight loss and fighting cancer to boosting your sex drive."[11] If they were alive today, Jingu Eizō and his colleagues who had promoted Japanese green tea by emphasizing its high vitamin C content and other health benefits would probably be bemused by the recent American "discovery" of green tea as a health beverage.

Why after World War II did Americans seemingly forget the practice of drinking green tea, a practice born in the early days of the republic and continued for a century and a half? To consider a more specific example, why did my maternal grandmother not perpetuate the custom of green tea consumption prevalent during her formative years in rural Illinois and continue a daily practice of drinking green tea after moving across the country to Washington State? One answer is availability. As we have seen, since 1941 green tea has not been imported in any significant volume. My grandmother would therefore have found it difficult to obtain, explaining why she would reserve her cache for guests. Like other Americans, at her local supermarket she would have chosen mainly from name-brand teas, which increasingly dominated the U.S. consumer landscape after World War II. As with coffee, Americans came mostly to purchase packaged teas, especially those sold in convenient tea bags.

As noted in previous chapters, during the late nineteenth century Americans began to enjoy more iced teas, a consumption pattern that expanded during the second half of the twentieth century. In 1992, the *New York Times* speculated that iced tea, already popular in southern states, would soon become a mainstay at New York restaurants. It cited the manager of the posh Four Seasons hotel, who proclaimed: "These days at lunch every other table is drinking iced tea." The article noted that in 1960 less than half the tea consumed was iced; that surged to 70 percent in 1980 before increasing to around 80 percent of all the tea drank in the United States in the early 1990s. During that decade, Americans started to purchase more ready-made iced teas in cans and bottles. As with the renewed consumption of green tea, young Americans particularly viewed iced tea as a "healthy" alternative to soft drinks.[12]

After World War II, sweet tea—black tea served cold with sugar added—gained popularity and emerged as a regional icon in the U.S. South. The artist and scholar E. Patrick Johnson notes that "the preference for sweet tea transcends racial and class boundaries, and every family (and even different people within the same family) has its own recipe." He uses sweet tea as a lens to present the perspectives of Black gay men across the South today. Drawing on numerous interviews, Johnson chronicles the wide range of methods for making sweet tea, which include using tea bags as well as instant and bottled varieties of black tea. Along with additions of juices and, of course, some amount of sugar or sweetener, many prefer to use name-brand teas, such as Lipton, to make their versions of sweet tea, underscoring how name brands have themselves become part of the fabric of today's U.S. teaways.[13]

Sweet tea's prominence in Southern culture has spawned origin stories. In 2010, Will Rizzo, a booster in the town of Summerville near Charleston, South Carolina, published a magazine article proclaiming that his town was the birthplace of sweet tea. He based his conclusion on reports that a French botanist brought tea plants, reputed to be the first planted in North America, to a nearby garden in the 1780s. In addition, in the 1880s Summerville was home to a short-lived experimental tea farm funded by the U.S. federal government. When the government decided to close it, an entrepreneur purchased the farm, expanding it into a successful tea plantation that operated until 1915. Rizzo also cites references to iced tea consumption in the South in the 1890s as allowing him to "step out on a pretty thick limb" and deem Summerville as the birthplace of sweet tea.[14] Summerville civic leaders thereafter embraced Rizzo's claim, creating a Sweet Tea Trail in the town's center and an annual festival centered on the beverage.

Robert F. Moss, a Charleston-based food writer, has strongly disputed Rizzo's bold assertion. He shows, as I noted earlier, the prevalence of iced tea, often sweetened, in Northern states dating back to the 1860s. Moss defines sweet tea as the "now-ritual Southern way of saturating large quantities of tea with sugar while it's still hot and then cooling and serving it over ice instead of letting each imbiber sweeten to taste at the time of serving." He argues that this now common teaway most likely emerged soon after World War II in Georgia and Alabama. People throughout the South have embraced it as part of "an ever-creeping pan-Southernism" that has brought the rise of a food culture marked by a "homogenous, aw-shucks blanket of cornbread, fried chicken, biscuits, and sweet tea."[15] Yet as a town news outlet recently noted, the veracity of Summerville's origin story is now beside the point. Interested tourists continue to flock to the annual festival, and Summerville has gained notoriety and a resulting economic stimulus from its now widely held renown as the "birthplace of Southern sweet tea."[16]

The Summerville sweet-tea story places focus on the domestic foundations of an American teaway. As this book has demonstrated, such domestic origins are vitally important, as throughout the history of their nation, Americans have chosen types of teas and ways of consuming them because of a range of domestic cultural, economic, social, and regional factors. Soon after independence from Britain, they took to green tea, deeming it more sophisticated. The taste for green tea would diversify, with the Midwest becoming the key consumption zone. As with so much of the American experience, racial prejudices also shaped teaways. Prejudice against Chinese teas and Chinese people in the United States contributed to Japanese teas gaining market share. Subsequent campaigns by lobbies promoting India and Ceylon black teas effectively used racial suspicions to sow seeds of doubt about Chinese and Japanese green teas, helping the United States become a predominately black tea–consuming nation.

Nonetheless, a problematic aspect in the Summerville sweet-tea story is the emphasis on the role of domestic tea production. Commercial tea farms founded in South Carolina in the late nineteenth century produced only modest amounts of the leaf. Moreover, they faced labor and transportation costs that made it difficult to compete with consistently lower-priced and better-known Asian teas.[17]

Throughout most of their nation's history, Americans have overwhelmingly consumed teas imported first from East Asia and, later, South Asia. The perspectives of the Chinese and, later, the Japanese who farmed, processed, and packed teas for U.S. consumers are therefore integral parts of the story of tea in the United States. Most of all, the American cup of green tea is emblematic of the international connections that shaped the American experience and simultaneously the course of modern Japan as well.

ACKNOWLEDGMENTS

I n researching and writing this book, I received help from colleagues, friends, and strangers. Kira Yoshie encouraged me when I first conceived of this project as a graduate student and has remained interested ever since. Sugiyama Shinya, whose comprehensive book on tea exports was an early inspiration, also offered ideas and advice. David Howell and Kären Wigen both gave support and suggestions in the early stages of the project.

I could begin archival research in earnest thanks to a Smithsonian Postdoctoral Fellowship, which allowed me to spend a summer at the National Museum of American History (NMAH). While there, I benefited from the guidance of Pete Daniel, who generously shared his vast knowledge of U.S. history and pointed me toward many valuable research avenues. The staff of the NMAH's Archive Center patiently answered my numerous questions and introduced sources that helped me expand my understanding of tea in U.S. history. During my stay in Washington, I simultaneously plumbed visual and textual sources at the National Museum of Asian Art, receiving assistance and advice from Louise Cort.

Thanks to a Japan Foundation Fellowship, I subsequently spent a fruitful year based at the Historiographical Institute, University of Tokyo. I thank Matsukata Fuyuko, a trusted colleague for many years, for helping make that stay possible. Hōya Tōru, Ono Shō, Sugimoto Fumiko,

Yokoyama Yoshinori, and many others in the University of Tokyo community guided me in locating many document collections.

An Association for Asian Studies Northeast Asia Council Research Travel Grant permitted me to return to Tokyo to delve into tea-related documents at the Diplomatic Archives, Ministry of Foreign Affairs in Tokyo. During that summer, Jason Karlin generously secured a desk for me at the Graduate School of Interdisciplinary Information Studies, University of Tokyo.

A fellowship from the National Endowment for the Humanities allowed me to research tea in the Midwest during a wonderfully productive year at the Newberry Library in Chicago. I appreciated the advice offered by Diane Dillon, Danny Greene, Liesl Olsen, and the incredibly helpful Newberry Library staff. Lunch conversations with Leon Fink and Ellie Tandy Shermer were always a pleasure, and I valued the input of other fellows, especially Sarah Weicksel and David Miller.

I gained fresh insights on using visual sources in this book during a summer as a Robert and Lisa Sainsbury Fellow at the Sainsbury Institute for the Study of Japanese Arts and Cultures (SISJAC) in Norwich, United Kingdom. I thank Mami Mizutori, Simon Kaner, Nicole Coolidge Rousmaniere, and the SISJAC staff for their help. During my time in Britain, I also benefited from fruitful exchanges with Meghen Jones, Christine Guth, and Rupert Faulkner.

A research fellowship from the International Research Center for Japanese Studies (Nichibunken) and the Hakuhodo Foundation allowed me to complete the research for this book. I thank Sano Mayuko for helping make that year in Kyoto possible and for inviting me to join Expos and Human History, her stimulating research group. Takii Kazuhiro also offered terrific advice, as did John Breen and Inaga Shigemi. In addition, I thank Mutō Yukari and Kumakura Isao for their interest in my work and suggestions on it.

During my time in Kyoto, I was fortunate to participate in a research group on the history of Japan's tea export trade convened by Sakurai Ryōju of Reitaku University. I appreciated the lively discussions and sharing of ideas among the group's members, which included Nakatake

Kanami, Awakura Daisuke, Nishizawa Mihoko, Ōnishi Hiroshi, Kira Yoshie, and Oyama Mizuyo.

Hamashita Takeshi also kindly invited me to participate in stimulating seminars on tea in Shizuoka held at the Global Center for Asian and Regional Research, University of Shizuoka. Many others in Shizuoka helped me learn more about tea, especially Yoshino Ako, Ide Nobuko, Ikeda Namiko, Konita Seiji, and Nakamura Yōichirō. Over the years, Tanimoto Isam and his son, Kotaro, of Hellyer and Company have been extremely generous with their time and helped me in numerous ways.

I also benefited from grants provided by the Wake Forest History Department, the Archie Fund from the Office of the Dean of the College, and Dingledine Faculty Fund for the Support of International Activities (which supported research in Australia); these proved instrumental in keeping this project moving forward.

In addition, I thank the individuals who invited me to give talks and join panels at academic conferences that aided me in refining conclusions about tea in Japan and the United States. That list includes Tim Amos, Jocelyn Celero, Karl Ian Cheng Chua, Fred Dickinson, Martin Dusinberre, Luke Franks, Furuta Kazuko, Linda Grove, Robert Hori, Iijima Mariko, Yoshiko Jo, Brenda Jordan, Kanda Sayako, David Leheny, Jay Lewis, Wolfram Manzenreiter, Murakami Ei, Nakamura Naofumi, Izumi Nakayama, Dael Norwood, Peter Perdue, Martin Ramos, Helen Siu, Shiroyama Tomoko, Nancy Stalker, Suzuki Keiko, Ken Pinnow, Morgan Pitelka, Jun Uchida, Eric Tagliacozzo, Sarah Thal, Silvio Vita, David Wank, and Samuel Yamashita. I appreciated Harald Fuess inviting me to participate in thought-provoking symposia on Japanese and global history and providing a generous welcome during a summer in residence at Heidelberg University. Julie Edelson cheerfully read numerous grant proposals and made each one better. Others who offered tips, suggestions, and encouraging words included Gary Albert, Dani Botsman, Tina Clemente, Ben Coates, Steve Ericson, Ted Fishman, Tom Frank, Michele Gillespie, Andrew Gordon, Hirano Masahiro, Mark Jones, Barak Kushner, Bonnie Campbell Lilienfeld, David Lubin, David Lurie, Brent Malin, David Odo, Akiko Ohta, Kenneth Pechter, the late

Maggie Shelton, Shibata Kaoru, Henry Smith, Lee Taniguchi, Julia Adeney Thomas, Nobuko Toyosawa, Sarah Watts, and Michael Wright. Akiyama Takayasu, who passed away in February 2021, remained a friend and true source of encouragement as I researched and wrote this book.

I thank Jordan Sand and two anonymous reviewers for their valuable input, as well as Paul Escott, who took the time to read an early draft and provided many helpful suggestions. Connie Hellyer gave generously of her editorial acumen to weed out my many awkward phrases. Christine Dunbar of Columbia University Press guided me to improve this book in numerous ways, while her colleague, Christian Winting, kindly answered numerous questions about images.

A great joy in researching and writing this book has been the opportunity to get to know family members around the world. While in Britain, Tessa Montgomery kindly permitted me access to the letters of William Alt, which allowed me to better understand the early years of the Japan-U.S. tea trade. A trip to Galva, Illinois, and the surrounding towns helped me not only learn about the area's history but connect with members of the Ingels clan. I give special thanks to Lynn Mathias, who shared family records and who, along with many others in the extended Hellyer family, made me feel welcome during my time in Chicago. My sisters, Martha and Tirrell, and my grandmother, Margaret, have remained supportive during the long maturation of this book. I valued the time reading Edo-period documents with my late father-in-law, Ayabe Isamu, and of the encouragement of many in the Ayabe family, most of all the love and constant support of my wife, Miho. My mother, Nancy Ingels Hellyer, has always been a guiding influence through her discipline, love of learning, and generosity to others—it is to her that I dedicate this book.

NOTES

INTRODUCTION

1. Victor H. Mair and Erling Hoh, *The True History of Tea* (London: Thames and Hudson, 2009), 23–39.
2. Bret Hinsch, *The Rise of Tea Culture in China: The Invention of the Individual* (Latham, MD: Rowman and Littlefield, 2015), 71–103.
3. Mair and Hoh, *The True History of Tea*, 71–83, 124–50.
4. Mary Lou Heiss and Robert J. Heiss, *The Tea Enthusiast's Handbook* (Berkeley, CA: Ten Speed, 2010).
5. "Afternoon Tea" menu at the Palm Court, The Plaza Hotel, New York City, https://www.theplazany.com/dining/the-palm-court/.
6. Guidebooks for children to refine good manners at a tea party are still published today. Dorothea Johnson, John Harney, and Ann Noyes, *Children's Tea and Etiquette: Brewing Good Manners in Young Minds* (Danville, KY: Benjamin, 2014).
7. In her recent lifestyle/recipe book, the actor Reese Witherspoon recommends that a family always keep a pot of sweet tea on hand to serve to guests who might drop by unexpectedly. Reese Witherspoon, *Whiskey in a Teacup: What Growing Up in the South Taught Me About Life, Love, and Baking Biscuits* (New York: Atria, 2018), 19–22.
8. So entrenched has been this idea that one of the more noted scholars of tea in the twentieth century, William Ukers, asserted that "amid the roar of musketry, a great republic was born—one that was soon to become the wealthiest consumer-nation in the world, but with a prenatal disinclination for tea." W. H. Ukers, *All About Tea* (New York: Tea and Coffee Trade Journal, 1935), 1:65.
9. Thomas J. Lipton, *Lipton's Autobiography* (New York: Duffield and Green, 1932), 189–90.
10. Erika Rappaport, *A Thirst for Empire: How Tea Shaped the Modern World* (Princeton, NJ: Princeton University Press, 2017), 193–207.

11.   The interest that Midwesterners held in products produced around the world has been explored in depth: Kristin L. Hoganson, *Consumers' Imperium: The Global Production of American Domesticity, 1865–1920* (Chapel Hill: University of North Carolina Press, 2007).

1. THE FOUNDATIONS OF TEAWAYS IN JAPAN AND THE UNITED STATES

1.   Sen Sōshitsu XV, *The Japanese Way of Tea: From Its Origins in China to Sen Rikyū*, trans. V. Dixon Morris (Honolulu: University of Hawai'i Press, 1998), 47–56, 50.

2.   The Japanese title of Eisai's text is *Kissa yōjōki*. Murai Yasuhiko, "The Development of *Chanoyu*: Before Rikyū," trans. Paul Varley, in *Tea in Japan: Essays of the History of Chanoyu*, ed. Paul Varley and Kumakura Isao (Honolulu: University of Hawai'i Press, 1989), 5–9.

3.   Murai, "The Development of *Chanoyu*: Before Rikyū," 10–12; Sen Sōshitsu, *The Japanese Way of Tea*, 75–115.

4.   Murai, "The Development of *Chanoyu*: Before Rikyū," 11. Wayne Farris recently published a study of tea in Japan focusing on cultivation and production in the medieval and early modern periods, with a concluding chapter that details aspects of modern production and consumption. In chapter 2 of his book, he explores the gradual transformation of tea from a medicinal product to a widely consumed commodity, which transpired from circa 1300 to 1600. William Wayne Farris, *A Bowl for a Coin: A Commodity History of Japanese Tea* (Honolulu: University of Hawai'i Press, 2019), 34–72.

5.   Kumakura Isao, "Sen no Rikyū: Inquires Into His Life and Tea," trans. Paul Varley, in Varley and Kumakura, *Tea in Japan*, 33–69; Sen Sōshitsu, *The Japanese Way of Tea*, 119–76. For more on the subsequent development of the tea ceremony, see Morgan Pitelka, ed., *Japanese Tea Culture: Art, History, and Practice* (London: Taylor & Francis, 2003); Rebecca Corbett, *Cultivating Femininity: Women and Tea Culture in Edo and Meiji Japan* (Honolulu: University of Hawai'i Press, 2018).

6.   Taka Oshikiri, "The Shogun's Tea Jar: Ritual, Material Culture, and Political Authority in Early Modern Japan," *Historical Journal* 59, no. 4 (2016): 932–37; Tsuru-shi Hakubutukan, Myu-jiamu Tsuru, *Heisei 14 nendo shuki tokubetsu ten: Chatsubo dōchū ten* [The autumn special exhibit for the 2002 fiscal year: an exhibit on the tea jar procession] (Tsuru City: Tsuru-shi Hakubutukan, Myu-jiamu Tsuru, 2002), 13–14.

7.   Kyōto-fu Chagyō Hyakunen-shi Hensan Iinkai, ed., *Kyōto-fu chagyō hyakunen-shi* [A history of one hundred years of tea production in Kyoto] (Uji-shi: Kyōto-fu Chagyō Kaigisho, 1994), 74–75; Hirao Michio, "Tosa chagyō-shi zakki" [Miscellaneous notes on the history of the Tosa tea industry], appendix in *Tosa-han ringyō keizai-shi* [An economic history of Tosa forestry] (Kōchi-shi: Kōchi Shiritsu Shimin Toshokan, 1956), 209–11.

8.   Luke Roberts, *Mercantilism in a Japanese Domain: The Merchant Origins of Economic Nationalism in Eighteenth-Century Tosa* (Cambridge: Cambridge University Press, 1998), 181; Hirao Michio, *Tosa-han shōgyō keizai-shi* [An economic history of

commerce in the Tosa domain] (Kōchi: Kōchi Shiritsu Shimin Toshokan, 1960), 214–22; Tsuzuki Kenkō, "Hansei jidai chūki kara Meiji no Ōtomo no chagyō nit-suite" [Tea production of Ōtomo from the mid-Edo to the Meiji periods], *Tosa shidan* 182 (December 1989): 106–9.

9. Masuda Yoshiaki, "Shoku seikatsu to ocha: mō hitotsu no cha—kinsei shomin no cha shōhi" [Tea and dietary habits: one more type of tea—consumption by commoners in the early modern period], in *Ocha to seikatsu, Nihon no ocha*, ed. Hayashi Eiichi (Tokyo: Gyōsei, 1988), 2:233.

10. Daigo Hachirō, *Cha no rekishi: Kawagoe cha to Sayama cha* [The history of tea: Kawa-goe tea and Sayama tea], *Kawagoe sōsho* 9 (Kawagoe-shi: Kawagoe Sōsho Kankōkai, 1982), 41–59.

11. Sashima Chōshi Hensan Iinkai, ed., *Sashima chōshi, tsūshi* [The history of Sashima Town, general history] (Sashima-chō: Sashima Chōshi Hensan Iinkai, 1998), 444–81; Chiba Kenritsu Sekiyadojō Hakubutsukan, ed., *Sashima-cha to suiun: Edo kōki kara Meiji ki o chūshin ni, Heisei 23 nendo Chiba kenritsu Sekiyadojō hakubutsukan kikaku tenji zuroku* [Sashima tea and water transport: a focus on the late Edo and Meiji peri-ods, a pictorial record of the exhibit project of the Chiba Prefectural Sekiyadojō Museum during the 2011 fiscal year] (Noda-shi, Chiba-ken: Chiba Kenritsu Sekiyadojō Hakubutsukan, 2011), 16, 35.

12. Farris details the process of making stir-roasted tea that originated in the sixteenth century. Farris, *A Bowl for a Coin*, 67–68.

13. Kyōto-fu Chagyō Hyakunen-shi Hensan Iinkai, ed., *Kyōto-fu chagyō hyakunen-shi*, 131–40; Iruma-shi Hakubutsukan, *Tokubetsu ten, Ocha to Nihon-jin—sono rekishi to gendai* [Tea and Japanese—historical and contemporary perspectives] (Iruma City: Iruma-shi Hakubutsu-kan, 1996), 50; Nakamura Yōichirō, *Bancha to Nihonjin* [Jap-anese and bancha] (Tokyo: Yoshikawa Kōbunkan, 1998), 144–47; Sashima Chōshi Hensan Iinkai, ed., *Sashima chōshi, tsūshi*, 465.

14. Kyōto-fu Chagyō Hyakunen-shi Hensan Iinkai, ed., *Kyōto-fu chagyō hyakunen-shi*, 136–42; Hayashiya Tatsusaburō and Fujioka Kenjirō eds., *Uji shishi 3: kinsei no reki-shi to haikan* [The history of Uji City, vol. 3: The landscape and history of the early modern period] (Uji-shi, 1976), 398–403; Patricia J. Graham, *Tea of the Sages: The Art of Sencha* (Honolulu: University of Hawai'i Press, 1998), 138–39.

15. Nakamura, *Bancha to Nihonjin*, 8–10, Nakamura Yōichirō, "The Origin of Tea Color," in *Encyclopedia of O-CHA*, O-CHA Net, World Green Tea Association, http://www .o-cha.net/english/encyclopedia/teacolor.html.

16. Ōkura Nagatsune, *Kōeki kokusan kō* [Treatise on expanding profits from domain products; 1859], in *Nihon nōsho zenshū* [Complete collection of works on Japanese agriculture], ed. Iinuma Jirō (Osaka: Nōsan Gyosan Bunka Kyōkai, 1978), 14:309–10.

17. "Gochasho, Ōhashi Jirōtarō, Edo" [The tea shop of Ōhashi Jirōtarō, Edo], pricelist, Siebold Collection, National Museum of Ethnology, Leiden. I thank Matti Forrer for kindly helping me view this and other parts of the collection.

18. Mitani Kazuma, *Meiji monōri zushū* [Collection of prints of Edo peddlers], *Kaisetsu* [Companion volume with analysis of the prints] (Tokyo: Rippu Shobō, 1975), 14, 62.

19. Cecilia Segawa Seigle, *Yoshiwara: The Glittering World of the Japanese Courtesan* (Honolulu: University of Hawai'i Press, 1993), 169–75, 234.

20. Jilly Traganou, *The Tōkaidō Road: Traveling and Representation in Edo and Meiji Japan* (New York: Routledge, 2004), 14.

21. Yamawaki Teijirō, *Kinsei Nihon no iyaku bunka* [The medicinal culture of early modern Japan] (Tokyo: Heibonsha, 1995), 7–74.

22. Yamada Shinichi, *Edo no ocha—haikai cha no saijiki* [Tea of Edo—as seen through glossaries of tea-related seasonal terms for *haikai* poetry] (Tokyo: Yasaka Shobō, 2007), 18–26.

23. Iwama Machiko, *Cha no igakushi—Chūgoku to Nihon* [The history of tea as medicine—China and Japan] (Kyoto: Shibunkaku, 2009), 187–89. Iwama gives the example of the botanist Ono Ranzan.

24. Masuda, "Shoku seikatsu to ocha," 232–33.

25. A more recent account is Markman Ellis, Richard Coulton, and Matthew Mauger, *Empire of Tea: The Asian Leaf That Conquered the World* (London: Reaktion, 2015), 32–51.

26. Research on China's dynamic economy during the Qing empire includes Kenneth Pomeranz, *The Great Divergence: China, Europe, and the Making of the Modern World Economy* (Princeton, NJ: Princeton University Press, 2000).

27. Richard Von Glahn, "Cycles of Silver in Chinese Monetary History," in *The Economic History of Lower Yangzi Delta in Late Imperial China: Connecting Money, Markets, and Institutions*, ed. Billy K. L. So (London: Routledge, 2012), 76–101.

28. For an excellent overview of the Canton system, see Peter C. Perdue, "The Rise and Fall of the Canton System: China in the World (1700–1860s), I–IV," MIT Visualizing Cultures, http://visualizingcultures.mit.edu/home/vis_menu.html.

29. Such a tea table was made in North Carolina between 1750 and 1780. It is today part of the collection of the Museum of Early Southern Decorative Arts, Winston-Salem, North Carolina, https://mesda.org/item/object/table-tea/3848/. For more about tilt-top tables, see Sarah Neale Fayen, "Tilt-Top Tables and Eighteenth-Century Consumerism," http://www.chipstone.org/html/publications/2003AF/Fayen/FayenIndex.html.

30. Rodris Roth, *Tea Drinking in Eighteenth-Century America: Its Etiquette and Equipage* (Washington, DC: Smithsonian Institution, 1961), 63–89.

31. John Francis Davis, *The Chinese: A General Description of the Empire of China and Its Inhabitants* (London: Charles Knight, 1836), 2:436–42. An explanation of these categories later in the nineteenth century is provided in Joseph M. Walsh and William Saunders, *"A Cup of Tea" Containing a History of the Tea Plant from Its Discovery to the Present Time, Including Its Botanical Characteristics . . . and Embracing Mr. William Saunders' Pamphlet on "Tea-Culture—a Probable American Industry"* (Philadelphia: By the Author, 1884), 101–4.

32. Jane Pettigrew and Bruce Richardson, *A Social History of Tea* (Danville, KY: Benjamin, 2015), 47, 51.

33. Gary Albert, "Pioneer Refinement: Kentucky's Mitchum Family Silver Purchased from Asa Blanchard," *Journal of Early Southern Decorative Arts* 35 (2014), http://www

.mesdajournal.org/2014/pioneering-refinement-kentuckys-mitchum-family-silver-purchased-asa-blanchard/. Silversmiths seem to have begun making separate tea pots in the late eighteenth century, a trend that continued in Britain and the United States into the first decades of the nineteenth century. I thank Gary Albert for bringing this reference to my attention.

34. "Tea Act, 1773," in *Understanding U.S. Military Conflicts Through Primary Sources*, ed. James R. Arnold and Roberta Wiener (Santa Barbara, CA: ABC-CLIO, 2015), 33–36.

35. John Adams Diary, December 17, 1773, in *Diary and Autobiography of John Adams*, vol. 2: *Diary 1771–1781*, ed. L. H. Butterfield (Cambridge, MA: Belknap, 1961), 85; Pettigrew and Richardson, *A Social History of Tea*, 95–96.

36. Jane T. Merritt, *The Trouble with Tea: The Politics of Consumption in the Eighteenth-Century Global Economy* (Baltimore, MD: Johns Hopkins University Press, 2017), 108–21.

37. James Fichter explores the antimonopolist stance espoused by many American merchants and the role such sentiments played in shaping the nature of U.S. maritime commerce with Asia after the American Revolution. James Fichter, *So Great a Profit: How the East Indies Trade Transformed Anglo-American Capitalism* (Cambridge, MA: Harvard University Press, 2010), 7–30.

38. Leonard Blussé, *Visible Cities: Canton, Nagasaki, and Batavia and the Coming of the Americans* (Cambridge, MA: Harvard University Press, 2009), 60–64.

39. Dan Du, "Green Gold and Paper Gold: Seeking Independence Through the Chinese-American Tea Trade, 1784–1815," *Early American Studies: An Interdisciplinary Journal* 16, no. 1 (2018): 168–86.

40. James R. Gibson, *Otter Skins, Boston Ships, and China Goods: The Maritime Fur Trade of the Northwest Coast, 1785–1841* (Seattle: University of Washington Press, 1992), 97–104.

41. "Tariff of 1789," in *Encyclopedia of Tariffs and Trade in U.S. History: The Texts of the Tariffs*, ed. Cynthia Clark Northrup and Elaine C. Prange Turney (Westport, CT: Greenwood, 2003), 3:1–3.

42. Timothy Pitkin, *A Statistical View of the Commerce of the United States of America: Its Connection with Agriculture and Manufactures: and an Account of the Public Debt, Revenues, and Expenditures of the United States* (Hartford, CT: Printed by Charles Hosmer, 1816), 209.

43. *Gazette of the United States & Philadelphia Daily Advertiser*, April 30, 1798, 1.

44. "Private Life of Washington," *Monthly Magazine and American Review* 3 no. 1 (July 1800): 73.

45. R. B. Forbes, *Remarks on China and the China Trade* (Boston: Samuel Dickinson Printer, 1844), 25. As before, U.S. merchants continued to ship a portion of the imported teas to Britain and Europe.

46. "Philadelphia Prices Current," *United States' Gazette* 25, no. 3551 (February 25, 1804): 1.

47. "Prices Current," *Weekly Register* (Baltimore, MD), September 18, 1813, 9.

48.   *Portland Gazette and Maine Advertiser*, October 22, 1810; *Palladium of Knowledge, or the Carolina and Georgia Almanac, for the Year of our Lord 1818 of the Julian Period, and 42–43 years of American Independence* (Charleston, SC: W. P. Young, 1817), n.p.

49.   The poorhouse purchased 1,282 pounds of bohea but only 7.5 pounds of the pricier hyson. Guardians of the Poor (Philadelphia), *The Accounts of the Guardians of the Poor and Managers of the Alms-House and House of Employment, Philadelphia, from 23rd May, 1803 to 23rd May 1804* (Philadelphia: Printed by John Geyer, 1804), 2.

50.   James R. Comer, "Cups That Cheer: Folkways of Caffeinated Beverages in the Reconstruction South," *Gulf Coast Historical Review* 10, no. 1 (Fall 1994): 65.

51.   "From the *Trenton Federalist*. To Thomas Jefferson, President of the United States," *Newport Mercury* (RI), May 10, 1803, 2.

52.   "The Tea Table," from the *Trenton Emporium, Weekly Visitor and Ladies' Museum*, April 5, 1823, 362.

53.   "A Country Tea Party," from the *Boston Magazine, Weekly Visitor and Ladies' Museum*, July 10, 1819, 171.

54.   "Eastern Sketches—no. III: The Tea-Party," *Saturday Evening Post* 4, no. 16 (April 16, 1825).

55.   Comer, "Cups That Cheer," 63–65. Lettice Bryan, *The Kentucky Housewife* (Cincinnati, OH: Shepard and Stearns, 1839), 407.

56.   The emergence of chai in India is explained by Philip Lutgendorf, "Making Tea in India: Chai, Capitalism, Culture," *Thesis Eleven* 113, no. 1 (2012): 18–26.

57.   Lydia Marie Francis Child, *The American Frugal Housewife: Dedicated to Those Who Are Not Ashamed of Economy* (New York: Samuel S. & William Wood, 1838), 84.

58.   "Observations: Qualities of the Animal and Vegetable Food [*sic*] Commonly Used in Diet," *Boston Medical Intelligencer*, January 24, 1825, 149.

59.   "Tea," *New England Farmer, and Horticultural Register* 6, no. 17 (November 16, 1827): 134.

60.   "Tea Drinking, Paris's Treatise on Diet," *New England Farmer and Horticultural Register* 5, no. 20 (December 8, 1826): 156.

61.   "Strange Rumours Respecting Tea," *Journal of Health, Conducted by an Association of Physicians* 1, no. 2 (September 23, 1829): 19.

62.   "On Green Tea," *Boston Medical Intelligencer* 5, no. 26 (November 13, 1827): 416.

63.   Bryan, *The Kentucky Housewife*, 385.

64.   "On China: On the Tea Leaf. Black Teas. Green Teas," *The Port-Folio* 7, no. 2 (February 1819): 3.

65.   "Analysis of Tea," *New Jersey and Pennsylvania Agricultural Monthly Intelligencer and Farmer's Magazine* 1 (May 2, 1825): 32.

66.   "On China: On the Tea Leaf. Black Teas. Green Teas," 3.

67.   Kate Bailey, "Technical Note: A Note on Prussian Blue in Nineteenth-Century Canton," *Studies in Conservation* 57, no. 2 (2012): 116–19. I thank Henry Smith for bringing this reference to my attention.

68.   William A. Alcott, *Tea and Coffee* (Boston: Gordon W. Light, 1839), 56.

69. David Beman, *The Mysteries of Trade, or, The Great Source of Wealth: Containing Receipts and Patents in Chemistry and Manufacturing; with Practical Observations of the Useful Arts* (Boston: Printed for the Author by Wm. Bellamy, 1825), 115–17.

70. "Adulterations of Food," *The Plough Boy, and Journal of the Board of Agriculture* 2, no. 7 (July 15, 1820): 54.

71. "Different Species of Tea," *Saturday Evening Post* 7, no. 363 (July 12, 1828): 4.

72. "Description of the Tea Plant; Its Name; Cultivation; Mode of Curing the Leaves; Transportation to Canton; Sale and Foreign Consumption; Endeavors to Raise the Shrub in Other Countries, 1839–1840," *Chinese Repository* 8 (July 1840): 156–57.

73. Alcott, *Tea and Coffee*, 164–67; Reginald Hanson, *A Short Account of Tea and the Tea Trade: With a Map of the China Tea Districts* (London: Whitehead, Morris and Lowe, 1876; repr. New York: Adamant Media Corporation, 2005), 53.

74. United States Revenue Commission (1865–1866), *Revenue System of the United States: Letter from the Secretary of the Treasury Transmitting the Report of a Commission Appointed for the Revision of the Revenue System of the United States* (Washington, DC: January 29, 1866), 54, Samuel J. May Anti-Slavery Collection, Cornell University, http://ebooks.library.cornell.edu/m/mayantislavery/.

75. Ernest Hurst Cherrington, *The Evolution of Prohibition in the United States of America: A Chronological History of the Liquor Problem and the Temperance Reform in the United States from the Earliest Settlements to the Consummation of National Prohibition* (Westerville, OH: American Issue Press, 1920), 110. I thank Christopher McKee for generously sharing a series of documents detailing the foods and beverages consumed by retired sailors at the U.S. Naval Asylum, documents that he located in: Miscellaneous administrative papers related to Commodore George W. Storer's term as governor of the U.S. Naval Asylum, 1854–1857, Philadelphia Naval Home (Naval Asylum), ZE File, Naval Department Library, Washington, DC; Letters Received by the Chief, Bureau of Yards and Docks, from the Governor of the Naval Asylum, 1849–1885, Record Group 71, National Archives, Washington, DC.

76. Water was commonly served with meals throughout the South. Sam Hilliard, "Hog Meat and Cornpone: Food Habits in the Ante-Bellum South," *Proceedings of the American Philosophical Society* 113, no. 1 (February 1969): 11.

77. "Tea as a Summer Drink," *Hillsborough Recorder* (NC), September 2, 1857, 1. The article was also printed in the *Southern Sentinel* (Iberville, LA), September 19, 1857, 1.

78. Dan Du, "This World in a Teacup: Chinese-American Tea Trade in the Nineteenth Century," PhD diss., University of Georgia, 2017, 138–40. I thank Dan Du for kindly sharing her dissertation with me.

79. John M. Roberts Diary, 1831–1848, Book 4 of 7, Edward E. Ayer Manuscript Collection, Newberry Library, Chicago, Vault Ayer MS 3157.

80. Harry E. Pratt, "The Lincolns Go Shopping," *Journal of the Illinois State Historical Society* 48, no. 1 (Spring 1955): 70–74.

81. Fujian began to produce oolong tea for outside markets in the eighteenth century. Robert Gardella, *Harvesting Mountains: Fujian and the China Tea Trade, 1757–1937* (Berkeley: University of California Press, 1994), 30.

82. W. H. Ukers, *All About Tea* (New York: Tea and Coffee Trade Journal, 1935), 2:512.
Some credit Richard Davies, a New York tea merchant, with creating the first Eng-
lish breakfast blend. Kenneth J. Blume, *Historical Dictionary of the U.S. Maritime
Industry* (Lanham, MD: Scarecrow, 2012), 195.

83. *New York Daily Times*, June 5, 1862, 3.

84. John King Fairbank, Katherine Frost Bruner, and Elizabeth MacLeod Matheson, eds.,
The I.G. in Peking: The Letters of Robert Hart, Chinese Maritime Customs, 1868–1907,
vol. 1: *1868–1890* (Cambridge, MA: Belknap, 1975), 5–7.

85. Forbes, *Remarks on China and the China Trade*, 55–56.

86. Isaac Smith Homans and Isaac Smith Homans Jr., eds., *Cyclopedia of Commerce and
Commercial Navigation* (New York: Harper Brothers, 1858), 303.

87. Man-houng Lin, *China Upside Down: Currency, Society, and Ideologies, 1808–1856*
(Cambridge, MA: Harvard University Asia Center, 2006), 72–114.

88. Jardine, Matheson, and Company Archives, Cambridge University (hereafter JM),
"Miscellaneous invoices, 1823–1881," A8/62/2, invoices: *Sea Witch* 14 October 1848
(Lima); *Congress* 5 September 1850 (Valparaiso). I thank Matheson & Company for
permission to research the archive and to cite this and other documents from it.

89. David R. MacGregor, *The Tea Clippers: Their History and Development, 1833–1875*,
2nd ed. (Annapolis, MD: Naval Institute Press, 1983), 68.

90. MacGregor, *The Tea Clippers*, 68; "The Canton Ship Stingray Ashore at Fire Island
Light," *New York Daily Times*, January 14, 1856, 4.

91. Patrick V. Kirch and Marshall Sahlins, *Anahulu: The Anthropology of History in the
Kingdom of Hawaii* (Chicago: University of Chicago Press, 1992), 1:103, 101–15.

92. Herman Melville, *Moby-Dick; or, The Whale* (Boston, 1926), 107. A reference to this
quotation can be found in Foster Rhea Dulles, *Yankees and Samurai: America's Role
in the Emergence of Modern Japan, 1791–1900* (New York, 1965), 23–24. More recently,
the New Bedford Whaling Museum prominently used this Melville quotation in its
online exhibit "Pacific Encounters: Yankee Whalers, Manjiro, and the Opening of
Japan," http://www.whalingmuseum.org/online_exhibits/manjiro/index.html.

93. J. D. B. DeBow, ed. *The Seventh Census of the United States* (Washington, DC: Robert
Armstrong, 1853), ix, xxix, lii; James Nakamura and Matao Miyamoto, "Social Struc-
ture and Population Change: A Comparative Study of Tokugawa Japan and Ch'ing
China," *Economic Development and Cultural Change* 30, no. 2 (January 1982): 235.

94. Victor Lieberman, *Strange Parallels*, vol. 2: *Mainland Mirrors: Europe, Japan, China,
South Asia, and the Islands* (Cambridge: Cambridge University Press, 2009), 459.

95. Joseph C. G. Kennedy, *Preliminary Report on the Eighth Census, 1860* (Washington,
DC: Government Printing Office, 1862), 3.

96. "Millard Fillmore, President of the United States of America, to His Imperial Majesty, the Emperor of Japan," in Robert Tomes, *The Americans in Japan: An Abridgement of the Government Narrative of the U.S. Expedition to Japan, Under Commodore Perry* (New York: D. Appleton and Company, 1857), 383–86.

97. John W. Dower, "Introduction, Yokohama Boomtown: Foreigners in Treaty-Port
Japan (1859–1872)" MIT Visualizing Cultures, https://visualizingcultures.mit.edu
/yokohama/index.html.

2. TEA AMID CIVIL WARS

1. "The First Cargo of Tea from Japan," *Chicago Tribune*, February 13, 1863, 2. For more about shipments of Japanese tea to the United States in the early 1860s, see Yoshino Ako, "Meiji ishin izen no Amerika ni okeru Nihoncha shijō no kaitaku: Amerika kōkoku shiryō kara yomitoku" [Pioneering efforts to market Japanese tea in the United States before the Meiji Restoration: an analysis through U.S. advertisements], *Shizuoka sangyō daigaku jōhō gakubu kenkyū kiyō* 21 (March 2019): 55–76.

2. *The British Metropolis in 1851. A Classified Guide to London, Etc. [with Maps and Plans.]* (London: Arthur Hall, Virtue, 1851), 158.

3. William Alt to Mother, November 16 and 20, 1853, personal correspondence of William John Alt (hereafter WA), 1854–1885. I thank Tessa Montgomery, a direct descendant of William Alt, for generously allowing me access to the letters and to publish excerpts from them.

4. For example, the ship delivered a group of Britons to the Canterbury colony in New Zealand in 1850. Edward Ward, *The Journal of Edward Ward, 1850–1851: Being His Account of the Voyage to New Zealand in the* Charlotte Jane *and the First Six Months of the Canterbury Settlement* (Christchurch: Pegasus, 1951).

5. "'The Charlotte Jane,'" *South Australian Register* (Adelaide), July 27, 1852, 2; "Cargo of the 'Charlotte Jane,'" *South Australian Register*, July 28, 1852, 2.

6. WA to Mother, May 30, 1854, Port Adelaide; WA to Mother, November 1854; WA to Mother, Barbados (date unknown, probably 1854).

7. WA to Mother, October 2, 1857, Shanghai.

8. WA to Mother, November 6, 1857, Shanghai.

9. WA to Mother, February 3, 1860, Nagasaki.

10. *North-China Herald* (Shanghai), January 14, 1860, 6.

11. Rutherford Alcock, *The Capital of the Tycoon: A Narrative of a Three Years' Residence in Japan* (London: Longman, Green, Longman, Roberts and Green, 1863), 2:387; Kenneth Mackenzie to Hong Kong, May 9, July 9, 1860; Mackenzie to Shanghai, October 30, 1860, Jardine Matheson In-correspondence, "Business Letters: Nagasaki, 1859–1886," B10-4, Jardine, Matheson and Company Archives, Cambridge University.

12. Regina Salvio, "Ōura Kei, Nagasaki's Remarkable Tea Merchant," *Crossroads: A Journal of Nagasaki History and Culture* 6 (Autumn 1998), http://www.uwosh.edu/home _pages/faculty_staff/earns/ourakei.html; Honma Yasuko, *Ōura Kei joden nōto* [Biographical notes on Ōura Kei] (Nagasaki, 1990), 96–98.

13. Mogeki Gentarō, ed., *Ōtani Kahei ōden [denki] Ōtani Kahei* [The biography of the honorable Ōtani Kahei] (Tokyo: Ōzorasha, 2010), 15, 24–25.

14. Yokohama Kaikō Shiryōkan, ed., "Shōkan tsutome o keiken shita seicha bōekishō: Ōtani Kahei" [A tea trader with experience working for an export firm: Ōtani Kahei], in *Yokohama shōnin to sono jidai* [Yokohama traders and that period] (Yokohama: Yūrindō, 1994), 169–71.

15. A British report compiled in 1873 gives a good overview of the refining process. Great Britain, Parliament, *Reports on the Production of Tea in Japan* (London: Harrison and Sons, 1873), 3.

16. Nagasaki Kenshi Henshū Iinkai, *Nagasaki kenshi, taigai kōshōhen* [The history of Nagasaki Prefecture: interactions with the outside world] (Tokyo: Yoshikawa Kōbunkan, 1985), 849–50.

17. WA to Mother, February 3, 1860, Nagasaki.

18. Glover to Shanghai, March 19, July 25, 1862, Jardine Matheson In-correspondence, "Business Letters: Nagasaki, 1859–1886," B10-4.

19. Mizuta Susumu, "Gaigokujin kyoryūchi ni okeru cha saiseiba no kenchiku saiseisōchi kenchiku keishiki oyobi setsubi naiyō no haaku to kaigai jirei to no hikaku shiron" [Tea-firing establishments in foreign settlements: details of buildings and apparatus compared with those in foreign countries], *Nihon kenchikugakkai keikaku-kei ronbunshū* 74, no. 639 (May 2009): 1155–63.

20. WA to Mother, November 3, 1860, Nagasaki.

21. WA to Mother, June 21, 1862, Nagasaki.

22. For an engaging biography of George Windsor Earl, see Ranald Noel-Paton, *An Eastern Calling: George Windsor Earl and a Vision of Empire* (London: Ashgrove, 2018). Noel-Paton describes the onboard romance of Elisabeth and William and their subsequent marriage in chap. 20.

23. Phillis Alt, "An Extract from the Memoirs of Elisabeth Cristina Alt, Née Earl, Who Lived in Nagasaki from 1864–1868, Together with an Abridged Biographical Sketch of Her Parents." Tessa Montgomery presented this extract to the city of Nagasaki in October 1985; Shinya Sugiyama, "Thomas B. Glover: A British Merchant in Japan, 1861–1870," *Business History* 26 (July 1984): 117–18.

24. Such practices are detailed in "Description of the Tea Plant; Its Name; Cultivation; Mode of Curing the Leaves; Transportation to Canton; Sale and Foreign Consumption; Endeavors to Raise the Shrub in Other Countries," *Chinese Repository* 8 (1839–1840): 148–49.

25. WA to Mother, Nagasaki, December 21, 1862.

26. Kawaguchi Kuniaki, *Chagyō kaika: Meiji hatten shi to Tada Motokichi* [The creation of the tea industry: Tada Motokichi and the history of Meiji-era expansion] (Tokyo: Zenbō-sha, 1989), 18–19, 28–29.

27. Conrad Totman, *The Collapse of the Tokugawa Bakufu, 1862–1868* (Honolulu: University of Hawai'i Press, 1980), 18.

28. "Kaei, Meiji nenkanroku" [Records from the Kaei period through the Meiji period], 1862/06/10 (July 6, 1862, in the Gregorian calendar), BU041/0640 [record number], Dai Nihon ishin shiryō kōhon [Manuscript of historical records related to the Meiji Restoration of Japan] (hereafter DNISK), Unpublished Document Collection, Historiographical Institute, University of Tokyo.

29. "Rōjū tashi" [Edicts of Tokugawa senior councilors], 1862/07/05 (July 31, 1862, Gregorian calendar), DNISK, BU045-0088.

30. Sugiyama Shinya, *Meiji ishin to Igirusu shōnin: Tomasu Guraba no shōgai* [English merchants and the Meiji Restoration: the life of Thomas Glover] (Tokyo: Iwanami shoten, 1993), 85.

31. Sugiyama, "Thomas B. Glover," 120–21.

32. The shogunate's move to limit Chōshū marked a departure from its previous policy of placing minimal restrictions on the purchase of arms by domains. Arima Narisuke, "Bakumatsu ni okeru seiyō kaki no yunyū" [Imports of Western firearms during the Bakumatsu period], *Nihon rekishi* 120 (June 1958): 2–3.

33. Kawaguchi, *Chagyō kaika*, 31–33.

34. For an overview of the Tokugawa-Chōshū War in 1866, see Totman, *Collapse of the Tokugawa Bakufu*, 227–66.

35. Morita Toshihiko, "Kaiseikan shihō no tenkai to sono genkai" [The development and limits of procedures at the Kaiseikan], in *Bakumatsu ishinki no kenkyū* [Research on the Bakumatsu and Meiji Restoration periods], ed. Ishii Takashi (Tokyo: Yoshikawa Kōbunkan, 1978), 290–91.

36. Marius B. Jansen, *Sakamoto Ryōma and the Meiji Restoration* (Princeton, NJ: Princeton University Press, 1961), 241–48.

37. Iwasaki Yatarō, *Iwasaki Yatarō nikki* [The diaries of Iwasaki Yatarō] (Tokyo: Iwasaki Yatarō Denki Hensan-kai, 1975), 120, 128, 130–34.

38. Iwasaki, *Iwasaki Yatarō nikki*, 133–34. Such transactions may have begun earlier—in 1862, Alt described exporting a large amount of camphor and tea on two vessels departing Nagasaki. WA to Mother, Nagasaki, December 21, 1862.

39. Kawaguchi, *Chagyō kaika*, 34.

40. Kawaguchi, *Chagyō kaika*, 35–36.

41. Richard R. Duncan, *Beleaguered Winchester: A Virginia Community at War, 1861–1865* (Baton Rouge: LSU Press, 2006), 36.

42. *Southern Cultivator* 20, nos. 9 and 10 (September and October 1862): 179; qtd. in Helen Zoe Veit, ed., *Food in the Civil War Era: The South* (East Lansing: Michigan State University Press, 2015), 78; "From the Southern Confederacy: Delicious Tea!" *Daily Bulletin* (Winchester, TN), October 24, 1862, 1.

43. *Southern Watchman*, April 22, 1863, 1; qtd. in Veit, ed., *Food in the Civil War Era*, 86.

44. R. Douglas Hurt, *Food and Agriculture During the Civil War* (Santa Barbara, CA: ABC-CLIO, 2016), 3–6.

45. "The Tea Trade: History of Its Growth," *Chicago Tribune*, December 25, 1863, 2.

46. *Daily Evansville Journal* (IN), January 27, 1863, 3; Metropolitan Hotel Breakfast Menu, 1865, Research Center, Chicago History Museum.

47. Egbert L. Viele, *Hand-book for Active Service: Containing Practical Instructions in Campaign Duties, the Recruit, the Company, the Regiment, the March, the Camp, Guards and Guard-mounting, Rations and Mode of Cooking Them* (Richmond, VA: J. W. Randolph, 1861), 58–59, Samuel J. May Anti-Slavery Collection, Cornell University. Although published in Richmond, the author is described as a former officer of a U.S. Engineers regiment and includes a preface indicating that the volume was written in New York in March 1861. The publisher may therefore have been marketing the book for sale in both the North and the South.

48. C. L. Kilburn, *Notes on Preparing Stores for the United States Army: Also on the Care of the Same, etc. (Designed for the Use of Those Interested)* (Cincinnati, OH: Bradley & Webb, 1863), 29–30.

49.   George F. Noyes, *Bivouac and the Battle-Field, or Campaign Sketches in Virginia and Maryland* (New York: Harper and Brothers, 1863), 60; "Chicago Sanitary Commission, from the 72d Illinois Regiment," *Chicago Daily Tribune*, October 31, 1863, 1.

50.   U.S. Revenue Commission (1865–1866), *Revenue System of the United States*, 55.

51.   *Urbana Union* (OH), October 26, 1864, 4.

52.   Marc Levinson, *The Great A&P and the Struggle for Small Business in America* (New York: Hill and Wang, 2011), 13–22.

3. MAKING JAPAN TEA

1.   "Japan," *New York Herald*, September 18, 1869, 8.

2.   Megan Kate Nelson, "Urban Destruction During the Civil War," *Oxford Research Encyclopedia of American History* http://americanhistory.oxfordre.com.

3.   In his influential book, the anthropologist Sidney Mintz emphasized this practice to help explain the widespread consumption of sugar in nineteenth-century Britain. Sidney Mintz, *Sweetness and Power: The Place of Sugar in Modern History* (New York: Viking-Penguin, 1985).

4.   Marc Levinson, *The Great A&P and the Struggle for Small Business in America* (New York: Hill and Wang, 2011), 17.

5.   United States Revenue Commission (1865–1866), *Revenue System of the United States*, 52–61.

6.   Levinson, *The Great A&P*, 23–31. Levinson notes that for several decades, the A&P served as a "banner" for the Great American Tea Company, with the two enterprises operating simultaneously, a fact concealed by Gilman in the belief that public knowledge of the connection would harm sales. Great American Tea Company Price List, 1871, Tea, c. 1816–1963, Warshaw Collection of Business Americana, Archives Center, National Museum of American History, Smithsonian Institution, Washington, DC. This collection is organized according to prominent products, including coffee, tea, and sugar, as well as thematic folders, such as temperance. In subsequent references, I will give details about the specific document and note the relevant folder in which it is cataloged.

7.   Great American Tea Company Price List, 1871, Tea, Warshaw Collection.

8.   *The American and China Mail* (advertising newspaper published by the American and China Tea Company) 1, no. 8 (July 1870): 4.

9.   "Tea: Trickery in the 'Cup That Cheers but Not Inebriates,' " *Chicago Daily Tribune*, January 15, 1879, 12; F. B. Goddard, *Grocers' Goods: A Family Guide to the Purchase of Flour, Sugar, Tea, Coffee, Spices, Canned Goods, Cigars, Wines, and All Other Articles Usually Found in American Grocery Stores* (New York: Tradesmen's Publishing Company, 1888), 23–24; "Japanese Teas," *Chicago Daily Tribune*, September 28, 1873, 8.

10.   Joseph M. Walsh and William Saunders, *"A Cup of Tea" Containing a History of the Tea Plant from Its Discovery to the Present Time, Including Its Botanical Characteristics . . . and Embracing Mr. William Saunders' Pamphlet on "Tea-Culture—a Probable American Industry"* (Philadelphia: By the Author, 1884), 122.

11. "Tea: Exposure of Wholesale Adulterations," *Chicago Daily Tribune*, May 24, 1881, 11. Walsh and Saunders, "*A Cup of Tea*," 97–101, 118–24.

12. "Tea: Exposure of Wholesale Adulterations," 12.

13. "Tea," *Chicago Daily Tribune*, February 3, 1873, 4.

14. Thomas W. Knox, *The Boy Travellers in the Far East, Part First, The Adventures of Two Youths in a Journey to Japan and China* (New York: Harper and Brothers, 1881), 268. This was the first book in a multivolume series that introduced various parts of the world to young American audiences.

15. Hannah Mary (Bouvier) Peterson, *The Young Wife's Cook Book with Receipts of the Best Dishes for Breakfast, Dinner and Tea* (Philadelphia: T. B. Peterson & Brothers, 1870), 481.

16. Levinson, *The Great A&P*, 30.

17. Robert Jay, *The Trade Card in Nineteenth-Century America* (Columbia: University of Missouri Press, 1987), 34–36.

18. The Great Atlantic and Pacific Tea Company's Teas and Coffees have been my solace throughout my life, Grandmother, Great Atlantic and Pacific Tea Company, 1883; The Great Atlantic and Pacific Tea Co.'s Teas and Coffees Are the Best, series of six cards, Date unknown; Tea, Warshaw Collection.

19. The cards included "A Whiskey Straight," "A Gin Cocktail," "A Claret Punch," "A Brandy Smash," "Tom and Jerry," and "Bread and Water." Tea, Warshaw Collection. See, for example, *The Sparkling Stream: Temperance Melodies* (New York: Charles W. Harris, 1860?), Temperance, Warshaw Collection.

20. A Temperance Picnic with the Old Woman Who Lives in a Shoe, Masonic Hall Ardmore, date and location unknown, Temperance, Warshaw Collection.

21. F. Bret Harte, *That Heathen Chinee and Other Poems Mostly Humorous* (London: John Camden Hotten, 1871), 15–19.

22. Trade card, Union Pacific Tea Company, Tea, Warshaw Collection.

23. Jay, *The Trade Card in Nineteenth-Century America*, 72–74. The text of the Page Act can be found at Immigration and Ethnic History Society, Immigration History, Page Act (1875), https://immigrationhistory.org/item/page-act/.

24. Jay, *The Trade Card in Nineteenth-Century America*, 74–75.

25. C. H. Remer China and Japan Tea Store, Syracuse, NY, c. 1870s–1880s.

26. A&P trade cards, c. 1885–1895, Tea, Warshaw Collection.

27. Nobuko Ide, *Ranji: The Roots of Modern Japanese Commercial Graphic Design* (Tokyo: Dentsū, 1993), 88–93. This conclusion is based upon the selection of labels presented by Ide in her book.

28. Josephine Lee, *The Japan of Pure Invention: Gilbert and Sullivan's "The Mikado"* (Minneapolis: University of Minnesota Press, 2010), xiv–xv.

29. "Amusements," *Sacramento Daily Record-Union*, November 6, 1889, 3.

30. Ide, *Ranji*, 94–103, 105–12.

31. Japanese Village Company, *Explanation of Japanese Village and Its Inhabitants* (New York: J. B. Rose, 1886), 10–11.

32. Chocolate Menier, Cocoa & Chocolate; Runkel Bros. Chocolates and Cocoas, New York, c. 1885, Temperance, Warshaw Collection.

33. "Breaking the Camel's Back," *Evansville Daily Journal* (IN), January 31, 1867, 2.

34. "Schuyler Colfax on Tariff," *Manitowoc Tribune* (WI), September 29, 1870, 2.

35. United States and Francis Preston Blair, John C. Rives, Franklin Rives, and George A. Bailey, *The Congressional Globe, Senate, 42nd Congress*, March–April (Washington, DC: Blair & Rives, 1872), 1448.

36. "Free Tea and Coffee," *New York Times*, June 5, 1880, 4.

37. U.S. Bureau of the Census, *Historical Statistics of the United States: Colonial Times to 1970*, Bicentennial ed., volume *Part 2. House Document—93rd Congress, 1st Session, No. 93–78* (Washington, D.C.: U.S. Department of Commerce, Bureau of the Census, 1975), 902; Shinya Sugiyama, *Japan's Industrialization in the World Economy 1859–1899: Export Trade and Overseas Competition* (London: Athlone, 1988), 148.

38. Mitani Hiroshi, *Kokkyō o koeru rekishi ninshiki—hikaku-shi no hakken-teki kōyō* [Historical knowledge across borders—the heuristic utility of comparative history], Iwanami kōza Nihon-shi [Iwanami lectures on Japanese history] 22 (Tokyo: Iwanami Shoten, 2016), 267. I thank Dani Botsman for bringing this reference to my attention.

39. Specifics about this movement of Tokugawa retainers to Shizuoka is detailed in Shizuoka ken, ed., *Shizuoka kenshi tsūshi-hen 5 kingendai ichi* [The history of Shizuoka Prefecture: narrative history volume 5, modern and current history, part 1] (Shizuoka: Shizuoka Prefecture, 1996), 17–20.

40. Andrew Gordon, *A Modern History of Japan: From Tokugawa Times to the Present*, 3rd ed. (New York: Oxford University Press, 2014), 64–65.

41. Kawaguchi, *Chagyō kaika*, 47–49.

42. Ōishi Sadao, *Meiji ishin to chagyō: Makinohara kaitaku shi kō* [The tea industry and the Meiji Restoration: a history of the development of Makinohara] (Shizuoka: Shizuoka-ken Chagyō Kaigi-sho, 1974), 24–27.

43. Ōishi, *Meiji ishin to chagyō*, 52–60.

44. Inagaki Shisei, ed., *Edo seikatsu jiten* [A dictionary of life in Edo] (Tokyo: Seiabō, 1975), 74.

45. Shimada Shishi Hensan Iinkai, ed., *Shimada shishi* [The history of Shimada City] (Shimada, 1973), 2:80–81.

46. Martin Dusinberre details the significant financial contributions offered by village elites in a part of Yamaguchi Prefecture during the Meiji period. Martin Dusinberre, *Hard Times in the Hometown: A History of Community Survival in Modern Japan* (Honolulu: University of Hawai'i Press, 2012), 55–59; Yamashita Kyūtarō, ed., *Shizuoka-ken meishi retsuden* [Biographies of men of distinction in Shizuoka Prefecture] (Hamamatsu: Shizuoka, 1884), 2:14, National Diet Digital Library.

47. Shimada Shishi Hensan Iinkai, ed., *Shimada shishi*, 97–99.

48. "Tokyo-fu reisho" [Edicts of the Tokyo municipal government], 8/1869, DNISK, ME 164-0702.

49. "[Kyoto] Fukukosho" [Edicts of the Kyoto urban prefectural government], 1873, DNISK, ME 181-0039; "Chashōsha kisoku mikomi-sho" [Prospective guidelines for tea trading companies], 1869/11/9, DNISK, ME 174-0569.

50. Nōmūkyoku, ed., *Meiji 16 nen: dainikai seicha kyōshinkai hōkoku: shinsa no bu, sankō no bu* [1883: report on the second competitive exhibition of refined tea: section concerning the judging of teas, reference section] (Tokyo: Nōmūkyoku, 1884), in *Meiji zenki sangyō hattatsushi shiryō bessatsu* [Documents related to the development of industry in the early Meiji period, supplemental volumes], ed. Meiji Bunken Shiryō Kankōkai (Tokyo: Meiji Bunken Shiryō Kankōkai, 1971), 106 (2): 84–86.
51. Hayashiya and Fujioka, eds., *Uji shishi 3: kinsei no rekishi to haikan*, 602–6.
52. Eliza Ruhamah Scidmore, *Jinrikisha Days in Japan* (New York: Harper & Brothers, 1891), 307.
53. Hayashiya and Fujioka, eds., *Uji shishi 3: kinsei no rekishi to haikan.*, 607–13.
54. Tsuzuki, "Hansei jidai chūki kara Meiji no Ōtomo no chagyō nitsuite," 107–8.
55. Daigo, *Cha no rekishi: Kawagoe cha to Sayama cha*, 23.
56. Sashima Chōshi Hensan Iinkai, ed., *Sashima chōshi, tsūshi* [The history of Sashima Town, general history] (Sashima-chō: Sashima Chōshi Hensan Iinkai, 1998), 774–80; Shibusawa Keizō, ed., *Japanese Life and Culture in the Meiji Era*, trans. Charles S. Terry (Tokyo: Ōbunsha, 1958), 259–60.
57. Sashima Chōshi Hensan Iinkai, ed., *Sashima chōshi, tsūshi*, 763–67, 775–80.
58. Yukimasa Hattori, *The Foreign Commerce of Japan Since the Restoration, 1869–1900* (Baltimore, MD: Johns Hopkins University Press, 1904), 28–29.
59. Sugiyama, *Japan's Industrialization in the World Economy*, 154.
60. Awakura Daisuke, *Nihon cha no kindai shi—bakumatsu kaikō kara Meiji kōki made* [The modern history of Japanese tea—from the opening of the ports in the Bakumatsu period to the late Meiji period] (Tokyo: Sōtensha, 2017), 85; Shirato Hidetsugu, "Yokohama to seicha yushutsu arekore" [This and that about tea exports through Yokohama]; Kubota Eiji, "Fuji cha ni omou" [Considering Fuji tea], in *Yokohama chagyō shi* [Records of Yokohama's tea industry], ed. Yokohama-shi Chagyō Kumiai, in *Nihon chagyō shi shiryō shūsei*, ed. Ogawa Kōraku and Termamoto Yasuhide [Compilation of documents related to Japan's tea industry] (1958; Tokyo: Bunsei Shoin Digital Library, 2003, 4: 75–76, 88.
61. William Alt to Mother, April 4, 1862, personal correspondence of William John Alt (hereafter WA), Nagasaki.
62. *London Gazette*, November 16, 1875, *London Gazette for the Year of 1875*, no. 24267, 5500; *London Gazette*, January 14, 1876, *London Gazette for the Year 1876*, no. 24284, 192.
63. WA to Mother, July 17, 1861, Nagasaki; WA to Mother, December 29, 1861, Nagasaki.
64. Phillis Alt, "An Abridged Biographical Sketch of Her Parents," 3–4; Lane Earns and Brian Burke-Gaffney, "William J. Alt," entry in "Oura Biographies," Nagasaki: People, Places, and Scenes of the Nagasaki Foreign Settlement, 1859–1941, http://www.nfs.nias.ac.jp/page019.html.
65. JM In-correspondence, Unbound Letters Japan, Kobe, 1877–1881. Both Hellyer and Hunt are presented as prominent firms in a chapter on Japan's tea trade in W. H. Morton Cameron and W. Feldwick, *Present Day Impressions of Japan: The History, People, Commerce, Industries and Resources of Japan and Japan's Colonial Empire,*

Kwantung, Chosen, Taiwan, Karafuto (Chicago: Globe Encyclopedia Company, 1919), 335–40.

66. Henry Gribble, "The Preparation of Japan Tea," *Transactions of the Asiatic Society of Japan* 12, no. 1 (November 1883): 12.

67. Yokohama Shinpōsha Chosakubu, *Yokohama hanjō-ki* [A chronicle of Yokohama's prosperity] (Yokohama Shinpōsha Chosakubu, 1903), 277–83; Noriko Kamachi, "The Chinese in Meiji Japan: Their Interaction with the Japanese Before the Sino-Japanese War," in *Race, Ethnicity, and Migration in Modern Japan: Imagined and Imaginary Minorities*, ed. Michael Weiner (New York: Routledge/Curzon), 203.

68. In the 1870s, workers received payment in Tenpō silver coins, so called because the shogunate began to mint them in 1837, the eighth year of the Tenpō period (1830–1843). The shogunate issued the coins until 1854, and the markets of the treaty ports adopted them as a standard currency, especially because of the coins' high silver content. It is unclear when payment in Tenpō coins ended, but by 1900 workers received salaries in yen and *sen* (one-hundredth of a yen) issued by the Meiji government. Takizawa Takeo and Nishiwaki Yasushi, eds., *Kahei* [Currency] (Tokyo: Tokyo-dō Shuppan, 1999), 283–85.

69. Yokohama Kaikō Shiryō-kan, ed., *Yokohama uta monogatari* [The story of Yokohama through its songs], compact disc (Tokyo: King Records, 2009). The tea songs originated in the Yokohama district of Honmoku, and even during the Meiji period, workers from outside that area had difficulty following the unique cadences used in them. Yokohama Shinpōsha Chosakubu, *Yokohama hanjō-ki*, 285.

70. Yokohama Shinpōsha Chosakubu, *Yokohama hanjō-ki*, 283–84.

71. Hiroshi Hazama, "Historical Changes in Life Style of Industrial Workers," in *Japanese Industrialization and Its Social Consequences*, ed. Hugh Patrick (Berkeley: University of California Press, 1976), 31–32.

72. Yokohama Shinpōsha Chosakubu, *Yokohama hanjō-ki*, 283; Naitō Tomomi, "Meiji zenki no yōji kyōiku ni okeru 19 seiki Amerika no eikyō (2): ochaba gakkō no katsudō to sono imi" [The influence of the nineteenth-century United States on preschool education in the early Meiji period: the activities and significance of the tea factory school], *Nihon hoiku gakkai taikai kenkyū ronbunshū* 53 (April 2000): 458–59.

73. "The Tea Trade in Japan: How the Leaves Are Picked and Dried and Shipped," *Chicago Daily Tribune*, October 14, 1888, 30.

74. Ide, *Ranji*, 41–43.

75. Yokohama Shinpōsha Chosakubu, *Yokohama hanjō-ki*, 282.

76. Ide, *Ranji*, 42; Hazama, "Changes in Life Style of Industrial Workers," 26. Hazama gives examples of wages in 1900, 1903, and 1906, demonstrating how they increased for factory workers during that period. Drawing on newspapers and other accounts of the period, Awakura Daisuke provides a more detailed analysis of wages and offers multiple insights about the often harsh working lives of women employed in tea refining factories. Awakura Daisuke, *Nihon cha no kindai shi—bakumatsu kaikō kara Meiji kōki made* [The modern history of Japanese tea—from the opening of the ports in the Bakumatsu period to the late Meiji period] (Tokyo: Sōtensha, 2017), 111–66.

77. Henry D. Smith, *Kiyochika—Artist of Meiji Japan* (Santa Barbara, CA: Santa Barbara Museum of Art, 1988), 6–21.

78. John Breen, "Ornamental Diplomacy: Emperor Meiji and the Monarchs of the Modern World," in *The Meiji Restoration: Japan as a Global Nation*, ed. Robert Hellyer and Harald Fuess (Cambridge: Cambridge University Press, 2020), 232–48.

79. Kangyōryō (Industrial Promotion Bureau), *Kangyō hōkoku* [Report on industrial promotion] 1 (December 1874): i–ii.

80. Nihonbashi Suharaya Mobei, ed., *Kōcha seihōsho* [Manual for black tea manufacture] (Tokyo, 1874), Faculty of Economics, University of Tokyo, http://www.lib.e.u-tokyo.ac.jp/.

81. Zen Nihon Kōcha Shinkō-kai, ed., *Kōcha hyakunenshi* [The hundred-year history of black tea], in *Nihon chagyō shishiryō shūsei* [Collected sources on Japan's tea industry], ed. Ogawa Kōraku and Teramoto Yasuhide (Tokyo: Bunsei Shoin, 2003), 19:16–17.

82. Tada Motokichi, "Shinkoku shōkyō shisatsu hōkokusho" [Report of inspection tour of the business conditions of China], February 14, 1876, in *Ōkuma Shigenobu, Ōkuma monjo* [The papers of Ōkuma Shigenobu], ed. Waseda Daigaku Shakai Kagaku Kenkyūjo (Tokyo: Waseda Daigaku Shakai Kagaku Kenkyūjo, 1958), 4:196–218.

83. Tada would end up not traveling to Philadelphia for reasons we will explain in the next chapter.

84. Imperial Japanese Commission to the International Exhibition at Philadelphia, 1876, *Official Catalogue of the Japanese Section: and Descriptive Notes on the Industry and Agriculture of Japan, International Exhibition, 1876* (Philadelphia: Japanese Commission, 1876), 32–33.

85. John H. Catherwood, "Tea Exhibited by the Chinese Government," in *United States Centennial Commission, International Exhibition 1876, Reports and Awards, Group III*, ed. Francis A. Walker (Philadelphia: J. B. Lippincott & Co., 1878), 28–31.

86. William Alt to Madge (Daughter), June 22, 1876.

87. Mark Ravina, *The Last Samurai: The Life and Battles of Saigō Takamori* (Hoboken, NJ: John Wiley & Sons, 2004), 198–99.

88. Ravina, *The Last Samurai*, 201–14.

89. Eric Foner, *Reconstruction: America's Unfinished Revolution, 1863–1877* (New York: Harper and Row, 1988), 582.

90. Foner, *Reconstruction*, 412–59, 583–601.

4. THE MIDWEST: GREEN TEA COUNTRY

1. Oscar Riggs, "The Tea Commerce of New York," *Frank Leslie's Popular Monthly* 16, no. 3 (1883): 295.

2. "An Ocean Race: Tea-laden Steamers from Japan Anxiously Awaited by New York Dealers," *Daily Inter Ocean*, morning ed., July 22, 1887, 3.

3. W. H. Ukers, *All About Tea* (New York: Tea and Coffee Trade Journal, 1935), 2:230; Aizawa Kichiheibei, *Nihon chagyōkai hōkoku* [Report of Japan Tea Association] (Tokyo: Nihon chagyōkai chūō honbu, 1896), 45–46.

4.   Joseph M. Walsh and William Saunders, *"A Cup of Tea" Containing a History of the Tea Plant from Its Discovery to the Present Time, Including Its Botanical Characteristics . . . and Embracing Mr. William Saunders' Pamphlet on "Tea-Culture—a Probable American Industry"* (Philadelphia: By the Author, 1884), 156; Ukers, *All About Tea*, 2:268.

5.   Mrs. R. B. Edson, "A True Romance," *Ballou's Monthly Magazine* 29, no. 1 (January–June 1869): 74; New England Tea Company trade card, Hartford, Connecticut, c. 1870s–1880s, Tea, Warshaw Collection.

6.   *Western Sentinel* (Winston-Salem, NC), October 25, 1877, 4; *Farmer and Mechanic* (Raleigh, NC), March 12, 1884, 4; *Daily Citizen* (Asheville, NC), November 27, 1889, 4.

7.   *Daily Los Angeles Herald*, July 23, 1878, 2.

8.   Francis L. Fugate, *Arbuckles: The Coffee That Won the West* (El Paso: Texas Western Press, University of Texas at El Paso, 1994). In my research, I found limited information to indicate the level of tea consumption among African American communities. I hope a future researcher will be able to expand our knowledge of this aspect of tea in the American experience.

9.   "The Wholesale Trade, Groceries: The Business of the Past Year," *Chicago Daily Tribune*, January 1, 1875, 3; "Chicago as a Tea Centre: It Is Today the Largest Tea Mart in the United States," *Chicago Daily Tribune*, November 27, 1887, 26.

10. Other accounts contend that New York received upward of 75 percent of all tea imports. Riggs, "The Tea Commerce of New York," 295.

11. *Lakeside Annual Directory of the City of Chicago, 1888* (Chicago: Chicago Directory Company, 1888), 770, 2239; Year of 1892, 2012; Year of 1896, 1617–1619; Year of 1898, 2370.

12. Such an annual schedule was a common practice among U.S. tea merchants at the time. John H. Blake, *Tea Hints for Retailers, in Two Parts* (Denver: Williamson-Haffner Engraving Company, 1903), 163; Tai Reiko, *Gaikokujin kyoryūchi to Kōbe: Kōbe kaikō 150nen ni yosete* [The foreign settlement and Kobe: marking the approaching 150-year anniversary of the establishment of Kobe as a treaty port] (Kobe: Kobe Shinbun Sōgō Shuppan Sentā, 2013), 175.

13. "Beikokukō no ichibancha" [The season's first teas sent to the United States], *Asahi shinbun* (Osaka), morning ed., April 6, 1888, 1.

14. Aizawa, *Nihon chagyōkai hōkoku*, 5–7. A brief biography of the Dexter-Roundy family, prominent in the Milwaukee grocery business for over a century, accompanies the finding aid for the Dexter-Roundy Family Papers, 1772–1951, Digital Collections, University of Wisconsin-Madison Libraries, http://digicoll.library.wisc.edu/.

15. *Milwaukee, a Half Century's Progress, 1846–1896: A Review of the Cream City's Wonderful Growth and Development from Incorporation Until the Present Time* (Milwaukee, WI: Consolidated Illustrating Company, 1896), 207.

16. *Wisconsin State Gazetteer and Business Directory, 1891–1892*, vol. 7, part 2 (Chicago: R.L. Polk and Company, 1893), 658, 940.

17. Aizawa, *Nihon chagyōkai hōkoku*, 7–10. Although Aizawa, a tea association official, is listed as the report's author, Furuya Takenosuke and Komada Hikonojō conducted the survey.

18. *Worthington Advance* (Worthington, MN), June 3, 1897, 4.

19. Aizawa, *Nihon chagyōkai hōkoku*, 10–13.

20. *Galva Weekly News* (Galva, IL), October 25, 1879, 1; December 1, 1881, 8; August 22, 1895, 1.

21. *Chicago Daily Tribune*, December 20, 1891, 29.

22. Elliott Robert Barkan, ed. *Immigrants in American History: Arrival, Adaptation, and Integration* (Santa Barbara, CA: ABC-CLIO, 2012), 632.

23. Mark A. Lause, "'The Cruel Striker War': Rail Labor and the Broken Symmetry of Galesburg Civic Culturem 1877–1888," *Journal of the Illinois State Historical Society* 91, no. 3 (Autumn 1998): 81–112.

24. Until circa 1900, Americans bought most of their foods and beverages in bulk. Brian Greenberg and Linda S. Watts, *Social History of the United States*, vol. 1: *The 1900s* (Santa Barbara, CA: ABC-CLIO, 2009), 243.

25. Advertisement of C. H. Slack, grocer, Chicago, *Chicago Daily Tribune*, August 5, 1882, 11.

26. Hamlin Garland, "Under the Lion's Paw," in *Main-Travelled Roads* (New York: Harper and Brothers, 1893), 200. I thank David Miller for bringing this reference to my attention.

27. Hamlin Garland, "The Return of a Private," in *Main-travelled Roads*, 185–86.

28. Herrick wrote the book along with her mother. Marion Harland (pseud. of Mary Virginia Terhune) and Christine Terhune Herrick, *The National Cook Book* (New York: C. Scribner's Sons, 1896), 214–20.

29. Menu of Gardner House Restaurant, Chicago, 1873, Chicago History Museum.

30. *St. Paul Daily Globe, Supplement* (St. Paul, MN), June 17, 1894, 20.

31. Christine Terhune Herrick, "The Day's Outing, What to Take with One for a Day's Bicycle Ride or Drive—Small Afternoon Tea Equipage—How to Carry a Change of Clothing in Small Space," *Minneapolis Journal*, April 30, 1904, 2.

32. "The Household," *Rocky Mountain Husbandman* (Diamond City, Montana Territory), June 28, 1883, 1; John Shelton Reed, *Holy Smoke: The Big Book of North Carolina Barbecue* (Chapel Hill: University of North Carolina Press, 2008), 192–94.

33. Harland and Herrick, *The National Cookbook*, 217–18.

34. Herrick, "The Day's Outing," 2; "Japanese Paper Napkins. Before the U.S. General Appraisers at New York, April 13, 1895," in U.S. Treasury, *Synopsis of the Decisions of the Treasury Department on the Construction of the Tariff, Navigation, and Other Laws for the Year Ending December 31, 1895* (Washington, D.C.: Government Printing Office, 1896), 467.

35. "Jap Tea Table Novelties," *Minneapolis Journal*, April 30, 1904, 2.

36. Cynthia A. Brandimarte, "Japanese Novelty Stores," *Winterthur Portfolio* 26, no. 1 (Spring 1991): 1–25.

37. *Manitowoc Pilot*, December 8, 1892, 3; *Mineral Point Tribune*, December 13, 1894, 4.

38. *Wahpeton Times* (ND), November 26, 1891, 8; *Waterbury Evening Democrat* (CT), April 19, 1895, 4.

39. Marc Levinson, *The Great A&P and the Struggle for Small Business in America* (New York: Hill and Wang, 2011), 30, 36–37.

40. The term "poor-man's tea" was used in a 1916 editorial, penned by an unnamed industry insider, that analyzed trends in the tea trade over previous decades. "Some Pertinent Tea Questions," *Tea and Coffee Trade Journal* 30, no. 2 (February 1916): 155.

41. Joshua Fogel, *Articulating the Sinosphere: Sino-Japanese Relations in Space and Time* (Cambridge, MA: Harvard University Press, 2009), 84–85; Janet Hunter and Shinya Sugiyama, "Anglo-Japanese Relations in Historical Perspective, 1600–2000: Trade and Industry, Finance, Technology, and the Industrial Challenge," in *The History of Anglo-Japanese Relations, 1600–2000*, vol. 4: *Economic and Business Relations*, ed. Janet Hunter and Shinya Sugiyama (London: Palgrave, 2002), 17–20.

42. Christine M. E. Guth, *Art, Tea, and Industry: Masuda Takashi and the Mitsui Circle* (Princeton, NJ: Princeton University Press, 1993), 26–30, 72–99.

43. Shibusawa Keizō, ed., and Charles S. Terry, trans., *Japanese Life and Culture in the Meiji Era* (Tokyo: Ōbunsha, 1958), 335; Frank Akpadock, *City in Transition: Strategies for Economic Regeneration of Inner-City Communities, the Case of Youngstown, Ohio* (Victoria, BC: Friesen, 2012), 263.

44. Mikiso Hane, *Peasants, Rebels, Women, and Outcastes: The Underside of Modern Japan*, updated 2nd ed. (New York: Rowan & Littlefield, 2016), 79–108.

45. Ogi Shinzō, *Tokyo shomin seikatsushi kenkyū* [Research on the history of the lives of Tokyo's commoners] (Tokyo: Nihon Hōsō Shuppan Kyōkai, 1979), 148.

46. The Nippon Tea Association (Chagyō Kumiai Chūō Kaigisho), ed., *The Annual Statistical Tea Report of the Nippon Tea Association 1935* (Tokyo: Chagyō Kumiai Chūō Kaigisho, 1936), 80–81. *Sencha* production outpaced that of *bancha* into the first decade of the twentieth century. Hakurankwai Kyokukai (Société des Expositions), ed., *Japan and Her Exhibits at the Panama-Pacific International Exhibition, 1915* (Tokyo: Japan Magazine Company, 1915), 111.

47. Eliza Ruhamah Scidmore, *Jinrikisha Days in Japan* (New York: Harper & Brothers, 1891), 166.

48. Isabella Bird, *Unbeaten Tracks in Japan; an Account of Travels on Horseback in the Interior* (New York: G. P. Putnam's Sons, 1881), 1:91–92.

49. "Tea Drinking in Japan," *McIvor Times and Rodney Advertiser* (Heathcote, Victoria), February 11, 1904, 2.

50. Steven J. Ericson, "Kinoshita Yoshio: Revolutionizing Service on Japan's National Railroads," in *The Human Tradition in Modern Japan*, ed. Anne Walthall (Wilmington, DE: Scholarly Resources, 2002), 118–19.

51. Sorimachi Shōji, *Tetsudō no Nihonshi* [Japan's history through railroads] (Tokyo: Bunken Shuppan, 1982), 431–37.

52. Institute of Food Behavior Science Japan, "Tetsudō no tabi ni kakasenai sonzai: ekiben" [An essential for railroad travel: the station boxed lunch], May 26, 2013, http://ifbs.or.jp/cha/2013/05/26/.

53. Fukuhaku Printing Company, Ltd., "Tabi de ocha o ippuku: kisha chabin, kisha dobin" [A cup of tea during travel: train teapots and train earthenware teapots], in *Za Korekushon: Seikatsu no Naka no Yakimonotachi* [The collection: pottery in our daily lives], *umakato.jp* [Internet ceramic festival website], http://www.umakato.jp

/archive/coll/03_02.html. The train teapots displayed on the website are from the Yōgyōshi Hakubutsukan [Museum of the Ceramic Industry History] in Utsunomiya City, Japan.

54. J. E. De Becker, *The Nightless City; Or, The History of the Yoshiwara Yūkwaku* (Yokohama: Max Nössler, 1899), 28.

55. *Jiji shinpō*, 1900, qtd. in Shibusawa, *Japanese Life and Culture in the Meiji Era*, 86–87.

56. Alice Mabel Bacon, *Japanese Girls and Women* (New York: Houghton, Mifflin, 1902), 211–13.

57. Merry White, *Coffee Life in Japan* (Berkeley: University of California Press, 2012), 7–11, 44.

58. White, *Coffee Life in Japan*, 16–17.

59. Hoshida Shigemoto, *Chagyō zensho* [The complete books of the tea industry] (originally published in 1888), in *Meiji zenki sangyō hattatsushi shiryō bessatsu* [Documents related to the development of industry in the early Meiji period, supplemental volumes], ed. Meiji Bunken Shiryō Kankōkai (Tokyo: Meiji Bunken Shiryō Kankōkai: 1971), 107 (2): 5–7.

60. "Hiogo [Hyogo] and Osaka Chamber of Commerce and Osaka Native Chamber of Commerce," *Japan Gazette* 26, no. 1 (July 8, 1880): 12.

61. The U.S. consul in Yokohama included a translation of that document in a consular report. U.S. Department of State, *Commercial Relations of the United States: Cotton and Woolen Mills of Europe, Reports from the Consuls of the United States on the Cotton and Woolen Industries of Europe, in Answer to a Circular from the Department of State*, September 23, 1882 (Washington, D.C.: Government Printing Office, 1882), 435–36; "British Consular Trade Report for Kanagawa, for the Year 1876," *Japan Weekly Mail*, July 7, 1877, 580–81. Surprisingly I have found no references in Japanese sources to the economic downturn, which affected the United States in the years following the Panic of 1873, as a factor in shaping the fortunes of Japan Tea on the U.S. market.

62. "Tea Adulterations," *Hickman Courier* (Hickman, KY), October 6, 1882, 2.

63. Deborah Blum, *The Poison Squad* (New York: Penguin, 2018), 1–2.

64. "Poisoning Food," *Chicago Daily Tribune*, November 11, 1880, 11; "Condemned," *Harper's Weekly*, January 15, 1881, 46.

65. J. H. Kellogg, *Plain Facts for Old and Young* (Burlington, IA: Segner and Condit, 1881), 292.

66. U.S. House of Representatives, Committee on Ways and Means, "To Prevent the Importation of Adulterated Teas," 42nd Cong., 2nd Sess., report no. 1927 (February 3, 1883), 1–3.

67. Lewis Heyl, *United States Duties on Imports, 1883: Revised, Corrected, and Supplemented* (Washington, D.C.: W. H. Morrison, 1883), 2:136–37.

68. "Adulterated Teas: The Sale of Several Hundred Thousand Pounds Stopped by Injunction, from the *New York Herald*, May 4," *Chicago Daily Tribune*, May 6, 1883, 13.

69. "Health Paragraphs: Poison in the Tea Pot," *New York Evangelist*, February 15, 1883, 7.

70. "Cheap Tea Sales Enjoined: A War Upon the Importation of Inferior Teas Begun," *New York Times*, May 4, 1883, 3; "Adulteration of Teas: Several Shipments Rejected by

the Inspector. How the Article Is Prepared for the Market and Colored with Prussian Blue. Information for Buyers," *New York Times*, August 23, 1883, 3.

71. "The Tea-Packers' Trade: Is the Coloring Process Injurious to the Tea? The System Explained and Defended by Prominent Members of the Trade—Bad Teas Shut Out," *New York Times*, August 26, 1883, 8.

72. Tada Motokichi, "Beikoku seifu nise seicha no yunyū o seikin sen to suru no fūsetsu, daishūkai enjutsu" [Rumors surrounding the U.S. government act to prohibit the import of adulterated teas, a speech before an association gathering], *Dainihon nōkai hōkoku* 23 (May 15, 1883): 45–53.

73. Peter Kornicki, "Public Display and Changing Values. Early Meiji Exhibitions and Their Precursors," *Monumenta Nipponica* 49, no. 2 (Summer 1994): 167–96.

74. Ōkubo Toshimichi, "Naikoku kangyō hakurankai kaijō shukuji [Congratulatory address at the opening of the exhibition for the promotion of domestic industry], in *Shukubun sakurei* [Examples of congratulatory addresses], ed. Higashi Kanichi (Tokyo: published by author, 1882), 1:23–24.

75. Hattori Kazuma, "Kaidai: chagyōkai, nōji taikai" [Synopsis: tea industry meetings and large agricultural assemblies], in *Meiji chūki sangyō undō shiryō*, vol. 23: *Chagyōkai hōkoku, nōjikai hōkoku* [Documents related to industry in the mid Meiji period, vol. 23: Reports by tea industry organizations, reports from agricultural assemblies], ed. Osa Yukio and Shōda Kenichirō (Tokyo: Nihon Keizai Hyōronsha, 1979), 4–5; Matsukata Masayoshi, "Seicha kyōshinkai hōshō juyoshiki shukuji" [Congratulatory address at the presentation ceremony for awards conferred at the competitive exhibition for refined teas], in Higashi, ed., *Shukubun sakurei*, 1:35–36.

76. Taka Okishiri, *Gathering for Tea in Modern Japan: Class, Culture, and Consumption in the Meiji Period* (London: Bloomsbury Academic, 2018), 36–44.

77. Sashima Chōshi Hensan Iinkai, ed., *Sashima chōshi, tsūshi* [The history of Sashima Town, general history] (Sashima-chō: Sashima Chōshi Hensan Iinkai, 1998), 770–71.

78. Hoshida Shigemoto, *Chagyō zensho*, 5–13.

79. Ukers, *All About Tea*, 2:229.

80. Haru Matsukata Reischauer, *Samurai and Silk: A Japanese and American Heritage* (Cambridge, MA: Belknap, 1986), 190–93.

81. Sunaga Noritake, "Meiji zenki no seicha yushutsu to Sayama kaisha no katsudō" [The efforts of the Sayama Company to export tea during the early Meiji period], *Saitama-ken shi kenkyū* 30 (February 1995): 10–29; "Trade Mark," M. Sato, tea no. 4921, registered July 17, 1877, "Tea, ca. 1816–1963," Warshaw Collection; U.S. Department of State, *Commercial Relations of the United States: Cotton and Woolen Mills of Europe*, 435–36.

82. Fortune's travels through China have been chronicled in a recent monograph, Sarah Rose, *For All the Tea in China: Espionage, Empire, and the Secret Formula for the World's Favorite Drink* (New York: Viking, 2010); and documentary, Diane Perelsztejn, dir., *Robert Fortune: The Tea Thief* (2001).

83. Arthur Reade, *Tea and Tea Drinking* (London: Sampson, Low, Marston, Searle, and Rivington, 1884), 19–20.

84. Shizuoka ken chagyō kumiai rengō kaigisho, ed., *Shizuoka ken chagyō shi* [The history of Shizuoka Prefecture's tea industry] (Shizuoka: Shizuoka ken chagyō kumiai rengō kaigisho, 1926), 1:1196–97.

85. Tada Motokichi, ed., *Kōcha setsu* [Report on black tea], translation of Edward Money, *The Cultivation and Manufacture of Tea* [1871] (Tokyo: Kannōkyoku, 1878).

86. Ko Heisū [Hu Bingshu] and Shinichirō Takezoe, *Chamu sensai* [A comprehensive guide to tea production] (Tokyo: Naimushō Kannōkyoku, 1877), 1–4.

87. International Exhibition, *The Official Catalogue of the Exhibits: With Introductory Notices of the Countries Exhibiting* (Melbourne: Mason, Firth & M'Cutcheon, 1880), 2:172.

88. J. O. Moody, "Tea," *Williamstown Chronicle* (Victoria) Australia, May 26, 1883, 2 (supplement), Trove Digitized Newspaper Database, http://trove.nla.gov.au /newspaper.

89. Hattori, "Kaidai: chagyōkai, nōji taikai," 10–12.

90. Neil Harris, "All the World a Melting Pot? Japan at American Fairs, 1876–1904," in *Cultural Excursions: Marketing Appetites and Cultural Tastes in Modern America* (Chicago: University of Chicago Press, 1990), 29–55.

91. Moses P. Handy, ed., *The Official Directory of the World's Columbian Exposition, May 1st to October 30th, 1893: A Reference Book of Exhibitors and Exhibits, and of the Officers and Members of the World's Columbian Commission* (Chicago: W. B. Conkey Company, 1893), 606–8.

92. "Japanese Tea House," handbill from Columbian Exposition 1893, "Tea, ca. 1816–1963," Warshaw Collection; Eliza Ruhamah Scidmore, "Tea, Coffee, and Cocoa at the Fair," *Harper's Bazaar*, September 30, 1893, 813; M. Murayama and Agricultural Bureau, Japan Department of Agriculture and Commerce, *Brief History & Preparation of the Japanese Tea Exhibited in the World's Columbian Exposition* (Tokyo: Kokubunsha, 1893), 10–13.

93. Benjamin Cummings Truman, *History of the World's Fair: Being a Complete Description of the World's Columbian Exposition from Its Inception* (Chicago: Mammoth, 1898), 435–37. Tudor Jenks, *The Century World's Fair Book for Boys and Girls: Being the Adventures of Harry and Philip with Their Tutor, Mr. Douglass, at the World's Columbian Exposition*, 185.

94. Yamaguchi Tetsunosuke, "Kissaten haken iin no hōkoku" [Report of staff member dispatched to work in Japan teahouse], *Chagyō hōkoku* [Tea industry report, Japan Central Tea Association] 8 (July 1894): 14–22. I thank Yoshino Ako for kindly sharing this source with me.

95. Truman, *History of the World's Fair*, 435–37.

96. Rand McNally and Company, *The World's Fair Album: Containing Photographic Views of Buildings . . . at the World's Columbian Exposition, Chicago 1893* (Chicago: Rand, McNally & Co., 1893); "Queen of the Fair: The 'White City' Does Homage to the Infanta," *Chicago Daily Tribune*, June 9, 1893, 1; Ukers, *All About Tea*, 2:306.

97. Walsh, *A Cup of Tea*, 147–57.

98. Kawaguchi, *Chagyō kaika*, 424–26.

5. THE BLACK TEA WAVE HITS AMERICA

1. *Daily Picayune* (New Orleans), March 17, 1895, 16; "China's Tea Trade with England," *Daily Inter Ocean* (Chicago), February 16, 1895, 4.
2. "Description of the Tea Plant," *Chinese Repository* 8 (July 1840): 140–42, 162.
3. Erika Rappaport, *A Thirst for Empire: How Tea Shaped the Modern World* (Princeton, NJ: Princeton University Press, 2017), 120–32, 189, 207.
4. Henry Knollys, *English Life in China* (London: Smith, Elder, & Co., 1885), 156–57.
5. Frank G. Carpenter, "The Trade of China: How It Is Declining and the Effect of the War," *The Oregonian*, March 24, 1895, 19.
6. "Travels in Japan: Immorality Among All Classes—Peculiar Knack of Flavoring Green Tea," *Evening Bulletin* (San Francisco), July 11, 1890, 4.
7. Josephine Lee, *The Japan of Pure Invention: Gilbert and Sullivan's "The Mikado"* (Minneapolis: University of Minnesota Press, 2010), 54–64.
8. *Chicago Daily Tribune*, July 14, 1895, 43.
9. *The Oregonian*, April 15, 1895, 3.
10. Rappaport, *A Thirst for Empire*, 198–99, 203.
11. *St. Paul Daily Globe*, August 5, 1893, 2.
12. *Daily Picayune*, March 17, 1895, 16.
13. "China's Tea Trade with England."
14. W. H. Ukers, *All About Tea* (New York: Tea and Coffee Trade Journal, 1935), 2:306.
15. "Reciprocal Trade with Ceylon," *Chicago Daily Tribune*, January 29, 1894, 3.
16. "Tea Cultivation in Ceylon: A Commercial Agent Describes It. Adulteration Here," *Milwaukee Sentinel*, January 18, 1895, 5.
17. "Took Him for a Negro. Ceylon Tea Merchant Ejected from a Train in the South," *Milwaukee Sentinel*, February 6, 1895, 2.
18. "Settles with Tissera. Railroad Pays for a Conductor's Blunder. Cingalese Tea Merchant Gets $1,500 in Damages," *Milwaukee Sentinel*, March 1, 1895, 3.
19. *Chicago Daily Tribune*, January 2, 1898, 27.
20. "Pacific Ocean Path to Trade. Proposal to Shorten Route of Commerce from Oriental Countries," *Chicago Daily Tribune*, December 5, 1898, 9; "Seattle the Port for the Tea Trade. Present Atlantic Cargoes Destined to Come to Puget Sound. Every Facility at Hand. Chicago Importers of the Cingalese Product Recognize Natural Laws of Commerce and Prepare to Divert Shipments," *Seattle Post-Intelligencer*, November 16, 1898, 12.
21. "Refuses a Permit for the Killing. Chief Badenoch Will Not Allow the Public Electrocution of the Elephant Gypsy," *Chicago Daily Tribune*, December 13, 1896, 5; "Think Gypsy Is a Sacred Animal. Orientals of Chicago Protest Against the Contemplated Execution of Man-Killing Elephant," *Chicago Daily Tribune*, December 27, 1896, 6.
22. "Strikes a Supposed Spaniard. V. L. Tissera's Swarthy Skin Provokes an Attack on Him on State Street—Is an American Citizen," *Chicago Daily Tribune*, March 3, 1898, 1.
23. "Big Steamers Safe at Docks. Liners Belated by Rough Weather Bring Strange Sea Stories," *Chicago Daily Tribune*, November 26, 1900, 5; "Tissera Makes Complaint,

Naturalized Cingalese Merchant Says Customs Officials Were Harsh," *New York Times*, November 27, 1900, 13.

24. Ukers, *All About Tea*, 2:266.

25. "Chicago Tea Men Back Up New York: Meeting at the Commercial Exchange Endorses the Measure of Senator Hill to Regulate Importations," *Chicago Daily Tribune*, February 7, 1897, 5.

26. "Law to Insure Pure Tea. The Importation of Unwholesome or Impure Brands Prohibited by Congress," *New York Times*, March 3, 1897, 12.

27. U.S. Department of Treasury, *Treasury Decisions Under Customs and Other Laws*, vol. 36: *January–June 1919* (Washington, DC: Government Printing Office, 1919), 154–56. "Quality of Teas Improved—Secretary Gage Says So in Reappointing the Experts," *New York Times*, December 14, 1897, 3; "Personnel of U.S. Board of Tea Experts for 1915," *Simmons Spice Mill*, February 1915, 173.

28. *New York Times*, April 8, 1897, 5. The East Indies Tea Company used a similar image in an advertisement run in the February 1897 issue of *Ladies' World* magazine. Image is included in Kristin L. Hoganson, *Consumers' Imperium: The Global Production of American Domesticity, 1865–1920* (Chapel Hill: University of North Carolina Press, 2007), 129.

29. Ukers describes him thus. Ukers, *All About Tea*, 2:309.

30. "The Tea Trade: America Wants Pure Teas—Are Ceylon and India Teas Supplanting Chinese and Japanese?" *New York Times*, July 12, 1897, 6; "Too Much Dust in Teas. Government Regulations to Purify It Stir Up Opposition of Some Importers," *New York Times*, August 29, 1897, 5.

31. "Tribune Trade Review," *Chicago Daily Times*, September 22, 1897, 9; "Quality of Teas Improved."

32. Hattori Kazuma, "Kaidai: chagyōkai, nōji taikai" [Synopsis: tea industry meetings and large agricultural assemblies], in *Meiji chūki sangyō undō shiryō*, vol. 23: *Chagyōkai hōkoku, nōjikai hōkoku* [Documents related to industry in the mid Meiji period, vol. 23: Reports by tea industry organizations, reports from agricultural assemblies], ed. Osa Yukio and Shōda Kenichirō (Tokyo: Nihon Keizai Hyōronsha, 1979), 14–15.

33. "That Tea Inspector: Twin City Merchants Are Most Anxious to Have One Here," *St. Paul Daily Globe*, March 23, 1899, 2; "Gets a Tea Inspector: St. Paul Wins Out in Its Fight with Eastern Interests," *Madison Daily Leader* (SD), April 14, 1899, 4.

34. Ōtani Kahei, *Ōbei manyū nisshi* [Journal of a journey to the United States and Europe], in *Meiji Ōbei kenbunroku shūsei* [A compilation of records of personal experiences in the United States and Europe during the Meiji period], ed. Asakura Haruhiko (Tokyo: Yumani Shobō, 1987), 21:56–71, 158–59.

35. "Beer and Tea Taxes: Ways and Means Committee Hears Forcible Appeals," *Washington Post*, January 28, 1902, 4; "Senate Passes War Tax Repeal Bill: Goes Through Without Division or Yea or Nay Vote," *New York Times*, March 22, 1902, 1.

36. "Japan Losing Tea Trade: Changed Conditions in the Country Make Production Impossible," *New York Daily Tribune*, September 30, 1900, 8; Michelle Craig McDonald and Steven Topik, "Americanizing Coffee: The Refashioning of a Consumer

Culture," in *Food and Globalization: Consumption, Markets, and Politics in the Modern World*, ed. Alexander Nuetzenadel and Frank Trentmann (New York: Berg, 2008), 117–18; "Tea, Coffee, and Liquors. Consumption of Tea, Coffee, Wine, Distilled Spirits, and Malt Liquors in the United States, Per Capita of Population, 1870 to 1897," *Yearbook of the United States Department of Agriculture 1897* (Washington, D.C.: U.S. Government Printing Office, 1898), 754.

37. An overview of Post and his marketing strategies can be found in Mark Pendergrast, *Uncommon Grounds: The History of Coffee and How It Transformed Our World* (New York: Basic Books, 1999), 95–112.

38. "Correspondence, the Tea Industry," T. W. Hellyer letter to *Japan Times*, April 24, 1897, 3.

39. Guilford L. Spencer in collaboration with Ervin E. Ewell, *Foods and Food Adulterants. Investigations Under the Direction of H. W. Wiley, Chief Chemist, Part Seventh, Tea, Coffee, and Cocoa Preparations*, U.S. Department of Agriculture, Division of Chemistry, Bulletin no. 13 (Washington, D.C.: Government Printing Office, 1892), 878–88.

40. Hattori, "Kaidai: chagyōkai, nōji taikai," 3.

41. Sashima Chōshi Hensan Iinkai, ed., *Sashima chōshi, tsūshi* [The history of Sashima Town, general history] (Sashima-chō: Sashima Chōshi Hensan Iinkai, 1998), 770–72.

42. Ukers, *All About Tea*, 2:218–19; John H. Blake, *Tea Hints for Retailers, in Two Parts* (Denver: Williamson-Haffner Engraving Company, 1903), 138. Farris outlines many of the advances in mechanized refining technology during the early twentieth century. William Wayne Farris, *A Bowl for a Coin: A Commodity History of Japanese Tea* (Honolulu: University of Hawai'i Press, 2019), 139–40.

43. W. A. Withers and G. S. Fraps, *The Adulteration of Coffee and Tea Offered for Sale in North Carolina*, North Carolina Agricultural Experiment Station, Bulletin 154 (Raleigh, NC, 1898), 45.

44. *Godey's Magazine*, February 1898, 240.

45. The McCord-Brady Company apparently provided all the teas for the Chinese Tea Garden. Omaha Public Library, Trans Mississippi & International Exposition Digital Collection, https://omahalibrary.org/digital-collections/.

46. *Chicago Daily Tribune*, July 28, 1898, 4.

47. Chagyō Kumiai Chūō Kaigisho, ed., *Nihon chagyō shi* [The history of Japan's tea industry] (Tokyo: Chagyō Kumiai Chūō Kaigisho, 1914), 145–46.

48. F. A. Rinehart, "Lipton's Teas Display, 1898," Omaha Public Library, Trans Mississippi & International Exposition Digital Collection, https://omahalibrary.org/digital-collections/.

49. Thomas J. Lipton, *Lipton's Autobiography* (New York: Duffield and Green, 1932), 165.

50. Lipton, *Lipton's Autobiography*, 189–190.

51. Blake, *Tea Hints for Retailers*, 226.

52. Label in collection of the Chudnow Museum of Yesteryear, Milwaukee, WI, http://www.chudnowmuseum.org/.

53. *Galva Weekly News*, February 19, 1903, 1.

54. Records of the Hills Brothers Coffee Company, Hills Brothers Series 4, Advertising Materials, circa 1890s–1987, Subseries 4.2, Historical Albums, 1911–1967, Archives Center, National Museum of American History, Smithsonian Institution.

55. "Cotton Tea and Urn Bags, Information for Buyers, Pithy Suggestions as to Where and How to Buy to the Best Advantage," *Tea and Coffee Trade Journal* 32, no. 6 (June 1917): 550; "Non-Refillable Tea Ball: Expert Invents Epoch-Making Tea Device That Insures Sanitary Tea Service," *Tea and Coffee Trade Journal* 31, no. 1 (July 1916): 71. Many popular works cite Thomas Sullivan, an American, with inventing the tea bag sometime around 1910. However, Ukers notes that in 1896 the British government awarded the first patent for an individual tea bag to one A. V. Smith of London. Ukers also asserts that the tea bag gained popularity in the United States, first in restaurants and then in homes, after 1920. Ukers, *All About Tea*, 2:443, 507.

56. "Weddings Past and Yet to Come," *Chicago Daily Tribune*, February 28, 1897, 38; *Japan Weekly Mail*, May 3, 1890, 466; Tai Reiko, *Gaikokujin kyoryūchi to Kōbe: Kōbe kaikō 150nen ni yosete* [The foreign settlement and Kobe: marking the approaching 150-year anniversary of the establishment of Kobe as a treaty port] (Kobe: Kobe Shinbun Sōgō Shuppan Sentā, 2013), 178–81.

57. Imperial Japanese Commission to the Louisiana Purchase Exhibition, *The Exhibition of the Empire of Japan, Official Catalogue* (St. Louis: International Exposition, 1904), 2–6.

58. "Japan's Tea Garden at the World's Fair," *Washington Times*, April 25, 1904, 7.

59. "Native Japanese Dinner Party," *St. Louis Republic*, July 14, 1904, 6.

60. "Japs in Merry War Over Tea Girls," *St. Louis Republic*, August 16, 1904, 2.

61. Marietta Holley, *Samantha at the St. Louis Exposition* (New York: G. W. Dillingham, 1904), 197.

62. "'Fair Japan,'" *Rich Hill Tribune* (MO), June 30, 1904, 1.

63. "Supplemental Magazine, Missouri, the World's Host," *St. Louis Republic*, October 23, 1904, 1.

64. "Ceylon Tea Is Rapidly Displacing Other Brands," *St. Louis Republic*, May 27, 1904, 8.

65. "Patriotic Tea Drinking: The China and Japan Products Are Ousted by the British in Ceylon," *Lexington Intelligencer* (MO), June 18, 1904.

66. *St. Louis Republic*, December 16, 1904, 9.

67. Teramoto Yasuhide, "Senkanki Amerika shijō o meguru Nihoncha to Indo Seron kōcha: māketto no kaitaku kōkoku katsudō" [Japanese tea and India, Ceylon black teas on the U.S. market in the interwar period: advertising activities to expand the market], *Kwansei Gakuin Daigaku keizaigaku ronkyū* 51, no. 3 (November 1997): 54–55; "Japan's Tea Trade with U.S.," *Tea and Coffee Trade Journal* 34, no. 3 (March 1918): 218; "The Tea Trade of the U.S., Showing Its Growth During the Past Ninety-Seven Years, with Particular Reference to Japan and China Imports," *Tea and Coffee Trade Journal* 34, no. 4 (April 1918): 334–35; "Important Facts About Tea—Part VII," *Simmons Spice Mill* 38, no. 2 (February 1915): 158; Frank R. Rutter, *Rice and Tea in Japan, Supplement to Commerce Report* (Washington, DC: Government Printing Office, 1922), 9.

68. "India and Ceylon Tea. Tea Taste of the People Changing—Importations Into North America Show a Phenomenal Increase," *Richmond Palladium and Sun-Telegram* (IN) July 9, 1907, 3.
69. "Labels Required on Tea," *St. Louis Republic*, December 23, 1910 (?), clipping in "Beikoku ni okeru honpō seicha no hanro kakuchō ikken, chakushokucha mondai" [Expanding sales of our nation's teas in the United States—the issue of colored teas], 489, Diplomatic Record Office, Japan Ministry of Foreign Affairs, Tokyo.
70. Robert S. Fletcher, "'To Newspaper Advertising I Owe Success,' P. C. Larkin the Tea King of America, with No Capital Built a Business of Millions Exclusively Through the Medium of Newspapers," *Arizona Republican*, November 5, 1907, 9.
71. Hirata Tomo to Foreign Minister Komura, August 17, 1910, Calcutta, Chakankei zakken, zoku kohi, kokoa [Miscellaneous documents related to tea, including coffee and cocoa] from Meiji 41 (1908), Diplomatic Record Office, Japan Ministry of Foreign Affairs, Tokyo.
72. John Callan O' Laughlin, "Japanese Power Menaces America: Pre-eminence of Island Empire's Naval Strength in Far East Constantly Threatens This Country," *Chicago Daily Tribune*, September 9, 1905, 1.
73. Okakura Kakuzō, *The Book of Tea* (New York: G. P. Putnam's Sons, 1906), 6, 11–13, 157. *The Book of Tea* remains a staple of Asia sections of retail bookstores and Asian novelty corners in many museum gift shops.
74. Kendall H. Brown, "Rashōmon: The Multiple Histories of the Japanese Tea Garden at Golden Gate Park," *Studies in the History of Gardens and Designed Landscapes: An International Quarterly* 18, no. 2 (March 2012): 93–119.
75. Jan Whitaker, *Tea at the Blue Lantern Inn: A Social History of the Tea Room Craze* (New York: St. Martin's, 2002), 10–12.
76. "Social Features of Shrine Ceremonial," *Tulsa Daily World*, March 9, 1913, 10.
77. "Solons Visit University City and Are Delighted with Visit," *Daily Capital Journal* (Salem, OR), January 26, 1911, 1; *Evening Public Ledger* (Philadelphia), July 9, 1920, 11.
78. "Couple Married in Japanese Garb," *Washington Times*, February 4, 1910, 7; "1881 Club New Years Reception," *Jefferson Jimplecute* (TX), January 7, 1910, 2.
79. "The Tea Room Habit Has Come to Stay: Women Like These Homelike Restaurants, but the Fad Has Struck the Men, Too," *New York Times*, April 3, 1904.
80. "Monday Afternoon Teas: Ideal Weather Invites Many Callers to Social 'At Homes,'" *Evening Capital Annapolis*, January 23, 1912, 4; "Dartmouth's Junior Week: Festivities Began with Fraternities Teas and Ended with a Dance," *New York Times*, May 26, 1912.
81. Mariko Iijima, "Coffee Production in the Asia-Pacific Region: The Establishment of a Japanese Diasporic Network in the Early Twentieth Century," *Journal of International Economic Studies* (Institute of Comparative Economic Studies, Hosei University) 32 (2018): 77–79.
82. "Tea Board Shuts Out Artificially Colored Tea from This Country," *Grocery World and General Merchant* 51, no. 8 (February 20, 1911), 6. If so desired, a skeptical tea drinker could employ a test to detect Prussian blue in tea. Fred West, "The Detection

of Prussian Blue in Tea," *Journal of Industrial and Engineering Chemistry* 4, no. 7 (July 1912): 528. I thank Brenda Jordan for bringing this reference to my attention.

83. Chagyō Kumiai Chūō Kaigisho, ed., *Chagyō kumiai chūō kaigisho tōkei nenpō* [The annual statistical tea report of the Nippon Tea Association], 1935 (Tokyo: Chagyō Kumiai Chūō Kaigisho, 1936), 80–81.

84. Furuya Takenosuke, "Kitabei gasshūkoku oyobi Eiryō Kanada ni okeru Taiwan ūroncha hanro kakuchō ni kan suru kengi" [Proposals for expanding the market for Taiwan oolong tea in the United States and Canada], July 1915, in "Chakankei zak-ken, zoku kohi, kokoa," file of documents from Meiji 41 (1908), Diplomatic Archives of the Ministry of Foreign Affairs of Japan; *The Exposition Beautiful; Over One Hundred Views [of] the Panama-California Exposition and San Diego, the Exposition City* (San Diego: Pictorial Publishing Company, 1915).

85. Asiatic Exclusion League, *Third Annual Meeting of the Asian Exclusion League, San Francisco May 1908* (San Francisco: Organized Labor Print, 1908), 14.

86. Shizuoka Chashō Kōgyō Kyōdō Kumiai, ed., *Zadankai, Shizuoka de katsuyaku shita gaikoku chashō no koto* [A conversation about the activities of Western tea firms in Shizuoka] (Shizuoka: Shizuoka Chashō Kōgyō Kyōdō Kumiai, 2000), 30. The Tani-moto family became the owners of Hellyer and Company in the 1970s.

87. "Obituary, Frederick Hellyer," *Simmons Spice Mill* 38, no. 5 (May 1915): 538; "Vincent L. Tissera," *Simmons Spice Mill* 39, no. 11 (November 1916): 1247. A picture of Tissera's grave at the Oakdale Memorial Cemetery in Davenport can be viewed at https://iowagravestones.org/cemetery_list.php?CID=82&cName=Oakdale+Memorial+Gardens.

6. DAILY CUPS DEFINED: BLACK TEA IN THE UNITED STATES, *SENCHA* IN JAPAN

1. "Tea Drinking Increased 36 Percent in Past Year," *True Republican* (Sycamore, IL), January 18, 1919, 5.

2. "Comprehensive Summary of the World's Tea Industry," *Spice Mill* 44, no. 1 (January 1921): 59.

3. Teramoto Yasuhide, *Senzenki Nihon chagyō shi kenkyū* [A study of Japan's tea industry in the prewar period] (Tokyo: Yūhikaku, 1999), 162–97.

4. Chagyō Kumiai Chūō Kaigisho, ed., *Chagyō ihō, dai 12 shū: Beika ryōkoku ni tai suru Nihon cha kōkoku senden sankō shiryō* [Reports on the tea industry, vol. 12: Reference materials concerning advertising and publicity for Japan Tea in the United States and Canada] (Tokyo: Chagyō Kumiai Chūō Kaigisho, 1926), 50–93.

5. Miyamoto Yūichirō, "Beikoku ni okeru Nihon ryokucha eigyōsha nami ni shōhisha chōsa" [A survey of consumers and retailers of Japanese green tea in the United States], *Chagyōkai*, July 1926, 5–12.

6. S. Livingston Davis, "Talks to Tea Buyers," *Tea and Coffee Trade Journal* 31, no. 1 (July 1916): 145.

7.   The album's content indicates it was compiled during the 1910s. The Manternach Advertising Agency prepared the advertisement and ran it in the *Journal of Commerce and Commercial Bulletin*, August 19, 1920. Records of the Hills Brothers Coffee Company, Hills Brothers Series 4, Advertising Materials, circa 1890s–1987, Subseries 4.2, Historical Albums, 1911–1967, Archives Center, National Museum of American History, Smithsonian Institution.

8.   H. C. Grote, "How Retailers Can Profitably Study the Wagon Route Men's Methods and Apply Some of Them to Their Businesses," *Tea and Coffee Trade Journal* 31, no. 4 (October 1917): 372.

9.   "Speaking of Standard Lines," *The Jewel* 1, no. 12 (August 11, 1923): 14.

10.   O. B. Westphal, "A Talk with Jewel Salesmen: Increasing Earning Power," *The Jewel* 1, no. 5 (January 15, 1923): 3; O. B. Westphal, "The True Facts About the Premium," *The Jewel* 1, no. 6 (February 15, 1923): 3; John S. Wright, "A Brief Marketing History of the Jewel Tea Company," *Journal of Marketing* 22, no. 4 (April 1958): 369–71.

11.   W. H. Ukers, *All About Tea* (New York: Tea and Coffee Trade Journal, 1935), 2:302.

12.   *Farmer's Wife* 30, no. 6 (June 1927): 360.

13.   I thank Jason Petrulis for sharing with me these particular advertisements, which are from the Japan Tea Promotion Committee, J. Walter Thompson Company, 35mm Microfilm Proofs, 1906–1960, undated, J. Walter Thompson Company Collection, John W. Hartman Center for Sales, Advertising, and Marketing History, Duke University.

14.   Erika Rappaport, *A Thirst for Empire: How Tea Shaped the Modern World* (Princeton, NJ: Princeton University Press, 2017), 230–34; Ukers, *All About Tea*, 2:317–19.

15.   "Tea Drinking—a Growing American Habit," *Spice Mill* 44, no. 10 (October 1921): 1718.

16.   "Some Interesting New York Tea Rooms: These Establishments, Oddly Situated and Decorated, Serve Tea and Coffee and Have Wide Appeal," *Spice Mill* 44, no. 1 (January 1921): 23–29.

17.   *The Tea Room Booklet* (New York: Woman's Home Companion, c. 1922), 2–6, 8–13.

18.   Sherwood Anderson, *Winesburg, Ohio* (New York: Penguin, 1992), 70.

19.   Chagyō Kumiai Chūō Kaigisho, ed., *Chagyō kumiai chūō kaigisho tōkei nenpō 1935* [The annual statistical report of the Japan Central Tea Association, 1935] (Tokyo: Chagyō Kumiai Chūō Kaigisho, 1936), 81.

20.   Shibusawa Keizō, ed., *Japanese Life and Culture in the Meiji Era*, trans. Charles S. Terry (Tokyo: Ōbunsha, 1958), 334–37.

21.   Chagyō Kumiai Chūō Kaigisho, ed., *Chagyō ihō, dai 19 shū, Dai Tokyo ni okeru seicha jijyō* [Reports on the tea industry, vol. 19: The state of affairs of tea in the Tokyo metropolitan area] (Tokyo: Chagyō Kumiai Chūō Kaigisho, 1927), 27–48.

22.   Shizuoka-ken Chagyō Kumiai Rengō Kaigisho, ed., *Shizuoka-ken chagyō zokuhen* [The history of Shizuoka Prefecture's tea industry, sequel edition] (Shizuoka: Shizuoka-ken Chagyō Kumiai Rengō Kaigisho, 1937), 75–85.

23.   Michiyō Tsujimura and Masataro Miura, "On Vitamin C in the Green Tea," *Bulletin of the Agricultural Chemical Society of Japan* 1, no. 1 (1924–1925): 13–14.

24.   Sagara Bussan Kaisha Seichabu, *Cha no kaori* [The fragrance of tea] (Shizuoka: Shizuoka-ken Chagyō Kumiai Rengō Kaigisho, 1929?), n.p.

25. Yamashiro Seicha Kabushiki Gaisha, *Cha no chishiki* [The wisdom of tea] (Kyoto: Yamashiro Seicha Kabushiki Gaisha, 1926), front cover, 96–97.

26. *Farm Journal* 54, no. 2 (February 1930): 49.

27. "A Good Word for Tea," *The Jewel* 6, no. 8 (May 7, 1928): 19.

28. Ukers, *All About Tea*, 1:548–550, 2:300.

29. Hazel E. Munsell, Senior Nutrition Chemist, Bureau of Home Economics, offered these conclusions in a report, "Tea Not a Reliable Source of Vitamin C, Nutrition Tests Show," in *Yearbook of the United States Department of Agriculture 1930*, ed. Milton S. Eisenhower and Arthur P. Chew (Washington, DC: U.S. Government Printing Office, 1930), 508–9.

30. Merry White, *Coffee Life in Japan* (Berkeley: University of California Press, 2012), 44, 53–55.

31. Tadani Shinzō, "Kissaten keiei nitsuite" [On the management of coffee shops], *Kahō* [Confectionary treasures] 1, no. 10 (December 1928): 14. Published by Wayōgashi rengō gijutsu shōreikai [Group for the Promotion of Technical Knowledge, Association of Confectioners of Western and Japanese Sweets].

32. Ukers, *All About Tea*, 2:431.

33. Ippei Fukuda, *The Japanese at Home* (Tokyo: Hokuseido, 1936), 58–59.

34. Fukuhaku Printing Company, Ltd., "Tabi de ocha o ippuku: kisha chabin, kisha dobin," http://www.umakato.jp/archive/coll/03_03.html.

35. Ukers, *All About Tea*, 2:431.

36. H. S. K. Yamaguchi, K. M. Yamaguchi, Frederic De Garis, Atsuharu Sakai, and Fujiya Hotel, eds., *We Japanese: Being Descriptions of Many of the Customs, Manners, Ceremonies, Festivals, Arts and Crafts of the Japanese, Besides Numerous Other Subjects* (1934; Miyanoshita, Japan: Fujiya Hotel, 1950), 292.

37. "Will Rogers Says," *The Independent* (Elizabeth City, NC), January 22, 1932, section 2, 4.

38. Futō Kanja, "Kissa to heigai" [Tea drinking and its ill effects], *Shokumotsu no yōjō* 6, no. 11 (November 1920): 36.

39. Ueda Seifū, "Kantan na ocha no irekata, nomikata" [Simple ways to brew and drink tea], in *Gendai jyosei to Nihon-cha* [Contemporary women and Japanese tea], ed. Katō Yūya (Shizuoka: Japan Central Tea Association, 1938), 12–18.

40. "Bancha no irekata" [How to brew *bancha*], *Asahi shinbun* (Tokyo), January 21, 1938, evening ed., 6.

41. Nakamura Chikushirō, "Bancha, sencha o oishiku ireru hiketsu" [Secrets for brewing delicious *bancha* and *sencha*], *Fujokai* 41, no. 1 (January 1930): 372; "Seikatsu no sumizumi kara muda wo nakusau" [Eliminating wasteful practices in every nook and cranny of one's life], *Fujin no tomo* 31, no. 2 (February 1937): 176–77.

42. "Watashi ga einen aiyō shite iru: ocha gawari no kenkō inyō" [Things I have used habitually for years: health drinks to replace tea], *Fujin kurabu* 20, no. 11 (September 1939): 230–31.

43. Oral account relayed by a Shizuoka tea merchant. According to another account, a Kyoto tea merchant developed an initial version of this type of tea by mixing green tea with pieces of a rice cake (*kagamimochi*) often consumed as part of New Year's

celebrations. An Osaka merchant later substituted roasted rice, creating the *genmai* tea consumed today. Takano Minoru et al. and Nihon Chagyō Chūōkai, eds., *Ryoku-cha no jiten* [The dictionary of green tea], 3rd rev. ed. (Tokyo: Shibata Shoten, 2002), 87.

44. Chagyō Kumiai Chūō Kaigisho, ed., *Chagyō kumiai sōritsu 50 shūnen kinen ronbunshū* [A collection of articles to commemorate the fiftieth anniversary of the creation of the Japan Central Tea Association], 4 vols. (Tokyo: Chagyō Kumiai Chūō Kaigisho, 1938).

45. Shizuoka-ken Naichishō Chagyō Kumiai Shūchi Iwata Shibu, *Cha no kaori* [The fragrance of tea] (Shizuoka: Shizuoka-ken Chagyō Kumiai Rengō Kaigisho, 1940?).

46. Ōyama Yasunari, "Jikkayōcha no shōhinka—[hōjicha] tōjō no igi" [The commercialization of a household tea—the significance of the appearance of *hōjicha*], *Saita chabunka shinkō zaidan kiyō* 6 (2006): 87–128.

47. Hayashiya Seicha mail-order postcard, author's collection; *Asahi shinbun* (Tokyo), morning ed., June 11, 1940, 5; *Asahi shinbun* (Tokyo), morning ed., February 8, 1941, 2.

48. Chagyō Kumiai Chūō Kaigisho, ed., *Chagyō ihō, dai 18shū, naigai seicha jijō* [Reports on the tea industry, vol. 18: Market conditions for tea at home and abroad] (Tokyo: Chagyō Kumiai Chūō Kaigisho, 1927), charts included before page 1.

49. *Evening World* (New York), October 14, 1920, 14; *New Britain Herald* (New Britain, CT), October 21, 1921, 4.

50. *Wisconsin Tobacco Reporter* (Edgerton), October 6, 1922, 3; *Galva News* (IL), June 16, 1927, 3; *Chicago Daily Tribune*, March 21, 1928, 12.

51. Shizuoka Chashō Kōgyō Kyōdō Kumiai, ed., *Zadankai, Shizuoka de katsuyaku shita gaikoku chashō no koto*, 27–28.

52. Nihon sangyō kyōkai, ed., *Beikoku dokuritsu hyaku gojū nen kinen Firaderufia bankoku hakurankai Nihon sangyō kyōkai jimu hōkoku* [Report of the Office of the Japan Industrial Association concerning the Philadelphia Sesquicentennial International Exhibition] (Tokyo: Nihon sangyō kyōkai, 1927), 274–82.

53. "Japan Tea Hall Menu," Japan Official, July–December 1933, Century of Progress Government Correspondence #2, Box 63, Japan, Chicago Circle Library, University of Illinois-Chicago (Hereafter CPGC); "Notes of a Century of Progress," *Chicago Daily Tribune*, June 15, 1933, 7.

54. Inter-Office Correspondence, January 23, 1933, Japan Official, January–June 1933, #2, CPGC.

55. "Freshman Girls and N.U. Boycott Japanese Tea," *Chicago Daily Tribune*, February 12, 1932, 4.

56. "Five Shot by Red in Anti-Jap Riot in Michigan Ave.: 3 Policemen and Woman Among Injured," *Chicago Daily Tribune*, March 13, 1932, 3.

57. "The Progress of Manchuria," South Manchuria Railway Company pamphlet, Japan Official, January-June 1933, #2, CPGC.

58. "Oriental Travelogues by Garner Curran"; "Japan Our Trans-Pacific Neighbor," text of lecture delivered in Hall of Science at A Century of Progress, Sunday, July 2, 1933, by Garner Curran; Chew Low, President, Chinese Consolidated Benevolent Association to Rufus Dawes, President of A Century of Progress, July 4, 1933; U.S. Grant Smith, Chief of Protocol of Century of Progress to Stanley Hornbeck, U.S. Department of State, July 20, 1933; all in "Japan Official, July–December 1933," #2, CPGC.

59. Inter-Office Correspondence, Publications Division, undated, Japan Official, January–June 1933, #2, CPGC.

60. Ruth De Young, "A Cup of Tea Is Ceremony to Japanese," *Chicago Daily Tribune*, July 15, 1933, 11.

61. Katō Tokusaburō and Nihon Ryokucha Hanro Kakuchō Rengō Tokubetsu Iinkai., eds., *Shikago shinpo isseiki bankoku hakurankai kinen shashinchō* [A commemorative picture book of A Century of Progress Chicago World Exposition, 1933] (Tokyo: Nihon Ryokucha Hanro Kakuchō Rengō Tokubetsu Iinkai, 1934), n.p.

62. Susan Hasegawa for the Japanese American Historical Society of San Diego, *Images of America: Japanese Americans in San Diego* (Charleston, SC: Arcadia, 2008), 16–17.

63. California Pacific International Exposition, *Official Guide, Souvenir Program, California Pacific International Exposition, San Diego* (San Diego, 1936), 3, 44–45.

64. Jingu Eizō, "Kitabei San de-go-haku to Nihoncha no senden" [Publicizing Japanese tea and the San Diego International Exposition], in *Chagyō ihō, dai 32shū kaigai seicha shijō chōsa shohōkoku* [Reports on the tea industry, vol. 32: Various reports on surveys of foreign tea markets], ed. Chagyō Kumiai Chūō Kaigisho (Tokyo: Chagyō Kumiai Chūō Kaigisho, 1939), 34.

65. Jack Morgan, "How World War II Changed History at San Antonio's Japanese Tea Garden," *Kera News*, October 6, 2015, https://www.keranews.org/post/incredible -story-behind-san-antonios-japanese-tea-garden.

66. *Galva News*, May 13, 1937, 9; *Chicago Daily Tribune*, October 16, 1938, 7.

67. Elizabeth La Hines, "Career Evolves as Tea Blender: Gertrude Ford Has Devoted 30 Years to Her 'Contribution to Gracious Living,'" *New York Times*, February 18, 1940, D6.

68. Rappaport, *A Thirst for Empire*, 285–88.

69. "Advertising Advised as Spur to Tea Sales: Forum Told It Is Second Only to Lemonade," *New York Times*, June 2, 1939, 38; Mrs. Gaynor Maddox, "Try Iced or Hot Tea Right After a Tennis Session," *Wilmington Morning Star* (NC), June 11, 1940, 6.

70. "No Hard Tack in U.S. Camps This Time," *Daily Missourian* (Columbia), August 30, 1917, 2; Charles E. Tracewell, "This and That," *Evening Star* (Washington, DC), October 8, 1928, 8.

71. "Household News by Eleanor Howe," *McDowell Times* (Keystone, WV), September 13, 1940, n.p.

72. Emily Post, "Woman May Not Accept Expenses," *Evening Star*, March 27, 1939, B8.

73. "Advertising Advised as Spur to Tea Sales."

74. Joseph Tetley & Company, *Tea Goes American: Do You Know What "Tea in the American Manner" Means? Did You Know America Is Doing Things to Tea? Here's the Story with New Recipes, Table-settings and Other Things* (New York: Tea Bureau, 1939), 6–7.

75. Chagyō Kumiai Chōūkaigisho, ed., *Kita Afurika ni okeru chagyō chōsa* [A survey of the tea industry in North Africa] (Tokyo, 1930).

76. Nakamura Enichirō, "Shin hanro Manshūkoku" [The new Manchurian market], *Chagyōkai*, September 1933, 4-1-4-4.

77. Ikegaya Keisaku and Koizumi Takeo, "Fuyu no Manshūkoku shijō o shisatsu shite" [An inspection of the market in Manchukuo during the winter], *Chagyōkai*, March 1936, 15–18.

78. Yamaguchi Chūgorō, "Manshūkoku seicha juyō gaikan" [An overview of demand for refined tea in Manchukuo], *Chagyōkai*, November 1936, 10–14.

79. Tomatsu Yasuko, "Gyōshubetsu kōkoku shrīzu, 7 inryō" [A series on advertisements of various businesses, no 7: Beverages], *Ad Studies* (Advertising Museum Tokyo) 45 (2011): 50.

80. Chagyō Kumiai Chūō Kaigisho, ed., *Chagyō kumiai chūō kaigisho tōkei nenpō* [The annual statistical report of the Japan Central Tea Association] (Tokyo: Chagyō Kumiai Chūō Kaigisho, 1940), 38–39.

81. Editorial, "Ōshū seiran no suii to yushutsu Nihon: cha no shōrai" [The wartime transition in Europe and Japan as an export state: the future of tea], *Cha*, June 1940, 6–8.

82. Editorial, "Nichibei kokkō no henka ni sho shi: Nihon cha o dō kangaebeki ka" [Confronting changes in the diplomatic relations of the United States and Japan: what must we consider about Japan Tea], *Cha*, February 1941, 6–7.

83. "Chagara kennō undō no zenkokuka" [The nationalization of the movement to donate tea leaves], *Cha*, February 1941, 10–14.

84. Haruko Taya Cook and Theodore F. Cook, *Japan at War: An Oral History* (New York: New Press, 1992), 177.

85. "Finds Japanese People Opposed to War with U.S.: Chicago Tea Man Tells of Life in Nippon," *Chicago Daily Tribune*, August 2, 1941, 3.

86. Morgan, "How World War II Changed History at San Antonio's Japanese Tea Garden."

87. Mitsuhashi Shirōji, "Kaitō shūnin ni sai shite" [Statement on assuming the office of association president], *Cha*, April 1942, 6.

88. Oda Nobugaki, "Senjishita ni okeru chagyō kyōkai no shimei" [The mission of the tea industry during this time of war], *Cha*, January 1943, 9.

89. *Cha*, September 1943, 4–11.

90. "Kore de yakedo ga naoru: shikai to sencha ōkyūyaku—rikugunshō imu tōkyokudan" [How to quickly treat burns: medicine made from paper ash and *sencha*, advice from the Army Ministry Medical Affairs Office], *Asahi shinbun*, morning ed., November 16, 1943, 3.

91. "Kyō ha bōkū kyōkabi: seishoku ni nareyo, hi mo mizu mo tsukawazu, hijōji no shokuryō ni—kono kokorogamae—natsu no bōkū fukusō, atama ya teashi ni mo, ima hitokufū" [Today is Air Raid Awareness Day: get used to uncooked emergency foods that are not prepared with fire and water, always be ready, wear your summer air raid clothes, be extra careful to protect your head and limbs], *Asahi shinbun*, morning ed., August 19, 1944, 4.

92. Shizuoka-ken Chagyō Kaigisho, ed., *Shin chagyō zensho* [A complete record of the new tea industry] (Shizuoka, Shizuoka-ken Chagyō Kaigisho, 1966), 20.

93. "Future Outlook Seen Rosy for Japanese Tea Exports: Efforts Being Made to Recapture Prewar Ranking as Leading Supplier of Vitamin-Rich Beverage," *Nippon Times Magazine, Foreign Trade Series* 11 (June 17, 1948): 1–2.

94. Warren H. Leonard and Raymond Roberts, *Tea in Japan*, National Resources Section Report 125 (Tokyo: General Headquarters, Supreme Commander for Allied Powers, 1949), 13–15.

95.   William A. Millen, "The Army Travels on Whose Stomach?" *Evening Star*, March 12, 1951, A8.

96.   Kathleen McLaughlin, "Tea Moves Ahead as a Global Drink: World Production Up 57% Since Before the War, F.A.O. Report Says," *New York Times*, April 18, 1960, 43.

97.   Shizuoka-ken Chagyō Kaigisho, ed., *Shin chagyō zensho*, 507–8.

98.   Yabu Mitsuo and Nakamura Yoriyuki, *Wagashi to Nichoncha* [Japanese tea and Japanese sweets] (Kyoto: Shibunkaku, 2017), 65.

99.   Susan Hanley, "The Material Culture: Stability in Transition" in *Japan in Transition: From Tokugawa to Meiji*, ed. Marius B. Jansen and Gilbert Rozman (Princeton, NJ: Princeton University Press, 1986), 460. Hanley cites the economic boom of World War I as a key factor in reshaping the Japanese diet.

100. "Are Green Tea Users True to the Brews Dealers Hope," *Wall Street Journal*, September 25, 1946, 8.

101. Nihoncha yushutsu kumiai (Shizuoka), *Tea News* 41 (February 1954): 16.

102. Hellyer and Company retained its Chicago office until the 1970s. Tanimoto Isam, whose family had moved with the Hellyers from Kobe to Shizuoka in the 1910s, subsequently purchased the firm. He and his son, Kotaro, still operate it in Shizuoka today.

103. Wright, "A Brief Marketing History of the Jewel Tea Company," 368.

104. *Galva News*, April 18, 1946, 9; August 4, 1949, 11; June 21, 1951, 2; August 6, 1953, 2.

105. Marge Dickinson, "Active Among Japanese—Galvan Back After a Year in Tokyo," *Galva News*, July 30, 1959, 1, 5; "Open House Set for Mrs. Blout," *Galva News*, July 30, 1959, 5.

CONCLUSION

1.   Nihon Television, *Dokusen tokuban! Mikeru Jakuson: 1440 jikan zenkiroku* [Exclusive edition! Michael Jackson: a complete record of 1,440 hours], YouTube video, 1987, https://www.youtube.com/watch?v=NGS2mm3-Ifo.

2.   Tea Industry Research Division, Agriculture and Forestry Technology Department, Kyoto Prefectural Agriculture, Forestry and Fisheries Technology Center, http://www.pref.kyoto.jp/chaken/bitamin.html.

3.   Mitsukoshi Online Store, https://mitsukoshi.mistore.jp/sogogift/drink/list?categoryId=11_030500&pageNo=1; Takashimaya Online Store, https://www.takashimaya.co.jp/shopping/gift/food/0400000042/0400000047/.

4.   Ezra F. Vogel, *Japan as Number One: Lessons for America* (Cambridge, MA: Harvard University Press, 1979).

5.   Kenneth A. Wantuck, *Just-in-Time for America: A Common Sense Production Strategy* (Milwaukee, WI: Forum, 1989).

6.   "Research Discovers Green Tea Inhibits Cancer of Esophagus," *New York Times*, June 1, 1994; Suzanne Hamlin, "Green Tea: More Than Just a Soothing Beverage," *New York Times*, June 15, 1994.

7. Armand Gilinsky Jr. and Wakako Kusumoto, "Koots Green Tea," in *Comparative Entrepreneurship Initiatives: Studies in China, Japan and the USA*, ed. Chikako Usui (London: Palgrave Macmillan, 2011), 282–85.

8. AriZona Beverages, https://www.drinkarizona.com/about.

9. Martin Fackler, "Americans Are Bracing for Green Tea Latte," *International Herald Tribune*, October 27, 2006; Gilinsky and Kusumoto, "Koots Green Tea," 285–96.

10. For a summary of recent research on green tea's health benefits, see Caroline Dow, *The Healing Power of Tea* (Woodbury, MN: Llewellyn, 2014), 37–45. See also the National Center for Complementary and Integrative Health (NCCIH) factsheet "Green Tea," https://nccih.nih.gov/health/greentea.

11. Ian Gallagher, "The Army That Will Help Meghan Look Her Best on Her Big Day— and the Strict List of Do's and Don'ts for Her Wedding Guests," *Daily Mail Online*, May 5, 2018, https://www.dailymail.co.uk/femail/article-5695351/The-army-help -Meghan-look-best-big-day-strict-dos-donts-list.html.

12. Florence Fabricant, "Iced Tea's New Popularity as a Pour That Refreshes," *New York Times*, June 10, 1992.

13. E. Patrick Johnson, *Black Gay Men of the South* (Chapel Hill: University of North Carolina Press, 2013), 29, 559–64.

14. Will Rizzo, "The Birthplace of Sweet Tea: Summerville's Unique Role in the South's Most Refreshing Cultural Phenomenon," *Azalea Magazine*, Spring 2010, 44–51, https://issuu.com/azaleamagazine/docs/spring_flipbook.

15. Robert F. Moss, "Summerville Can't Squeeze the Facts Out of Sweet Tea's Murky History," *Charleston City Paper*, November 13, 2013, https://www.charlestoncitypaper .com/charleston/summerville-cant-squeeze-the-facts-out-of-sweet-teas-murky -history/Content.

16. Joy Bonala, "Summerville's Popular Sweet Tea Festival and Trail Receiving a Revamp," *Summerville Journal Scene*, May 7, 2019, https://www.journalscene.com/news /summerville-s-popular-sweet-tea-festival-and-trail-receiving-a/article_2322a540 -7105-11e9-9f9d-8fa08996b26b.html.

17. "American Tea Culture: Costs Eight Times as Much to Pick a Pound Here as in China," *New York Times*, July 6, 1897; Susan M. Walcott, "Tea Production in South Carolina," *Southeastern Geographer* 34, no. 1 (May 1999): 65–70.

SELECTED BIBLIOGRAPHY

This bibliography does not include internet websites, newspaper articles, and early nineteenth-century U.S. periodicals, which are cited in the notes.

Aizawa Kichiheibei. *Nihon chagyōkai hōkoku* [Report of Japan Tea Association]. Tokyo: Nihon Chagyōkai Chūō Honbu, 1896.

Akpadock, Frank. *City in Transition: Strategies for Economic Regeneration of Inner-City Communities, the Case of Youngstown, Ohio.* Victoria, BC: Friesen, 2012.

Albert, Gary. "Pioneer Refinement: Kentucky's Mitchum Family Silver Purchased from Asa Blanchard." *Journal of Early Southern Decorative Arts* 35 (2014), http://www.mesdajournal .org/2014/pioneering-refinement-kentuckys-mitchum-family-silver-purchased-asa -blanchard/.

Alcock, Rutherford. *The Capital of the Tycoon: A Narrative of a Three Years' Residence in Japan.* 2 vols. London: Longman, Green, Longman, Roberts and Green, 1863.

Alcott, William A. *Tea and Coffee.* Boston: Gordon W. Light, 1839.

Alt, Phillis. "An Extract from the Memoirs of Elisabeth Cristina Alt, Née Earl, Who Lived in Nagasaki from 1864–1868, Together with an Abridged Biographical Sketch of Her Parents." Unpublished manuscript.

Alt, William John. Personal Correspondences, 1853–1884.

Anderson, Sherwood. *Winesburg, Ohio.* New York: Penguin, 1992.

Arima Narisuke. "Bakumatsu ni okeru seiyō kaki no yunyū" [Imports of Western firearms during the Bakumatsu period]. *Nihon rekishi* 120 (June 1958): 2–13.

Asiatic Exclusion League. *Third Annual Meeting of the Asian Exclusion League, San Francisco May 1908.* San Francisco: Organized Labor Print, 1908.

Awakura Daisuke. *Nihon cha no kindai shi—bakumatsu kaikō kara Meiji kōki made* [The modern history of Japanese tea—from the opening of the ports in the Bakumatsu period to the late Meiji period]. Tokyo: Sōtensha, 2017.

Bacon, Alice Mabel. *Japanese Girls and Women*. New York: Houghton, Mifflin, 1902.

Bailey, Kate. "Technical Note: A Note on Prussian Blue in Nineteenth-Century Canton." *Studies in Conservation* 57, no. 2 (2012): 116–21.

Barkan, Elliott Robert, ed. *Immigrants in American History: Arrival, Adaptation, and Integration*. Santa Barbara: ABC-CLIO, 2012.

"Beikoku ni okeru honpō seicha no hanro kakuchō ikken, chakushokucha mondai" [Expanding sales of our nation's teas in the United States—the issue of colored teas]. 489. Diplomatic Record Office, Japan Ministry of Foreign Affairs, Tokyo.

Beman, David. *The Mysteries of Trade; or, The Great Source of Wealth: Containing Receipts and Patents in Chemistry and Manufacturing; with Practical Observations of the Useful Arts*. Boston: Printed for the Author by Wm. Bellamy, 1825.

Bird, Isabella. *Unbeaten Tracks in Japan: An Account of Travels on Horseback in the Interior*. Vol. 1. New York: G. P. Putnam's Sons, 1881.

Blake, John H. *Tea Hints for Retailers, in Two Parts*. Denver: Williamson-Haffner Engraving Co., 1903.

Blum, Deborah. *The Poison Squad: One Chemist's Single-Minded Crusade for Food Safety at the Turn of the Twentieth Century*. New York: Penguin, 2018.

Blume, Kenneth J. *Historical Dictionary of the U.S. Maritime Industry*. Lanham, MD: Scarecrow, 2012.

Blussé, Leonard. *Visible Cities: Canton, Nagasaki, and Batavia and the Coming of the Americans*. Cambridge, MA: Harvard University Press, 2009.

Brandimarte, Cynthia A. "Japanese Novelty Stores." *Winterthur Portfolio* 26, no. 1 (Spring 1991): 1–25.

Breen, John. "Ornamental Diplomacy: Emperor Meiji and the Monarchs of the Modern World." In *The Meiji Restoration: Japan as a Global Nation*, ed. Robert Hellyer and Harald Fuess, 232–48. Cambridge: Cambridge University Press, 2020.

British Metropolis in 1851. A Classified Guide to London, Etc. [with Maps and Plans]. London: Arthur Hall, Virtue, 1851.

Brown, Kendall H. "Rashōmon: The Multiple Histories of the Japanese Tea Garden at Golden Gate Park." *Studies in the History of Gardens and Designed Landscapes: An International Quarterly* 18, no. 2 (March 2012): 93–119.

Brown, Sidney DeVere. "Nagasaki in the Meiji Restoration: Choshu Loyalists and British Arms Merchants." *Crossroads: A Journal of Nagasaki History and Culture* 1 (Summer 1993): 1–18.

Bryan, Lettice. *The Kentucky Housewife*. Cincinnati, OH: Shepard and Stearns, 1839.

Butterfield, L. H., ed. *Diary and Autobiography of John Adams*. Vol. 2: *Diary, 1771–1781*. Cambridge, MA: Belknap, 1961.

California Pacific International Exposition. *Official Guide, Souvenir Program, California Pacific International Exposition, San Diego*. San Diego, 1936.

Cameron, W., H. Morton, and W. Feldwick. *Present Day Impressions of Japan: The History, People, Commerce, Industries and Resources of Japan and Japan's Colonial Empire, Kwantung, Chosen, Taiwan, Karafuto*. Chicago: Globe Encyclopedia Co., 1919.

Catherwood, John H. "Tea Exhibited by the Chinese Government." In *United States Centennial Commission, International Exhibition 1876, Reports and Awards, Group III*, ed. Francis A. Walker, 28–31. Philadelphia: J. B. Lippincott & Co., 1878.

Century of Progress Government Correspondence #2, Box 63, Japan. A Century of Progress records, Special Collections and University Archives, University of Illinois at Chicago.

Cha [Magazine of Japan Central Tea Association]. "Chagara kennō undō no zenkokuka" [The nationalization of the movement to donate tea leaves]. February 1941, 10–14.

——. "Editorial, Nichibei kokkō no henka ni sho shi: Nihon cha o dō kangaebeki ka" [Confronting changes in the diplomatic relations of the United States and Japan: what must we consider about Japanese Tea]. February 1941, 6–7.

——. "Editorial, Ōshū seiran no suii to yushutsu Nihon: cha no shōrai" [The wartime transition in Europe and Japan as an export state: the future of tea]. June 1940, 6–8.

Chagyō Kumiai Chūō Kaigisho, ed. *Chagyō kumiai chūō kaigisho tōkei nenpō* [The annual statistical report of the Japan Central Tea Association]. Tokyo: Chagyō Kumiai Chūō Kaigisho, 1940.

——, ed. *Chagyō kumiai sōritsu 50 shūnen kinen ronbunshū* [A collection of articles to commemorate the fiftieth anniversary of the creation of the Japan Central Tea Association]. 4 vols. Tokyo: Chagyō Kumiai Chūō Kaigisho, 1938.

——, ed. *Chagyō kumiai chūō kaigisho tōkei nenpō* [The annual statistical tea report of the Nippon Tea Association]. 1935. Tokyo: Chagyō Kumiai Chūō Kaigisho, 1936.

——, ed. *Kita Afurika ni okeru chagyō chōsa* [A survey of the tea industry in North Africa]. Tokyo, 1930.

——, ed. *Chagyō ihō, dai 19 shū, Dai Tokyo ni okeru seicha jijyō* [Reports on the tea industry, vol. 19: The state of affairs of tea in the Tokyo metropolitan area]. Tokyo: Chagyō Kumiai Chūō Kaigisho, 1927.

——, ed. *Chagyō ihō, dai 18 shū, naigai seicha jijō* [Reports on the tea industry, vol. 18: Market conditions for tea at home and abroad]. Tokyo: Chagyō Kumiai Chūō Kaigisho, 1927.

——, ed. *Chagyō ihō, dai 12 shū: Beika ryōkoku ni tai suru Nihon cha kōkoku senden sankō shiryō* [Reports on the tea industry, vol. 12: Reference materials concerning advertising and publicity for Japan Tea in the United States and Canada]. Tokyo: Chagyō Kumiai Chūō Kaigisho, 1926.

——, ed. *Nihon chagyō shi* [The history of Japan's tea industry]. Tokyo: Chagyō Kumiai Chūō Kaigisho, 1914.

Cherrington, Ernest Hurst. *The Evolution of Prohibition in the United States of America: A Chronological History of the Liquor Problem and the Temperance Reform in the United States from the Earliest Settlements to the Consummation of National Prohibition*. Westerville, OH: American Issue, 1920.

Chiba Kenritsu Sekiyadojō Hakubutsukan, ed., *Sashima-cha to suiun: Edo kōki kara Meiji ki o chūshin ni, Heisei 23 nendo Chiba kenritsu Sekiyadojō hakubutsukan kikaku tenji zuroku* [Sashima tea and water transport: a focus on the late Edo and Meiji periods, a pictorial record of the exhibit project of the Chiba Prefectural Sekiyadojō Museum during the 2011 fiscal year]. Noda-shi, Chiba-ken: Chiba Kenritsu Sekiyadojō Hakubut-sukan, 2011.

Child, Lydia Marie Francis. *The American Frugal Housewife: Dedicated to Those Who Are Not Ashamed of Economy*. New York: Samuel S. & William Wood, 1838.

Comer, James R. "Cups That Cheer: Folkways of Caffeinated Beverages in the Reconstruction South." *Gulf Coast Historical Review* 10, no. 1 (Fall 1994): 61–71.

Cook, Haruko Taya, and Theodore F. Cook. *Japan at War: An Oral History*. New York: New Press, 1992.

Corbett, Rebecca. *Cultivating Femininity: Women and Tea Culture in Edo and Meiji Japan*. Honolulu: University of Hawai'i Press, 2018.

Cronon, William. *Nature's Metropolis: Chicago and the Great West*. New York: Norton, 1991.

Dai Nihon ishin shiryō kōhon [Manuscript of historical records related to the Meiji Restoration of Japan]. Unpublished document collection, Historiographical Institute, University of Tokyo.

Daigo Hachirō. *Cha no rekishi: Kawagoe cha to Sayama cha* [The history of tea: Kawagoe tea and Sayama tea]. *Kawagoe sōsho* 9. Kawagoe-shi: Kawagoe Sōsho Kankōkai, 1982.

Davis, John Francis. *The Chinese: A General Description of the Empire of China and Its Inhabitants*. Vol. 2. London: Charles Knight, 1836.

Davis, S. Livingston. "Talks to Tea Buyers—The Practical Tea Man Column." *Tea and Coffee Trade Journal* 31, no. 1 (July 1916): 145.

De Becker, J. E. *The Nightless City; or, The History of the Yoshiwara Yūkwaku*. Yokohama: Max Nössler, 1899.

DeBow, J. D. B., ed. *The Seventh Census of the United States*. Washington, DC: Robert Armstrong, 1853.

"Description of the Tea Plant; Its Name; Cultivation; Mode of Curing the Leaves; Transportation to Canton; Sale and Foreign Consumption; Endeavors to Raise the Shrub in Other Countries, 1839–1840." *Chinese Repository* 8 (July 1840): 132–64.

Dexter-Roundy Family Papers, 1772–1951. Digital Collections, University of Wisconsin–Madison Libraries. http://digicoll.library.wisc.edu/.

Dow, Caroline. *The Healing Power of Tea*. Woodbury, MN: Llewellyn, 2014.

Dower, John W. "Introduction, Yokohama Boomtown: Foreigners in Treaty-Port Japan (1859–1872)." MIT Visualizing Cultures. https://visualizingcultures.mit.edu/yokohama/index.html.

Du, Dan. "Green Gold and Paper Gold: Seeking Independence Through the Chinese-American Tea Trade, 1784–1815." *Early American Studies: An Interdisciplinary Journal* 16, no. 1 (2018): 151–91.

——. "This World in a Teacup: Chinese-American Tea Trade in the Nineteenth Century." PhD diss., University of Georgia, 2017.

Dulles, Foster Rhea. *Yankees and Samurai: America's Role in the Emergence of Modern Japan, 1791–1900*. New York, 1965.

Duncan, Richard R. *Beleaguered Winchester: A Virginia Community at War, 1861–1865*. Baton Rouge: Louisiana State University Press, 2006.

Dusinberre, Martin. *Hard Times in the Hometown: A History of Community Survival in Modern Japan*. Honolulu: University of Hawai'i Press, 2012.

Earns, Lane, and Brian Burke-Gaffney. "Nagasaki: People, Places, and Scenes of the Nagasaki Foreign Settlement, 1859–1941." http://www.nfs.nias.ac.jp/index.html.

Edson, Mrs. R. B. "A True Romance." *Ballou's Monthly Magazine* 29, no. 1 (January–June 1869): 74.

Ellis, Markman, Richard Coulton, and Matthew Mauger. *Empire of Tea: The Asian Leaf That Conquered the World*. London: Reaktion, 2015.

Ericson, Steven J. "Kinoshita Yoshio: Revolutionizing Service on Japan's National Railroads." In *The Human Tradition in Modern Japan*, ed. Anne Walthall, 115–36. Wilmington, DE: Scholarly Resources, 2002.

Ewell, Ervin E. *Foods and Food Adulterants. Investigations Under the Direction of H. W. Wiley, Chief Chemist, Part Seventh, Tea, Coffee, and Cocoa Preparations*. U.S. Department of Agriculture, Division of Chemistry, Bulletin 13. Washington, DC: Government Printing Office, 1892.

Exposition Beautiful; Over One Hundred Views [of] the Panama-California Exposition and San Diego, the Exposition City. San Diego: Pictorial Publishing Co., 1915.

Fairbank, John King, Katherine Frost Bruner, and Elizabeth MacLeod Matheson, eds. *The I.G. in Peking: The Letters of Robert Hart, Chinese Maritime Customs, 1868–1907*. Vol. 1: *1868–1890*. Cambridge, MA: Belknap, 1975.

Farmer's Wife 30, no. 6 (June 1927): 360.

Farris, William Wayne. *A Bowl for a Coin: A Commodity History of Japanese Tea*. Honolulu: University of Hawai'i Press, 2019.

Fayen, Sarah Neale. "Tilt-Top Tables and Eighteenth-Century Consumerism." http://www.chipstone.org/html/publications/2003AF/Fayen/FayenIndex.html.

Fichter, James. *So Great a Proffit: How the East Indies Trade Transformed Anglo-American Capitalism*. Cambridge, MA: Harvard University Press, 2010.

Fogel, Joshua. *Articulating the Sinosphere: Sino-Japanese Relations in Space and Time*. Cambridge, MA: Harvard University Press, 2009.

Foner, Eric. *Reconstruction: America's Unfinished Revolution, 1863–1877*. New York: Harper and Row, 1988.

Forbes, R. B. *Remarks on China and the China Trade*. Boston: Samuel Dickinson Printer, 1844.

Fugate, Francis L. *Arbuckles: The Coffee That Won the West*. El Paso: Texas Western Press, University of Texas at El Paso, 1994.

Fujin kurabu. "Watashi ga einen aiyō shite iru: ocha gawari no kenkō inyō" [Things I have used habitually for years: health drinks to replace tea]. *Fujin kurabu* 20, no. 11 (September 1939): 230–31.

Fujin no tomo. "Seikatsu no sumizumi kara muda o nakusau" [Eliminating wasteful practices in every nook and cranny of one's life]. *Fujin no tomo* 31, no. 2 (February 1937): 176–77.

Fukuda, Ippei. *The Japanese at Home*. Tokyo: Hokuseido, 1936.

Fukuhaku Printing Company, Ltd. "Tabi de ocha o ippuku: kisha chabin, kisha dobin" [A cup of tea during travel: train teapots and train earthenware teapots]. http://www.umakato.jp/archive/coll/03_02.html.

Futō Kanja. "Kissa to heigai" [Tea drinking and its ill effects]. *Shokumotsu no yōjō* 6, no. 11 (November 1920): 36.

Gardella, Robert. *Harvesting Mountains: Fujian and the China Tea Trade, 1757–1937*. Berkeley: University of California Press, 1994.

Garland, Hamlin. *Main-Travelled Roads*. New York: Harper and Brothers, 1893.

Gibson, James R. *Otter Skins, Boston Ships, and China Goods*. Seattle: University of Washington Press, 1992.

Gilinsky, Armand Jr., and Wakako Kusumoto. "Koots Green Tea." In *Comparative Entrepreneurship Initiatives: Studies in China, Japan and the USA*, ed. Chikako Usui, 276–300. London: Palgrave Macmillan, 2011.

Graham, Patricia J. *Tea of the Sages: The Art of Sencha*. Honolulu: University of Hawai'i Press, 1998.

Great Britain, Parliament. *Reports on the Production of Tea in Japan*. London: Harrison and Sons, 1873.

Greenberg, Brian, and Linda S. Watts. *Social History of the United States*. Vol. 1: *The 1900s*. Santa Barbara, CA: ABC-CLIO, 2009.

Gribble, Henry. "The Preparation of Japan Tea." *Transactions of the Asiatic Society of Japan* 12, no. 1 (November 1883): 1–32.

Grote, H. C. "How Retailers Can Profitably Study the Wagon Route Men's Methods and Apply Some of Them to Their Businesses." Practical Retail Grocer Column. *Tea and Coffee Trade Journal* 31, no. 4 (October 1917): 372.

Gochasho, Ōhashi Jirōtarō, Edo. [The tea shop of Ōhashi Jirōtarō, Edo] pricelist. Siebold Collection, National Museum of Ethnology, Leiden, Netherlands.

Goddard, F. B. *Grocers' Goods: A Family Guide to the Purchase of Flour, Sugar, Tea, Coffee, Spices, Canned Goods, Cigars, Wines, and All Other Articles Usually Found in American Grocery Stores*. New York: Tradesmen's Publishing Co., 1888.

Gordon, Andrew. *A Modern History of Japan: From Tokugawa Times to the Present*. 3rd ed. New York: Oxford University Press, 2014.

Guardians of the Poor (Philadelphia). *Accounts of the Guardians of the Poor and Managers of the Alms-House and House of Employment, Philadelphia, from 23rd May, 1803, to 23rd May 1804*. Philadelphia: Printed by John Geyer, 1804.

Guth, Christine M. E. *Art, Tea, and Industry: Masuda Takashi and the Mitsui Circle*. Princeton, NJ: Princeton University Press, 1993.

Haddad, John R. *America's First Adventure in China: Trade, Treaties, Opium, and Salvation*. Philadelphia: Temple University Press, 2013.

Hakurankwai Kyokwai (Société des Expositions), ed. *Japan and Her Exhibits at the Panama-Pacific International Exhibition, 1915*. Tokyo: Japan Magazine Co., 1915.

Handy, Moses P., ed. *The Official Directory of the World's Columbian Exposition, May 1st to October 30th, 1893: A Reference Book of Exhibitors and Exhibits, and of the Officers and Members of the World's Columbian Commission*. Chicago: W. B. Conkey Co., 1893.

Hane, Mikiso. *Peasants, Rebels, Women, and Outcastes: The Underside of Modern Japan*. Updated 2nd ed. New York: Rowan & Littlefield, 2016.

Hanley, Susan. "The Material Culture: Stability in Transition." In *Japan in Transition: From Tokugawa to Meiji*, ed. Marius B. Jansen and Gilbert Rozman, 447–70. Princeton, NJ: Princeton University Press, 1986.

Hanson, Reginald. *A Short Account of Tea and the Tea Trade: With a Map of the China Tea Districts*. London: Whitehead, Morris and Lowe, 1876; Elibron Classics replica ed. New York: Adamant Media Corporation, 2005.

Harland, Marion [pseud. of Mary Virginia Terhune] and Christine Terhune Herrick. *The National Cook Book*. New York: C. Scribner's Sons, 1896.

Harper's Weekly. "Condemned." January 15, 1881, 46.

Harris, Neil. "All the World a Melting Pot? Japan at American Fairs, 1876–1904." In *Cultural Excursions: Marketing Appetites and Cultural Tastes in Modern America*, ed. Neil Harris, 29–55. Chicago: University of Chicago Press, 1990.

Harte, F. Bret. *That Heathen Chinee and Other Poems Mostly Humorous*. London: John Camden Hotten, 1871.

Hasegawa, Susan, for the Japanese American Historical Society of San Diego. *Images of America: Japanese Americans in San Diego*. Charleston, SC: Arcadia, 2008.

Hattori Kazuma. "Kaidai: chagyōkai, nōji taikai" [Synopsis: tea industry meetings and large agricultural assemblies]. In *Meiji chūki sangyō undō shiryō*, vol. 23: *Chagyōkai hōkoku, nōjikai hōkoku* [Documents related to industry in the mid Meiji period, vol. 23: Reports by tea industry organizations, reports from agricultural assemblies], ed. Osa Yukio and Shōda Kenichirō. Tokyo: Nihon Keizai Hyōronsha, 1979.

Hattori, Yukimasa. *The Foreign Commerce of Japan Since the Restoration, 1869–1900*. Baltimore, MD: Johns Hopkins University Press, 1904.

Hayashiya Tatsusaburō and Fujioka Kenjirō eds. *Uji shishi 3: kinsei no rekishi to haikan* [The history of Uji City, vol. 3: The landscape and history of the early modern period]. Uji-shi, 1976.

Hazama, Hiroshi. "Historical Changes in the Life Style of Industrial Workers." In *Japanese Industrialization and Its Social Consequences*, ed. Hugh Patrick, 21–51. Berkeley: University of California Press, 1976.

Heiss, Mary Lou, and Robert J. Heiss. *The Tea Enthusiast's Handbook*. Berkeley, CA: Ten Speed, 2010.

Hellyer, Robert. "1874: Tea and Japan's New Trading Regime." In *Asia Inside Out: Trading Empires of the South China Coast, South Asia, and the Gulf Region*, vol. 1: *Critical Times*, ed. Eric Tagliacozzo, Helen Siu, and Peter Perdue, 186–206. Cambridge, MA: Harvard University Press, 2015.

——. "On the Dining Car, in the Station Restaurant, and from the Platform Peddler: Tea on Railways in the United States and Japan, 1860–1960." In *Railway Catering Between Imaginary and Consumption: Consumers, Images, and Markets*, ed. Jean-Pierre Williot, 267–82. New York: Peter Lang, 2017.

——. "Quality as a Moving Target: Japanese Tea, Consumer Preference, and Federal Regulation on the U.S. Market." In *Imitation, Counterfeiting, and the Quality of Goods in Modern Asian History*, ed. Kazuko Furuta and Linda Grove, 93–106. Singapore: Springer, 2017.

——. "The West, the East, and the Insular Middle: Trading Systems, Demand, and Labour in the Integration of the Pacific, 1750–1875." *Journal of Global History* 8, no. 3 (November 2013): 391–413.

Heyl, Lewis. *United States Duties on Imports, 1883: Revised, Corrected, and Supplemented.* Vol. 2. Washington, DC: W. H. Morrison, 1883.

Hilliard, Sam. "Hog Meat and Cornpone: Food Habits in the Ante-Bellum South." *Proceedings of the American Philosophical Society* 113, no. 1 (February 1969): 1–13.

Hinsch, Bret. *The Rise of Tea Culture in China: The Invention of the Individual.* Latham, MD: Rowman and Littlefield, 2015.

Hirao Michio. *Tosa-han shōgyō keizai-shi* [An economic history of commerce in the Tosa domain]. Kōchi: Kōchi Shiritsu Shimin Toshokan, 1960.

——. *Tosa-han ringyō keizai-shi* [An economic history of Tosa forestry]. Kōchi-shi: Kōchi Shiritsu Shimin Toshokan, 1956.

Hoganson, Kristin L. *Consumers' Imperium: The Global Production of American Domesticity, 1865–1920.* Chapel Hill: University of North Carolina Press, 2007.

Holley, Marietta. *Samantha at the St. Louis Exposition.* New York: G. W. Dillingham, 1904.

Homans, Isaac Smith and Isaac Smith Homans Jr., eds. *Cyclopedia of Commerce and Commercial Navigation.* New York: Harper Brothers, 1858.

Honma Yasuko. *Ōura Kei joden nōto* [Biographical notes on Ōura Kei]. Nagasaki, 1990.

Hoshida Shigemoto. *Chagyō zensho* [A complete account of the tea industry]. In *Meiji zenki sangyō hattatsushi shiryō bessatsu* [Documents related to the development of industry in the early Meiji period, supplemental volumes], 107 (2), ed. Meiji Bunken Shiryō Kankōkai. 1888; Tokyo: Meiji Bunken Shiryō Kankōkai, 1971.

Hunter, Janet, and Shinya Sugiyama, eds. *The History of Anglo-Japanese Relations, 1600–2000.* Vol. 4: *Economic and Business Relations.* London: Palgrave, 2002.

Hurt, R. Douglas. *Food and Agriculture During the Civil War.* Santa Barbara, CA: ABC-CLIO, 2016.

Ide, Nobuko. *Ranji: The Roots of Modern Japanese Commercial Graphic Design.* Tokyo: Dentsū, 1993.

Iijima, Mariko. "Coffee Production in the Asia-Pacific Region: The Establishment of a Japanese Diasporic Network in the Early Twentieth Century." *Journal of International Economic Studies* (Institute of Comparative Economic Studies, Hosei University) 32 (2018): 75–88.

Ikegaya Keisaku and Koizumi Takeo. "Fuyu no Manshūkoku shijō o shisatsu shite" [An inspection of the market in Manchukuo during the winter]. *Chagyōkai* (March 1936): 15–18.

Imperial Japanese Commission to the International Exhibition at Philadelphia, 1876. *Official Catalogue of the Japanese Section: and Descriptive Notes on the Industry and Agriculture of Japan, International Exhibition, 1876.* Philadelphia: Japanese Commission, 1876.

Imperial Japanese Commission to the Louisiana Purchase Exhibition. *The Exhibition of the Empire of Japan, Official Catalogue.* St. Louis: International Exposition, 1904.

Inagaki Shisei, ed. *Edo seikatsu jiten* [A dictionary of life in Edo]. Tokyo: Seiabō, 1975.

Institute of Food Behavior Science Japan. "Tetsudō no tabi ni kakasenai sonzai: ekiben" [An essential for railroad travel: the station boxed lunch]. May 26, 2013. http://ifbs.or.jp/cha /2013/05/26/.

International Exhibition. *The Official Catalogue of the Exhibits: With Introductory Notices of the Countries Exhibiting*. Vol. 2. Melbourne: Mason, Firth & M'Cutcheon, 1880.

Iruma-shi Hakubutsukan. *Tokubetsu ten, ocha to Nihon-jin—sono rekishi to gendai* [Special exhibition, Japanese and tea—historical and contemporary perspectives]. Iruma City: Iruma-shi Hakubutsu-kan, 1996.

Iwama Machiko. *Cha no igakushi—Chūgoku to Nihon* [The history of tea as medicine—China and Japan]. Kyoto: Shibunkaku, 2009.

Japan Tea Promotion Committee, J. Walter Thompson Company, 35mm Microfilm Proofs, 1906–1960 and Undated. J. Walter Thompson Company Collection, John W. Hartman Center for Sales, Advertising, and Marketing History, Duke University, Durham, NC.

Japanese Village Company. *Explanation of Japanese Village and Its Inhabitants*. New York: J. B. Rose, 1886.

Jardine, Matheson, and Company Archives. "Miscellaneous Invoices, 1823–1881," "In-correspondence, Business Letters: Nagasaki, 1859–1886." University Library, Cambridge University, Cambridge, United Kingdom.

Jay, Robert. *The Trade Card in Nineteenth-Century America*. Columbia: University of Missouri Press, 1987.

Jenks, Tudor. *The Century World's Fair Book for Boys and Girls: Being the Adventures of Harry and Philip with Their Tutor, Mr. Douglass, at the World's Columbian Exposition*. New York: Century Company, 1893.

Jewel [magazine]. "A Good Word for Tea." *Jewel* 6, no. 8 (May 7, 1928): 19.

——. "Speaking of Standard Lines." *Jewel* 1, no. 12 (August 11, 1923): 14.

Jingu Eizō. "Kitabei San de-go-haku to Nihoncha no senden" [Publicizing Japanese tea and the San Diego International Exposition]. In *Chagyō ihō, dai 32shū kaigai seicha shijō chōsa shohōkoku* [Reports on the tea industry, vol. 32: Various reports on surveys of foreign tea markets], ed. Chagyō Kumiai Chūō Kaigisho, 34. Tokyo: Chagyō Kumiai Chūō Kaigisho, 1939.

Johnson, Dorothea, John Harney, and Ann Noyes. *Children's Tea and Etiquette: Brewing Good Manners in Young Minds*. Danville, KY: Benjamin, 2014.

Johnson, E. Patrick. *Sweet Tea: Black Gay Men of the South*. Chapel Hill: University of North Carolina Press, 2013.

Joseph Tetley & Company. *Tea Goes American: Do You Know What "Tea in the American Manner" Means? Did You Know America Is Doing Things to Tea? Here's the Story with New Recipes, Table-Settings and Other Things*. New York: Tea Bureau, 1939.

Kamachi, Noriko. "The Chinese in Meiji Japan: Their Interaction with the Japanese Before the Sino-Japanese War." In *Race, Ethnicity and Migration in Modern Japan*, vol. 3: *Imagined and Imaginary Minorities*, ed. Michael Weiner, 199–212. New York: Routledge/ Curzon, 2004.

Kangyōryō [Industrial Promotion Bureau]. *Kangyō hōkoku* [Report on industrial promotion] 1 (December 1874): i–ii, 1–22.

Katō Tokusaburō and Nihon Ryokucha Hanro Kakuchō Rengō Tokubetsu Iinkai, eds. *Shikago shinpo isseiki bankoku hakurankai kinen shashinchō* [A commemorative picture book of the Century of Progress Chicago World Exposition, 1933]. Tokyo: Nihon Ryokucha Hanro Kakuchō Rengō Tokubetsu Iinkai, 1934.

Kawaguchi Kuniaki. *Chagyō kaika: Meiji hatten shi to Tada Motokichi* [The creation of the tea industry: Tada Motokichi and the history of Meiji-era expansion]. Tokyo: Zenbō-sha, 1989.

Kellogg, J. H. *Plain Facts for Old and Young.* Burlington, IA: Segner and Condit, 1881.

Kennedy, Joseph C. G. *Preliminary Report on the Eighth Census, 1860.* Washington, DC: Government Printing Office, 1862.

Kilburn, C. L. *Notes on Preparing Stores for the United States Army: Also on the Care of the Same, etc. (Designed for the Use of Those Interested).* Cincinnati, OH: Bradley & Webb, 1863.

Kirch, Patrick V., and Marshall Sahlins. *Anahulu: The Anthropology of History in the Kingdom of Hawaii.* Vol. 1. Chicago: University of Chicago Press, 1992.

Knollys, Henry. *English Life in China.* London: Smith, Elder, & Co., 1885.

Knox, Thomas W. *The Boy Travellers in the Far East, Part First, The Adventures of Two Youths in a Journey to Japan and China.* New York: Harper and Brothers, 1881.

Kornicki, Peter. "Public Display and Changing Values. Early Meiji Exhibitions and Their Precursors." *Monumenta Nipponica* 49, no. 2 (Summer 1994): 167–96.

Kumakura Isao. "Sen no Rikyū: Inquiries into His Life and Tea." Trans. Paul Varley. In *Tea in Japan: Essays of the History of Chanoyu*, ed. Paul Varley and Kumakura Isao, 33–69. Honolulu: University of Hawaiʻi Press, 1989.

Kyōto-fu Chagyō Hyakunen-shi Hensan Iinkai, ed. *Kyōto-fu chagyō hyakunen-shi* [A history of one hundred years of tea production in Kyoto]. Uji-shi: Kyōto-fu Chagyō Kaigisho, 1994.

Lakeside Annual Directory of the City of Chicago. Chicago: Chicago Directory Co., 1875–1917.

Lause, Mark A. "'The Cruel Striker War': Rail Labor and the Broken Symmetry of Galesburg Civic Culture, 1877–1888." *Journal of the Illinois State Historical Society* 91, no. 3 (Autumn 1998): 81–112.

Lee, Josephine. *The Japan of Pure Invention: Gilbert and Sullivan's "The Mikado."* Minneapolis: University of Minnesota Press, 2010.

Levinson, Marc. *The Great A&P and the Struggle for Small Business in America.* New York: Hill and Wang, 2011.

Lieberman, Victor. *Strange Parallels.* Vol. 2: *Mainland Mirrors: Europe, Japan, China, South Asia, and the Islands.* Cambridge: Cambridge University Press, 2009.

Lin, Man-houng. *China Upside Down: Currency, Society, and Ideologies, 1808–1856.* Cambridge, MA: Harvard University Asia Center, 2006.

Lipton, Thomas J. *Lipton's Autobiography.* New York: Duffield and Green, 1932.

List of Commercial Menus, Mostly from Hotels and Restaurants, 1853–[ongoing]. Research Center, Chicago History Museum, Chicago.

Liu, Yong. *The Dutch East India Company's Tea Trade with China, 1757–1781.* Leiden: Brill, 2007.

Lutgendorf, Philip. "Making Tea in India: Chai, Capitalism, Culture." *Thesis Eleven* 113, no. 1 (2012): 11–31.

MacGregor, David R. *The Tea Clippers: Their History and Development, 1833–1875*. 2nd ed. Annapolis, MD: Naval Institute Press, 1983.

Mair, Victor H., and Erling Hoh. *The True History of Tea*. London: Thames and Hudson, 2009.

Masuda Yoshiaki. "Shoku seikatsu to ocha: mō hitotsu no cha—kinsei shomin no cha shōhi" [Tea and dietary habits: one more type of tea—consumption by commoners in the early modern period]. In *Ocha to seikatsu*, vol. 2: *Nihon no ocha* [Japanese tea, vol. 2: Tea and life], ed. Hayashi Eiichi. Tokyo: Gyōsei, 1988.

Matsukata Masayoshi. "Seicha kyōshinkai hōshō juyoshiki shukuji" [Congratulatory address at the presentation ceremony for awards conferred at the competitive exhibition for refined teas]. In *Shukubun sakurei* [Examples of congratulatory addresses], vol. 1, ed. Higashi Kanichi. Tokyo: published by author, 1882.

McDonald, Michelle Craig, and Steven Topik. "Americanizing Coffee: The Refashioning of a Consumer Culture." In *Food and Globalization: Consumption, Markets, and Politics in the Modern World*, ed. Alexander Nuetzenadel and Frank Trentmann, 109–28. New York: Berg, 2008.

Melville, Herman. *Moby-Dick; or, The Whale*. Boston, 1926.

Merchants' Magazine and Commercial Review. "China Trade for 1862." March 1, 1863, 262.

Merritt, Jane T. *The Trouble with Tea: The Politics of Consumption in the Eighteenth-Century Global Economy*. Baltimore, MD: Johns Hopkins University Press, 2017.

Miyamoto Yūichirō. "Beikoku ni okeru Nihon ryokucha eigyōsha nami ni shōhisha chōsa" [A survey of consumers and retailers of Japanese green tea in the United States]. *Chagyōkai* (July 1926): 5–12.

Miscellaneous Administrative Papers Related to Commodore George W. Storer's Term as Governor of the U.S. Naval Asylum, 1854–1857. Philadelphia Naval Home (Naval Asylum), ZE File, Naval Department Library, Washington, DC; Letters Received by the Chief, Bureau of Yards and Docks, from the Governor of the Naval Asylum, 1849–1885, Record Group 71, National Archives, Washington.

Mitani Hiroshi. *Kokkyō o koeru rekishi ninshiki—hikaku-shi no hakken-teki kōyō* [Historical knowledge across borders—the heuristic utility of comparative history]. Iwanami kōza Nihon-shi [Iwanami Lectures on Japanese History] 22. Tokyo: Iwanami Shoten, 2016.

Mitani Kazuma. *Meiji monōri zushū* [Collection of prints of Edo peddlers]; *Kaisetsu* [Companion volume with analysis of the prints]. Tokyo: Rippu Shobō, 1975.

Mitsuhashi Shirōji. "Kaitō shūnin ni sai shite" [Statement on assuming the office of association president]. *Cha*, April 1942, 6.

Mizuta Susumu. "Gaigokujin kyoryūchi ni okeru cha saiseiba no kenchiku saiseisōchi kenchiku keishiki oyobi setsubi naiyō no haaku to kaigai jirei to no hikaku shiron [Tea firing establishments in foreign settlements: details of buildings and apparatus compared with those in foreign countries]. *Nihon kenchikugakkai keikaku-kei ronbun-shū* 74, no. 639 (May 2009): 1155–63.

Mogeki Gentarō, ed. *Ōtani Kahei ōden [denki] Ōtani Kahei* [The biography of the honorable Ōtani Kahei]. Denki Sōsho 354. Tokyo Ōzorasha, 2010.

Morita Toshihiko. "Kaiseikan shihō no tenkai to sono genkai" [The development and limits of procedures at the Kaiseikan]. In *Bakumatsu ishinki no kenkyū* [Research on the Bakumatsu and Meiji Restoration periods], ed. Ishii Takashi, 271–321. Tokyo: Yoshikawa Kōbunkan, 1978.

Munsell, Hazel E. "Tea Not a Reliable Source of Vitamin C, Nutrition Tests Show." In *Yearbook of the United States Department of Agriculture 1930*, ed. Milton S. Eisenhower and Arthur P. Chew, 508–9. Washington, DC: U.S. Government Printing Office, 1930.

Murai, Yasuhiko. "The Development of *Chanoyu*: Before Rikyū." Trans. Paul Varley. In *Tea in Japan: Essays of the History of Chanoyu*, ed. Paul Varley and Kumakura Isao, 3–32. Honolulu: University of Hawai'i Press, 1989.

Murayama, M., and Agricultural Bureau, Japan Department of Agriculture and Commerce. *Brief History & Preparation of the Japanese Tea Exhibited in the World's Columbian Exposition*. Tokyo: Kokubunsha, 1893.

Nagasaki Kenshi Henshū Iinkai. *Nagasaki kenshi, taigai kōshōhen* [The history of Nagasaki Prefecture: interactions with the outside world]. Tokyo: Yoshikawa Kōbunkan, 1985.

Naitō Tomomi. "Meiji zenki no yōji kyōiku ni okeru 19 seiki amerika no eikyō (2): ochaba gakkō no katsudō to sono imi" [The influence of the nineteenth-century United States on preschool education in the early Meiji period]. *Nihon hoiku gakkai taikai kenkyū ronbunshū* 53 (April 2000): 458–59.

Nakamura Chikushirō. "Bancha, sencha o oishiku ireru hiketsu" [Secrets for brewing delicious *bancha* and *sencha*]. *Fujokai* 41, no. 1 (January 1930): 372.

Nakamura Enichirō. "Shin hanro Manshūkoku" [The new Manchurian market]. *Chagyōkai* (September 1933): 4-1-4-4.

Nakamura, James, and Matao Miyamoto. "Social Structure and Population Change: A Comparative Study of Tokugawa Japan and Ch'ing China." *Economic Development and Cultural Change* 30, no. 2 (January 1982): 229–69.

Nakamura Yōichirō. "The Origin of Tea Color." In *Encyclopedia of O-CHA*. O-CHA Net, World Green Tea Association. http://www.o-cha.net/english/encyclopedia/teacolor.html.

——. *Bancha to Nihonjin* [Japanese and *bancha*]. Tokyo: Yoshikawa Kōbunkan, 1998.

Nelson, Megan Kate. "Urban Destruction During the Civil War." In *Oxford Research Encyclopedia of American History*. http://americanhistory.oxfordre.com.

New Bedford Whaling Museum. "Pacific Encounters: Yankee Whalers, Manjiro, and the Opening of Japan." http://www.whalingmuseum.org/online_exhibits/manjiro/index.html.

Nihon sangyō kyōkai, ed. *Beikoku dokuritsu hyaku gojū nen kinen Firaderufia bankoku hakurankai Nihon sangyō kyōkai jimu hōkoku* [Report of the office of the Japan Industrial Association concerning the Philadelphia Sesquicentennial International Exhibition]. Tokyo: Nihon sangyō kyōkai, 1927.

Nihon Television. *Dokusen tokuban! Mikeru Jakuson: 1440 jikan zenkiroku* [Exclusive edition! Michael Jackson: a complete record of 1,440 hours]. 1987. https://www.youtube.com/watch?v=NGS2mm3-Ifo.

Nihonbashi Suharaya Mobei, ed. *Kōcha seihōsho* [Manual for black tea manufacture]. Tokyo, 1874. Online at Faculty of Economics, University of Tokyo, http://www.lib.e.u-tokyo.ac .jp/.

Nippon Tea Association [Chagyō Kumiai Chūō Kaigisho], ed. *The Annual Statistical Tea Report of the Nippon Tea Association 1935*. Tokyo: Chagyō Kumiai Chūō Kaigisho, 1936.

Nippon Times Magazine, Foreign Trade Series. "Future Outlook Seen Rosy for Japanese Tea Exports: Efforts Being Made to Recapture Prewar Ranking as Leading Supplier of Vitamin-Rich Beverage." *Nippon Times* 11 (June 17, 1948): 1–2.

Noel-Paton, Ranald. *An Eastern Calling: George Windsor Earl and a Vision of Empire*. London: Ashgrove, 2018.

Nōmūkyoku, ed. *Meiji 16 nen: dainikai seicha kyōshinkai hōkoku: shinsa no bu, sankō no bu* [1883: report on the second competitive exhibition of refined tea: section concerning the judging of teas, reference section]. Tokyo: Nōmūkyoku, 1884. In Meiji Bunken Shiryō Kankōkai, ed., *Meiji zenki sangyō hattatsushi shiryō bessatsu* [Documents related to the development of industry in the early Meiji period, supplemental volumes]. 106 (2). Tokyo: Meiji Bunken Shiryō Kankōkai, 1971.

Northrup, Cynthia Clark, and Elaine C. Prange Turney, eds. *Encyclopedia of Tariffs and Trade in U.S. History: The Texts of the Tariffs*. Vol. 3. Westport, CT: Greenwood, 2003.

Noyes, George F. *Bivouac and the Battle-Field; or, Campaign Sketches in Virginia and Maryland*. New York: Harper and Brothers, 1863.

Oda Nobugaki. "Senjishita ni okeru chagyō kyōkai no shimei" [The mission of the tea industry during this time of war]. *Cha*, January 1943, 9.

Ogi Shinzō. *Tokyo shomin seikatsushi kenkyū* [Research on the history of the lives of Tokyo's commoners]. Tokyo: Nihon Hōsō Shuppan Kyōkai, 1979.

Ōishi Sadao. *Chosakushū* [Collected works]. 5 vols. Tokyo: Nōsangyoson Bunka Kyōkai, 2004.

——. *Meiji ishin to chagyō: Makinohara kaitaku shi kō* [The tea industry and the Meiji Restoration: a history of the development of Makinohara]. Shizuoka: Shizuoka-ken Chagyō Kaigi-sho, 1974.

Okakura Kakuzō. *The Book of Tea*. New York: G. P. Putnam's Sons, 1906.

Okishiri, Taka. *Gathering for Tea in Modern Japan: Class, Culture and Consumption in the Meiji Period*. London: Bloomsbury Academic, 2018.

——. "The Shogun's Tea Jar: Ritual, Material Culture, and Political Authority in Early Modern Japan." *Historical Journal* 59, no. 4 (2016): 927–45.

Ōkubo Toshimichi. "Naikoku kangyō hakurankai kaijō shukuji [Congratulatory address at the opening of the exhibition for the promotion of domestic industry]. In *Shukubun sakurei* [Examples of congratulatory addresses], vol. 1, ed. Higashi Kanichi. Tokyo: Published by author, 1882.

Ōkura Nagatsune. *Kōeki kokusan kō* [Treatise on expanding profits from domain products], 1859. In *Nihon nōsho zenshū* [Complete collection of works on Japanese agriculture], vol. 14, ed. Iinuma Jirō. Osaka: Nōsan Gyosan Bunka Kyōkai, 1978.

Omaha Public Library. Trans Mississippi & International Exposition Digital Collection. https://omahalibrary.org/digital-collections/.

Osaka Shōkō Kaigisho, ed. "Cha tonya" [Tea wholesalers]. In *Osaka shōgyōshi shiryō* [Documents on the commercial history of Osaka]. Osaka: Osaka Shōkō Kaigisho, 1964.

Ōtani Kahei. *Ōbei manyū nisshi* [Journal of a journey to the United States and Europe]. In *Meiji Ōbei kenbunroku shūsei* [A compilation of records of personal experiences in the United States and Europe during the Meiji period], vol. 21, ed. Asakura Haruhiko. Tokyo: Yumani Shobō, 1987.

Ōyama Yasunari. "Jikkayōcha no shōhinka—[*hōjicha*] tōjō no igi" [The commercialization of a household tea—the significance of the appearance of *hōjicha*]. *Saita chabunka shinkō zaidan kiyō* 6 (2006): 87–128.

Palladium of Knowledge, or the Carolina and Georgia Almanac, for the Year of our Lord 1818 of the Julian Period, and 42–43 Years of American Independence. Charleston, SC: W. P. Young, 1817. Early American Imprints, Series II: Shaw Shoemaker database.

Pendergrast, Mark. *Uncommon Grounds: The History of Coffee and How It Transformed Our World.* New York: Basic Books, 1999.

Perelsztejn, Diane, dir. *Robert Fortune: The Tea Thief.* Documentary film, 2001.

Peterson, Hannah Mary (Bouvier). *The Young Wife's Cook Book with Receipts of the Best Dishes for Breakfast, Dinner and Tea.* Philadelphia: T. B. Peterson & Brothers, 1870.

Pettigrew, Jane, and Bruce Richardson. *A Social History of Tea.* Danville, KY: Benjamin, 2015.

Pitelka, Morgan, ed. *Japanese Tea Culture: Art, History, and Practice.* London: Taylor & Francis, 2003.

Pitkin, Timothy. *A Statistical View of the Commerce of the United States of America: Its Connection with Agriculture and Manufactures: and an Account of the Public Debt, Revenues, and Expenditures of the United States.* Hartford, CT: Printed by Charles Hosmer, 1816.

Pomeranz, Kenneth. *The Great Divergence: China, Europe, and the Making of the Modern World Economy.* Princeton, NJ: Princeton University Press, 2000.

Pratt, Harry E. "The Lincolns Go Shopping," *Journal of the Illinois State Historical Society* 48, no. 1 (Spring 1955): 65–81.

Rappaport, Erika. *A Thirst for Empire: How Tea Shaped the Modern World.* Princeton, NJ: Princeton University Press, 2017.

——. "Packaging China: Foreign Articles and Dangerous Tastes in the Mid-Victorian Tea Party." In *The Making of the Consumer: Knowledge, Power, and Identity in the Modern World*, ed. Frank Trentmann, 125–46. Oxford: Berg, 2006.

Ravina, Mark. *The Last Samurai: The Life and Battles of Saigō Takamori.* Hoboken, NJ: John Wiley, 2004.

Reade, Arthur. *Tea and Tea Drinking.* London: Sampson, Low, Marston, Searle, and Rivington, 1884.

Records of the Hills Brothers Coffee Company. Archives Center, National Museum of American History. Smithsonian Institution, Washington, DC.

Reischauer, Haru Matsukata. *Samurai and Silk: A Japanese and American Heritage.* Cambridge, MA: Belknap, 1986.

Riggs, Oscar. "The Tea Commerce of New York." *Frank Leslie's Popular Monthly* 16, no. 3 (1883): 295.

Rizzo, Will. "The Birthplace of Sweet Tea: Summerville's Unique Role in the South's Most Refreshing Cultural Phenomenon." *Azalea Magazine*, Spring 2010, 44–51. https://issuu .com/azaleamagazine/docs/spring_flipbook.

Roberts, John M. Diaries [manuscript], 1831–1848. Book 4 of 7. Edward E. Ayer Manuscript Collection, Vault Ayer MS 3157, Newberry Library, Chicago.

Roberts, Luke. *Mercantilism in a Japanese Domain: The Merchant Origins of Economic Nationalism in Eighteenth-Century Tosa.* Cambridge: Cambridge University Press, 1998.

Rose, Sarah. *For All the Tea in China: Espionage, Empire, and the Secret Formula for the World's Favorite Drink.* New York: Viking, 2010.

Roth, Rodris. *Tea Drinking in Eighteenth-Century America: Its Etiquette and Equipage.* Washington, DC: Smithsonian Institution, 1961.

Rutter, Frank R. *Rice and Tea in Japan, Supplement to Commerce Report.* Washington, DC: Government Printing Office, 1922.

"Ryokucha sonohoka no shokuhin no bitamin ganyūno hikaku" [Comparing the vitamin content of various foods to green tea]. Kyōtofu Nōrinsuisan Gijutsu Sentā, Nōrin Sentā, Chagyō Kenkyūjo [Kyoto Prefectural Agriculture, Forestry and Fisheries Technology Center, Agriculture and Forestry Technology Department, Tea Industry Research Division]. http://www.pref.kyoto.jp/chaken/bitamin.html.

Sagara Bussan Kaisha Seichabu. *Cha no kaori* [The fragrance of tea]. Shizuoka: Shizuoka-ken Chagyō Kumiai Rengō Kaigisho, 1929(?).

Sashima Chōshi Hensan Iinkai, ed. *Sashima chōshi, tsūshi* [The history of Sashima town, general history]. Sashima-chō: Sashima Chōshi Hensan Iinkai, 1998.

Scidmore, Eliza Ruhamah. *Jinrikisha Days in Japan.* New York: Harper & Brothers, 1891.

——. "Tea, Coffee, and Cocoa at the Fair." *Harper's Bazaar*, September 30, 1893, 813.

Seigle, Cecilia Segawa. *Yoshiwara: The Glittering World of the Japanese Courtesan.* Honolulu: University of Hawai'i Press, 1993.

Sen Sōshitsu XV. *The Japanese Way of Tea: From Its Origins in China to Sen Rikyū.* Trans. V. Dixon Morris. Honolulu: University of Hawai'i Press, 1998.

Shibusawa Keizō, ed. *Japanese Life and Culture in the Meiji Era.* Trans. Charles S. Terry. Tokyo: Ōbunsha, 1958.

Shimada Shishi Hensan Iinkai, ed. *Shimada shishi* [The history of Shimada City]. Vol. 2. Shimada, 1973.

Shizuoka-ken, ed. *Shizuoka kenshi tsūshi-hen 5 kingendai ichi* [The history of Shizuoka Prefecture: narrative history, vol. 5: Modern and current history, part 1]. Shizuoka: Shizuoka Prefecture, 1996.

Shizuoka-ken Chagyō Kaigisho, ed. *Shin chagyō zensho* [A complete record of the new tea industry]. Shizuoka: Shizuoka-ken Chagyō Kaigisho, 1966.

Shizuoka-ken Chagyō Kumiai Rengō Kaigisho, ed. *Shizuoka ken chagyō shi* [The history of Shizuoka Prefecture's tea industry]. Vol. 1. Shizuoka: Shizuoka ken chagyō kumiai rengō kaigisho, 1926.

——, ed. *Shizuoka-ken chagyō zokuhen* [The history of Shizuoka Prefecture's tea industry, sequel edition]. Shizuoka: Shizuoka-ken Chagyō Kumiai Rengō Kaigisho, 1937.

Shizuoka Chashō Kōgyō Kyōdō Kumiai, ed. *Zadankai, Shizuoka de katsuyaku shita gaikoku chashō no koto* [A conversation about the activities of Western tea firms in Shizuoka]. Shizuoka: Shizuoka Chashō Kōgyō Kyōdō Kumiai, 2000.

Shizuoka-ken Naichishō Chagyō Kumiai Shūchi Iwata Shibu. *Cha no kaori* [The fragrance of tea]. Shizuoka: Shizuoka-ken Chagyō Kumiai Rengō Kaigisho, 1940(?).

Simmons Spice Mill. "Important Facts About Tea—Part VII." *Simmons Spice Mill* 38, no. 2 (February 1915): 158.

——. "Personnel of U.S. Board of Tea Experts for 1915." *Simmons Spice Mill* 38, no. 2 (February 1915): 173.

Smith, Andrew. *Drinking History: Fifteen Turning Points in the Making of American Beverages.* New York: Columbia University Press, 2012.

Smith, Henry D. *Kiyochika—Artist of Meiji Japan.* Santa Barbara, CA: Santa Barbara Museum of Art, 1988.

Sorimachi Shōji. *Tetsudō no Nihonshi* [Japan's history through railroads]. Tokyo: Bunken Shuppan, 1982.

Spencer, Guilford L., in collaboration with Ervin E. Ewell. *Foods and Food Adulterants. Investigations Under the Direction of H. W. Wiley, Chief Chemist, Part Seventh, Tea, Coffee, and Cocoa Preparations.* U.S. Department of Agriculture, Division of Chemistry, Bulletin 13. Washington, DC: Government Printing Office, 1892.

Spice Mill. "Some Interesting New York Tea Rooms: These Establishments, Oddly Situated and Decorated, Serve Tea and Coffee and Have Wide Appeal." *Spice Mill* 44, no. 1 (January 1921): 23-29.

——. "Tea Drinking—A Growing American Habit." *Spice Mill* 44, no. 10 (October 1921): 1718.

Sugiyama, Shinya. *Japan's Industrialization in the World Economy, 1859-1899: Export Trade and Overseas Competition.* London: Athlone, 1988.

——. *Meiji ishin to Igirusu shōnin: Tomasu Guraba no shōgai* [English merchants and the Meiji Restoration: the life of Thomas Glover]. Tokyo: Iwanami shoten, 1993.

——. "Thomas B. Glover: A British Merchant in Japan, 1861-1870." *Business History* 26, no. 2 (July 1984): 115-38.

Sunaga Noritake. "Meiji zenki no seicha yushutsu to Sayama kaisha no katsudō" [The efforts of the Sayama Company to export tea during the early Meiji period]. *Saitama-ken shi kenkyū* 30 (February 1995): 10-29.

Tada Motokichi. "Beikoku seifu nise seicha no yunyū o seikin sen to suru no fūsetsu, daishūkai enjutsu" [Rumors surrounding the U.S. government act to prohibit the import of adulterated teas, a speech before an association gathering]. *Dainihon nōkai hōkoku* 23 (May 15, 1883): 45-53.

——, supervising ed. *Kōcha setsu* [Report on black tea]. Translation of Edward Money, *The Cultivation and Manufacture of Tea* [1871]. Tokyo: Kannōkyoku, 1878.

——. "Shinkoku shōkyō shisatsu hōkokusho" [Report of inspection tour of the market conditions of China], February 14, 1876. In *Ōkuma monjo* [The papers of Ōkuma Shigenobu], vol. 4, ed. Waseda Daigaku Shakai Kagaku Kenkyūjo. Tokyo: Waseda Daigaku Shakai Kagaku Kenkyūjo, 1958.

Tadani Shinzō. "Kissaten keiei nitsuite" [On the management of coffee shops]. *Kahō* 1, no. 10 (December 1928): 14.

Tai Reiko. *Gaikokujin kyoryūchi to Kōbe: Kōbe kaikō 150nen ni yosete* [The foreign settlement and Kobe: marking the approaching 150-year anniversary of the establishment of Kobe as a treaty port]. Kobe: Kobe Shinbun Sōgō Shuppan Sentā, 2013.

Takano Minoru et al. and Nihon Chagyō Chūōkai, eds. *Ryokucha no jiten* [The dictionary of green tea]. 3rd rev. ed. Tokyo: Shibata Shoten, 2002.

Takizawa Takeo and Nishiwaki Yasushi, eds. *Kahei* [Currency]. Tokyo: Tokyo-dō Shuppan, 1999.

"Tea Act, 1773." In *Understanding U.S. Military Conflicts Through Primary Sources*, ed. James R. Arnold and Roberta Wiener. Santa Barbara, CA: ABC-CLIO, 2015.

Tea and Coffee Trade Journal. "Cotton Tea and Urn Bags, Information for Buyers, Pithy Suggestions as to Where and How to Buy to the Best Advantage." *Tea and Coffee Trade Journal* 32, no. 6 (June 1917): 550.

——. "Some Pertinent Tea Questions." *Tea and Coffee Trade Journal* 30, no. 2 (February 1916): 155.

——. "The Tea Trade of the U.S., Showing Its Growth During the Past Ninety-Seven Years, With Particular Reference to Japan and China Imports." *Tea and Coffee Trade Journal* 34, no. 4 (April 1918): 334–35.

"Tea, ca. 1816–1963." "Temperance" (Subject Categories), Warshaw Collection of Business Americana, Archives Center, National Museum of American History, Smithsonian Institution, Washington, DC.

Tea Room Booklet. New York: Woman's Home Companion, c. 1922.

Teramoto Yasuhide. "Senkanki Amerika shijō o meguru Nihoncha to Indo Seron kōcha: māketto no kaitaku kōkoku katsudō" [Japanese Tea and India, Ceylon black teas on the U.S. market in the interwar period: advertising activities to expand the market]. *Kwansei Gakuin Daigaku keizaigaku ronkyū* 51, no. 3 (November 1997): 51–88.

——. *Senzenki Nihon chagyō shi kenkyū* [A study of Japan's tea industry in the prewar period]. Tokyo: Yūhikaku, 1999.

Tokyo Daigaku Shiryōhensanjo Koshashin Kenkyū Purojekuto, ed. *Kōseisai gazō de yomigaeru 150-nenmae no bakumatsu, Meiji shoki Nihon: Burugā & Mōzā no garasu genban shashin korekushon* [Reviving Bakumatsu and early Meiji Japan of 150 years ago with high-definition images: the Burger & Moser original glass photo collections]. Tokyo: Yōsensha, 2018.

Tomatsu Yasuko. "Gyōshubetsu kōkoku shrīzu, 7 inryō" [A series on advertisements of various businesses, no. 7: Beverages]. *Ad Studies* (Advertising Museum Tokyo) 45 (2011): 48–51.

Tomes, Robert. *The Americans in Japan: An Abridgement of the Government Narrative of the U.S. Expedition to Japan, Under Commodore Perry*. New York: D. Appleton and Co., 1857.

Totman, Conrad. *The Collapse of the Tokugawa Bakufu, 1862–1868*. Honolulu: University of Hawai'i Press, 1980.

Traganou, Jilly. *The Tōkaidō Road: Traveling and Representation in Edo and Meiji Japan*. New York: Routledge, 2004.

Truman, Benjamin Cummings. *History of the World's Fair: Being a Complete Description of the World's Columbian Exposition from Its Inception.* Chicago: Mammoth, 1898.

Tsujimura, Michiyō, and Masataro Miura. "On Vitamin C in the Green Tea." *Bulletin of the Agricultural Chemical Society of Japan* 1, no. 1 (1924–1925): 13–14.

Tsuru-shi Hakubutukan, Myūjiamu Tsuru. *Heisei 14 nendo shuki tokubetsu ten: Chatsubo dōchū ten* [The autumn special exhibit for the 2002 fiscal year: an exhibit on the tea jar procession]. Tsuru City: Tsuru-shi Hakubutukan, Myūjiamu Tsuru, 2002.

Tsuzuki Kenkō. "Hansei jidai chūki kara Meiji no Ōtomo no chagyō nitsuite" [Tea production of Ōtomo from the mid-Edo to the Meiji periods]. *Tosa shidan* 182 (December 1989): 106–9.

Ueda Seifū. "Kantan na ocha no irekata, nomikata" [Simple ways to brew and drink tea]. In *Gendai jyosei to Nihon-cha* [Contemporary women and Japanese tea], ed. Katō Yūya, 12–18. Shizuoka: Chagyō Kumiai Chūō Kaigisho, 1938.

Ukers, W. H. *All About Tea.* 2 vols. New York: Tea and Coffee Trade Journal, 1935.

United States and Francis Preston Blair, John C. Rives, Franklin Rives, and George A. Bailey. *The Congressional Globe, Senate, 42nd Congress.* March–April. Washington: Blair & Rives, 1872.

U.S. Bureau of the Census. *Historical Statistics of the United States: Colonial Times to 1970.* Bicentennial ed. House Document, 93rd Cong., 1st sess., no. 93–78. Washington, DC: U.S. Department of Commerce, Bureau of the Census, 1975.

U.S. Department of State. *Commercial Relations of the United States: Cotton and Woolen Mills of Europe, Reports from the Consuls of the United States on the Cotton and Woolen Industries of Europe, in Answer to a Circular from the Department of State.* Washington, DC: Government Printing Office, 1882.

U.S. Department of the Treasury. *Treasury Decisions Under Customs and Other Laws.* Vol. 36: *January–June 1919.* Washington, DC: Government Printing Office, 1919.

U.S. House of Representatives, Committee on Ways and Means. "To Prevent the Importation of Adulterated Teas." 42nd Cong., 2nd sess., report no. 1927, February 3, 1883.

U.S. Revenue Commission (1865–1866). *Revenue System of the United States: Letter from the Secretary of the Treasury Transmitting the Report of a Commission Appointed for the Revision of the Revenue System of the United States.* Washington, DC: January 29, 1866. Samuel J. May Anti-Slavery Collection, Cornell University.

U.S. Treasury. *Synopsis of the Decisions of the Treasury Department on the Construction of the Tariff, Navigation, and Other Laws for the Year Ending December 31, 1895.* Washington, DC: Government Printing Office, 1896.

Veit, Helen Zoe, ed. *Food in the Civil War Era: The South.* East Lansing: Michigan State University Press, 2015.

Viele, Egbert L. *Hand-book for Active Service: Containing Practical Instructions in Campaign Duties, the Recruit, the Company, the Regiment, the March, the Camp, Guards and Guard-mounting, Rations and Mode of Cooking Them.* Richmond, VA: J. W. Randolph, 1861.

Vogel, Ezra F. *Japan as Number One: Lessons for America.* Cambridge, MA: Harvard University Press, 1979.

Von Glahn, Richard. "Cycles of Silver in Chinese Monetary History." In *The Economic History of Lower Yangzi Delta in Late Imperial China: Connecting Money, Markets, and Institutions*, ed. Billy K. L. So, 76–101. London: Routledge, 2012.

Walcott, Susan M. "Tea Production in South Carolina." *Southeastern Geographer* 34, no. 1 (May 1999): 61–74.

Walsh, Joseph M., and William Saunders. *"A Cup of Tea" Containing a History of the Tea Plant from Its Discovery to the Present Time, Including Its Botanical Characteristics . . . and Embracing Mr. William Saunders' Pamphlet on "Tea-Culture—a Probable American Industry."* Philadelphia: By the Author, 1884.

Wantuck, Kenneth A. *Just-in-Time for America: A Common Sense Production Strategy.* Milwaukee, WI: Forum, 1989.

Ward, Edward. *The Journal of Edward Ward, 1850–1851: Being His Account of the Voyage to New Zealand in the* Charlotte Jane *and the First Six Months of the Canterbury Settlement.* Christchurch: Pegasus, 1951.

West, Fred. "The Detection of Prussian Blue in Tea." *Journal of Industrial and Engineering Chemistry* 4, no. 7 (July 1912): 528.

Westphal, O. B. "A Talk with Jewel Salesmen: Increasing Earning Power." *Jewel* 1, no. 5 (January 15, 1923): 3.

——. "The True Facts About the Premium." *Jewel* 1, no. 6 (February 15, 1923): 3.

Whitaker, Jan. *Tea at the Blue Lantern Inn: A Social History of the Tea Room Craze.* New York: St. Martin's, 2002.

White, Merry. *Coffee Life in Japan.* Berkeley: University of California Press, 2012.

Wisconsin State Gazetteer and Business Directory, 1891–1892. Vol. 7, part 2. Chicago: R. L. Polk and Co., 1893.

Withers, W. A., and G. S. Fraps. *The Adulteration of Coffee and Tea Offered for Sale in North Carolina.* North Carolina Agricultural Experiment Station Bulletin 154. Raleigh, NC, 1898.

Witherspoon, Reese. *Whiskey in a Teacup: What Growing Up in the South Taught Me About Life, Love, and Baking Biscuits.* New York: Atria, 2018.

Wright, John S. "A Brief Marketing History of the Jewel Tea Company." *Journal of Marketing* 22, no. 4 (April 1958): 367–76.

Yabu Mitsuo and Nakamura Yoriyuki. *Wagashi to Nichoncha* [Japanese tea and Japanese sweets]. Kyoto: Shibunkaku, 2017.

Yamada Shinichi. *Edo no ocha—haikai cha no saijiki* [Teas of Edo—as seen through glossaries of tea-related seasonal terms for haikai poetry]. Tokyo: Yasaka Shobō, 2007.

Yamaguchi Chūgorō. "Manshūkoku seicha juyō gaikan" [An overview of demand for refined tea in Manchukuo]. *Chagyōkai*, November 1936, 10–14.

Yamaguchi, H. S. K, K. M. Yamaguchi, Frederic De Garis, Atsuharu Sakai, and Fujiya Hotel, eds. *We Japanese: Being Descriptions of Many of the Customs, Manners, Ceremonies, Festivals, Arts, and Crafts of the Japanese, Besides Numerous Other Subjects.* 1934; Miyanoshita, Japan: Fujiya Hotel, 1950.

Yamaguchi Tetsunosuke. "Kissaten haken iin no hōkoku" [Report of staff member dispatched to work in Japan teahouse]. *Chagyō hōkoku* 8 (July 1894): 14–22.

Yamashiro Seicha Kabushiki Gaisha. *Cha no chishiki* [The wisdom of tea]. Kyoto: Yamashiro Seicha Kabushiki Gaisha, 1926.

Yamashita Kyūtarō, ed. *Shizuoka-ken meishi retsuden* [Biographies of men of distinction in Shizuoka Prefecture]. Vol. 2. Hamamatsu, Shizuoka, 1884.

Yamawaki Teijirō. *Kinsei Nihon no iyaku bunka* [The medicinal culture of early modern Japan]. Tokyo: Heibonsha, 1995.

Yearbook of the United States Department of Agriculture 1897. Washington, DC: U.S. Government Printing Office, 1898.

Yokohama Kaikō Shiryōkan, ed. "Shōkan tsutome o keiken shita seicha bōekishō: Ōtani Kahei" [A tea trader with experience working for an export firm: Ōtani Kahei]. In *Yokohama shōnin to sono jidai* [Yokohama traders and that period]. Yokohama: Yūrindō, 1994.

——. *Yokohama uta monogatari* [The story of Yokohama through its songs]. Compact disc. Tokyo: King Records, 2009.

Yokohama Shinpōsha Chosakubu. *Yokohama hanjō-ki* [A chronicle of Yokohama's prosperity]. Yokohama Shinpōsha Chosakubu, 1903.

Yokohama-shi Chagyō Kumiai, ed. *Yokohama chagyō shi* [Records of Yokohama's tea industry]. In *Nihon chagyō shi shiryō shūsei* [Compilation of documents related to Japan's tea industry], vol. 4, ed. Ogawa Kōraku and Teramoto Yasuhide. 1958; Tokyo: Bunsei Shoin Digital Library, 2003.

Youth's Companion. "In a Japanese Tea-House." *Youth's Companion* 78, no. 45 (November 10, 1904): 572.

Zen Nihon Kōcha Shinkō-kai, ed. *Kōcha hyakunenshi* [The hundred-year history of black tea]. Vol. 19 of *Nihon chagyō shishiryō shūsei* [Collected sources on Japan's tea industry], ed. Ogawa Kōraku and Teramoto Yasuhide. Tokyo: Bunsei Shoin, 2003.

INDEX

women. *See* gendering of tea; Japanese
  women; tea parties
world fairs. *See* fairs and expositions
World War I, 93, 153–54, 183
World War II, 186–93

Yamaguchi Prefecture, 87. *See also* Chōshū
  domain
Yamashiro province, 13
Yamashiro Tea Company, 167, 172
Yamato court, 8
Yamauchi family, 12
Yamauchi Toyonori, 76

Yankee tea parties, 24, 30, 183. *See also* tea
  parties
Yokohama: adulteration and the value of
  exported teas, 109–10; as port city, 34–35,
  77; rail line to Tokyo, 72; tea brokers and
  wholesalers, 40; tea refining factories, 59,
  78–83, 138 (*see also* factories); tea shipped
  from, 56, 93; tea transported to, 77;
  unrest and anti-Western sentiment in, 45
Yoshinobu, Shogun, 47–48, 69–72
young hyson, 19, 23, 28–29

zaibatsu, 104

Printed in the USA
CPSIA information can be obtained
at www.ICGtesting.com
JSHW021935090424
60869JS00004B/18

9 780231 216678